THE COLTS' BALTIMORE

THE COLTS'

BALTIMORE

A CITY AND ITS LOVE AFFAIR
IN THE 1950S

MICHAEL OLESKER

THE JOHNS HOPKINS UNIVERSITY PRESS
BALTIMORE

© 2008 The Johns Hopkins University Press
All rights reserved. Published 2008
Printed in the United States of America on acid-free paper

9 8 7 6 5 4 3 2 1

The Johns Hopkins University Press
2715 North Charles Street
Baltimore, Maryland 21218-4363
www.press.jhu.edu

◀ LIBRARY OF CONGRESS CATALOGING-IN-PUBLICATION DATA

Olesker, Michael.
  The Colts' Baltimore : a city and its love affair in the 1950s / Michael Olesker.
  p. cm.
  Includes bibliographical references.
  ISBN-13: 978-0-8018-9062-8 (hardcover : alk. paper)
  ISBN-10: 0-8018-9062-4 (hardcover : alk. paper)
  1. Baltimore Colts (Football team)—History. 2. Football fans—United States—
Biography. I. Title.
  GV956.B3O54 2008
  796.332'64'097526—dc22   2008014463

A catalog record for this book is available from the British Library.

*Special discounts are available for bulk purchases of this book. For more informa-
tion, please contact Special Sales at 410-516-6936 or specialsales@press.jhu.edu.*

The Johns Hopkins University Press uses environmentally friendly book materi-
als, including recycled text paper that is composed of at least 30 percent post-
consumer waste, whenever possible. All of our book papers are acid-free, and our
jackets and covers are printed on paper with recycled content.

For my father, Lionel Olesker,
And my uncle, Dr. Richard Loebman,
And my brother Mitchell,
for all those afternoons at a ballpark on 33rd Street

CONTENTS

PREFACE:
THE GHOSTS OF BALL GAMES PAST

ON DECEMBER 28, 1958, the day the Baltimore Colts and New York Giants played their football game at Yankee Stadium, I was a thirteen-year-old kid having a heart attack with four of my friends. Simultaneous heart attacks, it's what we used to do on Sunday afternoons. We were two hundred miles from the Bronx, in my parents' living room in northwest Baltimore, watching the explosion of the whole world of American sports on a little black-and-white television set while our hearts did drum solos beneath our skinny adolescent chests.

A couple of us were there as a form of penance. We were supposed to go to New York with our fathers, but honesty got in the way. My father had two tickets, and one of them was for me, and then he decided it wasn't. The same with one of my friends and his father.

Since confession is good for the soul, even when it comes fifty years later, I will quickly brief you on the tragic story. Two weeks before the Colts met the Giants, half a dozen guys from my neighborhood bowled a game of duckpins at the Hilltop Bowling Lanes, across the street from the Hilltop Diner that Barry Levinson later made famous in the movies. One of the guys, not me, got a great idea: Let's sneak out without paying. What the hell, we'll save thirty cents apiece—we can run across the street and buy some french fries with gravy at the diner.

Five of us escaped, and one never made it.

Jakie Rubinstein.

I give you his name today because Jakie got caught and then finked on every one of us.

When my father, Lionel Olesker, heard what I had done, he suddenly became Judge Hardy.

"You're not going to the championship game," he said.

That was his best shot.

"But, Dad," I said.

That was my best shot.

"Let this be a lesson to you," said my father, a meticulously honest man.

"It is," I said.

"What's the lesson?"

"Never go bowling with Jakie Rubinstein."

So I didn't make it to Yankee Stadium. So what gives me the authority to write this fiftieth anniversary remembrance of the sudden-death game, and the Colts, and the Baltimore of that time?

For openers, I was part of the gang at Memorial Stadium, at that time the world's largest and most raucous outdoor semireligious congregation. Year after year there we were: my father, my younger brother Mitchell, my uncle Dr. Richard Loebman, and me.

Since then, I've spent forty years writing for newspapers. I came up as a sports reporter and wrote features on the Colts when John Unitas was still wearing his high-tops. I broke in under the sports editor John Steadman, who practically invented the Colts, and I spent bountiful hours across the decades listening to his insider's perspective on the team. His stories are here. I worked with N. P. "Swami" Clark, the beat reporter on the Colts at the *Baltimore News-Post* (which later became the *News American*). I've been friends across the years with Chuck Thompson and Vince Bagli, who were the team's great broadcast voices. Their stories are here.

I've spent more than three decades writing newspaper columns in Baltimore. Over those years I've spent lovely hours with the likes of

Unitas and Artie Donovan, Lenny Moore and Jim Mutscheller, Jim Parker and Raymond Berry, Alan Ameche and Andy Nelson. Their stories are here.

But they're not the only members of the cast of '58. It's been my delight through the years to write about Baltimore's great characters, who also make up this book: the political types of the Colts' greatest era such as Tommy D'Alesandro and Dominic "Mimi" DiPietro and Jack Pollack; the media types such as Buddy Deane and Royal Parker; the former street corner guys such as Nookie the Bookie Brown and Julius "Lord" Salsbury. And Philip "Pacey" Silbert and Constantine "Gussie" Huditean and Leonard "Boogie" Weinglass and the future filmmaker John Waters; and the free spirits Bill Gattus and Eugene "Reds" Hubbe, who circled the Memorial Stadium sidelines each Sunday and conducted cheers for the faithful. Their stories are here.

How intimate were the legendary ties between the Colts and Baltimore?

Well, when John Steadman died in 2001, seventeen years after the Colts departed, his mourners left the church that snowy morning to the stirring religious sounds of the Baltimore Colts marching song played at funereal tempo.

How close were the Colts to Baltimore?

When Reds Hubbe died in 2004, the funeral director's full name was Anthony Colt Connelly. He was born on that December 1959 day the Colts won their second straight National Football League championship. His parents thought his middle name was the least they could do to honor their football team.

So, like millions of Americans on December 28, 1958, my friends and I gathered in front of the television set and watched a football game, the first so-called sudden-death game, the one the writers called "the best game ever played."

That game is one of America's last great moments shot in glorious black and white, like *On the Waterfront* or World War II. Once in a while on the History Channel they'll dig up some old World War II stuff shot in color. But, let's face it, it never looks authentic. That war was fought in black and white, wasn't it?

It's the same way with the '58 Colts and Giants game. The black and white is part of its lingering aura. We're watching the turning of a civilization, the last visible evidence of a culture that's emerged from the cave but hasn't yet developed its preening self-awareness and the cynical marketing techniques to constantly remind everyone how wonderful it is. That alone marks it distinctly as belonging to another time.

There was no color TV coverage of the game. And there were no instant replays, split screens, fade-outs, slow motion, stop-actions, or reverse-angle shots. They hadn't been invented yet. You saw the play once, and then you waited to see the next play. How primitive it all seems fifty years later.

This was the moment that not only started pro football as the nation's game—it also changed television. Fifty years ago, TV really was a mass medium: three networks, and that was it. None of this cable TV, or satellite TV, with dozens of channels. You didn't have niche programming. You had the whole country watching one of three channels —meaning we all had pretty much the same points of reference.

And just as Milton Berle was the guy who cemented entertainment on TV and John Kennedy's assassination made TV the first place everybody would turn to for breaking news, the sudden-death game forever changed Sunday afternoons in America.

Now we watched John Unitas throw footballs instead of hearing Alistair Cooke talk shop with Bertrand Russell on *Omnibus*.

For better or worse.

Watching the game at my house that day were Joel Kruh, Ron Sallow, Phil Rubinstein, and Barry Director. We were like kids in every neighborhood back in '58. School's out, you put on your after-school clothes and get up a game. On Sundays when the Colts game was over, you got up another game until your mother called you to dinner. You wanted to imitate the thrilling thing you had just witnessed. You wanted to make the Colts' story your own. You were so hungry to be like those guys and hear the cheering of the crowd. You threw the ball downfield, or you caught it, and somewhere in your head you heard the voice of Chuck Thompson hollering your name on the radio.

We played our games of touch football in the street (three complete's a first down) and our games of tackle down at the Grove Park Elementary School, after the little kids went home. I still drive through the old neighborhood, out in northwest Baltimore, and pause when I spot the grassy area where we used to play.

In my mind's eye I still see the whole gang of us choosing up sides every afternoon—the ghosts of a thousand neighborhoods, racing breathlessly until the daylight fades and everyone's forced to go home. There's Joel Kruh zigging and zagging like Lenny Moore. There's Phil Rubinstein running his pass routes and then bending over to pick up his yarmulka because it flies off his head every time he runs a pass pattern. And Stan Nusenko's running, and Harvey Hyatt's throwing a block, and Rob Meyer's naturally better than anybody because he plays varsity ball for Forest Park High School, which lifts the status of our entire game. (Our entire neighborhood, actually.) And Barry Director's throwing the ball long, and that's me racing for it and reaching out as far as I can like Raymond Berry.

And now and then, when the wind is right, there's the voice of Chuck Thompson, saying, "One of the greatest catches these eyes have ever seen, by this Colts rookie who grew up right here in Baltimore . . . "

Fifty years later, bet me I'm not the only guy who hears it.

THE COLTS' BALTIMORE

THE LOST CITY

THEY'RE THE ONLY TWO MEN in America who would haul a football banner to a funeral service. Eugene "Reds" Hubbe and Bill Gattus, straight off the street corner, who else? On the day John Unitas goes to his grave, the two of them, Reds and Gattus, march up to the front steps of the stately Cathedral of Mary Our Queen as though they might conduct orchestrated cheers for the dearly departed. And everybody around Baltimore agrees this is a beautiful thing to behold.

The banner shows Unitas's shy grinning face and says, "Thanks for the memories." The picture goes back to the beginning of everything, back when they brought John down here from Pittsburgh. The poor guy was working full-time on a construction crew and playing semi-pro ball for six dollars a game after the Steelers cut him. Everybody at the cathedral knows the story by heart. The Steelers drafted him but never even let him see action, except for the silly publicity shot that made the papers up in Pittsburgh. It was John offering some insights about football to a Chinese nun.

But now even the nun can't save him. A week ago, Unitas was brought down by a heart attack, at sixty-nine. It must have been a blind-side hit. The man who put *sudden death* into the American language would have stared down the real thing if he had seen it coming.

He did it once upon a time, didn't he? December 28, 1958, in the frigid dusk at Yankee Stadium. It was that distant world where professional football was a scruffy postgraduate afterthought to the college boys' game and baseball was still reverently termed the national pastime by sports writers who hadn't looked up from their Underwoods long enough to notice the world shifting all around them. Wasn't it Unitas's Baltimore Colts who touched off the spark that changed America's sporting culture? Didn't they electrify the whole damned country in that famous sudden-death overtime game against the New York Giants?

Didn't they? It's all so long ago and the story so marvelous that it's killing everybody in Baltimore to see the way it finished. Like Reds and Gattus, members of the original cast of characters, perennial adolescents who arrive this morning with the echoes of a city's giddiest hour still ringing in their ears. Or those uniformed cops trying to deal with all the funeral traffic along sun-splashed Charles Street up in north Baltimore. Or the guy in that small plane doing laps overhead, looking as lonesome as some distant lunar module. He's trailing a banner behind him the way he did on all those long-ago Sundays at Memorial Stadium.

"Unitas We Stand," it says.

The old brick ballpark was down on 33rd Street, a ten-minute drive from here. "Miracle on 33rd Street," the newspaper headlines used to holler whenever Unitas pulled some last-minute victory out of defeat. Most of these mourners held season tickets there, back when six bucks got you a seat on the fifty-yard line. Some of them were part of that throng of twelve thousand who packed the special buses and trains running from Baltimore's Penn Station up to New York on the morning of the '58 game, when they spent four hours hollering back and forth across the aisles, "Gimme a C . . . ," while they downed their morning breakfast and beer and the Colts marching band went tootling through the cars. Or maybe they were part of the sea of thirty thousand swarming across the tarmac at the old Friendship International Airport to greet the returning world champion Colts that night, when it looked like Lindbergh landing in the darkened madness at Le Bourget.

It was innocent, distant 1958, and they still care about it. In fact, it's

The Baltimore Colts' fight song, the city's unofficial municipal anthem. The band struck up, "Let's go, you Baltimore Colts," and the people who packed 33rd Street's Memorial Stadium, "the world's largest outdoor insane asylum," roared to the heavens. *Courtesy Enoch Pratt Free Library*

still the sweetest grand-opera memory of a lot of their lives, the consummation of a municipal love affair that sprang from their hearts and not the marketing instinct of some NFL public relations manipulators. A simpler time, too, back in '58, when no terrorists flew airplanes into skyscrapers. And now it's Unitas, struck down on September 11, 2002, the first anniversary of the attacks.

What's happened to the world? In '58, Eisenhower's still steering the country through an eight-year sleepwalk. World War II is thirteen years over. There's a cold war, sure, but Russia's all the way over on the other side of the planet, and it isn't attacking American cities. In '58, you're sitting pretty with thirty cents in your pocket for a burger and a Coke at the Read's drugstore counter. Your dad buys gas at the Esso station without needing a bank loan to fill up his new Chevy Impala. For a hundred bucks a month to Union Trust, the family's finally situated in a pretty decent house. And the Colts are still in Baltimore.

These people gathered to say good-bye to Unitas—they remember all of it. And now they've lived to see the end of the story. Unitas goes, and so goes the heart of it. The whole country threw a spotlight on that '58 game, and a self-conscious city took unaccustomed bows in the glare. That's what Reds and Gattus and the rest of them are mourning today: not just Unitas but the memory of a brief moment when Baltimore emerged from its sense of itself as gawky and overlooked for a few breath-taking ticks of the clock. And then the town went back to being Baltimore again: this quirky burg, this oddball, self-conscious town caught between glittery New York and Washington and lost in the shadows of both. In fact, lost among the entire East Coast Big-Five megalopolis: Boston and New York, Philly and Washington, and, oh yeah, that other place: Baltimore.

Bal-tee-more.

Bawlamer.

Whatever.

It was always the easiest of the five to overlook. It has the least money and the puniest history. ("Baltimore: Home of the First Umbrella!" How's that for a municipal slogan to stir the heart?) It's a city of so many streets of endless row houses that somebody called it the Berlin Wall with windows. Most of 'em with formstone fronts. Formstone, which the hometown moviemaker John Waters always called the polyester of brick. Years ago, it's where all the Polish ladies and the German ladies and the colored ladies would get on their knees on Saturday mornings and scrub their white marble front stoops as if doing some kind of weekly religious penance. It's a city so hungry for heroes that, when the writer Garry Wills strolled down the aisle of the Cathedral of Mary Our Queen one Sunday, he noticed a picture of the young Babe Ruth. The Babe, who grew up in west Baltimore, was sketched in with a bevy of heavenly saints. In Baltimore, said Wills, who lived there at the time, "We do tend to mingle."

"We're an innocent city," a *Baltimore Sun* editorial writer, James Bready, once told the *New York Times*'s Russell Baker. Bready surely had his customary tender glint in his eye as he said it. "We never surrendered to the success dream," he said. "We are a city where people don't think they're very bright."

A municipal inferiority complex, some called it. Back in '58, New York nightlife meant Rodgers and Hammerstein on Broadway, and Baltimore's meant strippers on The Block. A generation of neighborhood guys in places like Little Italy and Highlandtown and Curtis Bay can still recite their names: Irma the Body and Patti Waggin. Ronnie Belle and her twin liberty bells, and Tempest Storm. And the famous Blaze Starr.

Back then, John Waters was a lad headed toward Calvert Hall, the Catholic school where the priests had no idea what was going through this weird kid's mind. Waters and a pal named Harris Glenn Milstead would cut class and run down to The Block to see a stripper named Lady Zorro. She was their favorite. They thought she looked like Johnny Cash. Or they'd watch Blaze strut her stuff. Waters went on to make underground classics like *Eat Your Makeup.* Then he had the big hit with *Hairspray.* Milstead learned to put on women's clothes, and he became a cross-dressing actor called Divine. Years later, Waters called Blaze Starr's agent and asked if Blaze would like a role in one of his movies. The agent was Blaze's sister.

"Would there be nudity?" the sister delicately asked.

"No," said Waters, figuring Blaze had to be seventy by then.

"Well, then," said the sister, "she wouldn't be interested."

Washington's Brooklyn, the wise guys called Baltimore. If they thought to call it anything at all. Manhattan had glitter and style, and Baltimore had high school dropouts in overalls spending the next thirty years down at the steel mills. The kids in their black high-top Keds and their PF Fliers, playing ball out there on the playground at south Baltimore's St. Mary's Star of the Sea School—they always knew when it was four o'clock because the whistle blew down at the Bethlehem Steel plant and all their old men came trudging home. They were the generation that turned out airplanes and armaments during the boom World War II years, when the city's population swelled to nearly a million. But the war was long over in '58, and the mills and the factories were losing their way and the jobs disappearing and the city feeling a little neglected, a little left behind.

Just a town on the way to another town, that's what they called Baltimore. Philadelphia happily cloaked itself in Benjamin Franklin and all of its great Declaration of Independence history. Baltimore had the body of John Wilkes Booth, lying in an unmarked grave at Green Mount Cemetery. *Loser's town,* the outsiders said. Washington had political power. Baltimore's politics was based on election-day walk-around money, handed over with a sly wink by the precinct bosses, ensuring everybody got out the neighborhood vote. Boston had the great literary tradition. Baltimore's most famous writer was Edgar Allan Poe. He knew about reading. Knew about walk-around money, too. Or its liquid variation. Russell Baker, who grew up in west Baltimore and graduated from Edgar Allan Poe Junior High, across the street from Poe's grave, remembered a classroom lesson about Poe spending his last hours being hustled from one east Baltimore polling place to another. The more he voted, the more drinks he earned. He drank himself stiff. Or so the story went.

In so many ways, Baltimore had a history of feeling outclassed, overmatched, not ready to mix in polite circles. And, until December 1958, with the Colts and the Giants at Yankee Stadium, pro football had the same problems.

Until that hour, hallowed baseball held the sweet spot in America's sentimental heart. The game had folklore and tradition on its side; football, in Jimmy Breslin's phrase, was a game invented to occupy coal miners on their days off. Baseball's poster child was Mickey Mantle; in him, the youth of America saw the precise reflections of their own boyish bubble-gum faces. Healthy ten-year-old boys gimped around the bases, trying to imitate Mickey on his poor battered legs; in pro football, everybody limped—from tearing each other's ligaments apart. The game had toothless Neanderthals, their wintry faces well hidden inside their helmets, throwing a few final forearm shivers before capitulating to serious livelihoods. "The pros are potbellies," Roger Kahn wrote. "A bunch of beer swizzlers playing lazy football. And the only thing worse is the bunch of beer swizzlers watching." Baseball had the New York Yankees waltzing through one triumphant summer after another in the nation's media capital; the football Colts' stars spent their off-hours on second jobs, even during the season. Some worked at Bethlehem Steel. Others sold liquor. A few of them sold cemetery plots, and a couple more tried professional wrestling. All were trying to stretch their paychecks. In '58, the National Football League was still a sport in search of an identity. Sure, there were pockets of provincial interest, but it was college football that held the country's deepest loyalties. Army and Navy still counted as big time. So did Harvard and Yale—*that's* how long ago we're talking. Baseball, wrote Philip Roth, was "our great secular nationalistic church." The World Series was an annual national celebration carried out in glorious sunlight. Pro football's championship contest? Hell, it couldn't compare with Notre Dame on a routine Saturday afternoon.

But the '58 Colts-Giants game went through the country like an electric shock. It changed everything. *Sports Illustrated* immediately called it "the best game ever played." Newspaper guys around the country wrote about it all that winter, when they'd previously gotten themselves all twittery over pitchers and catchers heading for spring training. And the memories had legs. At century's end, the TV sports network ESPN ranked the '58 game number 1 on its list of the greatest sporting events of all time. Football, baseball, quoits, whatever: The Greatest.

You said the words *sudden death* to sports fans of a certain age, and they knew precisely what you meant: the first game that refused to end when time expired. Nobody had ever heard of such a thing; even the players didn't know what to do. Across the years, parents passed the story down to their kids like family heirlooms. The Colts, down to their last minute, frantically driving the length of the field against a murderous Giants defense. The clock ticking away. The stadium crowd howling to the heavens, and Unitas, cool as could be, somehow finding Raymond Berry over and over in the fading twilight. In this hour of his ultimate greatness Johnny U wasn't just a quarterback. He was Elvis at the dawn of rock and roll, he was Al Jolson at the dawn of talkies, declaring, "You ain't heard nothin' yet."

That's Bill Gattus in his old Colts helmet, fifty years after he and Reds Hubbe circled the field and led cheers at Memorial Stadium. *Courtesy Baltimore News-American Collection, Marylandia and Special Collections, University of Maryland Libraries*

And the two ball clubs, the Baltimore Colts and the New York Giants, were ushering in a whole new ethos in American sports: faster, tougher. Bloodier, too. And wealthier beyond all previous imagining.

BUT NOW, ON THIS SUNLIT September morning forty-four years since Unitas first saw sudden death, the real thing has blind-sided him. Outside the church, it's the first line out of Reds Hubbe's mouth: "Remember the '58 game?" he says. It's not so much a question as a rhetorical twitch.

"Remember it?" everybody says. "*Remember it?*"

Instinctively, everyone performs his role in the ancient municipal ritual. The memory authenticates us; it says we're fully credentialed citizens.

"*Hell, I can tell you where I was.*"

So can Reds and Gattus. They were ad hoc cheerleaders for a whole era. They circled the field at Memorial Stadium every Sunday while

Unitas, oblivious to the roar around him, orchestrated his last-minute miracles. Reds and Gattus led cheers that sounded as if they were conducting the ocean.

"Gimme a C."

"C!"

"Gimme an O."

"O!"

"Gimme an L."

In those days, Jim DeWald was one of those fans cheering back at them as though the future of the free world depended on it. Now he's one of these sentimental souls gathering to say good-bye. It's like closing time for a generation. It's like a final weepy benediction for everybody's vanished youth, and for a Baltimore that fell fabulously in love with a football team and then lost it but never forgot how the love affair felt in that wonderful yesterday.

Outside the cathedral now, it feels like it's still that era. Jim DeWald stands in the funeral crowd and tells a little story. He is fifty-four. When Unitas was breaking in, DeWald went to Montebello Elementary School and had Miss Cohn in the second grade. There were three sacred classroom rituals each morning. One was the Our Father. One was the Pledge of Allegiance. The other was the Baltimore Colts marching song. "Let's go, you Baltimore Colts / And put that ball across the line . . . "

It was a roomful of seven-year-olds absorbing it each morning like an anthem, or a nonsectarian haftorah. I wander off when DeWald and a couple of pals finish singing the last bars of the song, and I bump into a friend from forty years ago named Rick Spiegel. He keeps videos at home. Not porno videos, like other respectable men his age. Videotape of the old Colts, stuff from the '50s all the way through to the bitter end. He has the video from the '58 title game and the '59 title game, and he has clips of Buddy Young and Big Daddy Lipscomb and Bert Rechichar that look like they date from the Pleistocene Era.

"Remember that game against the Bears?" he says.

Again, the ancient recitations: Half a minute left to play, the Colts down by four. The Bears' Doug Atkins levels Unitas, smashes his mouth, breaks his nose. The Colts call time out. They can't get Unitas to stop gushing blood. "You're coming out of the game," says Weeb

Ewbank, the Colts' coach. "You take me out," says Unitas through a face so grotesquely battered that his teammates can't bear to look at him, "and I'll kill you." They stop the bleeding only when the lineman Alex Sandusky reaches down for a clump of mud and shoves it up Unitas's nose. On the next play, with seconds left on the clock, John throws the touchdown bomb to Lenny Moore in the corner of the Bears' end zone.

"Sure, I remember," I tell Spiegel. "Art Donovan says that game was rougher than World War II. And he was with the marines in the Pacific." The two of us laugh at the very notion. But, at this moment, it's as if we all went off to war with the Colts, and Unitas was the guy who died for everybody's sins.

"Look at this," Spiegel says, sweeping a hand toward the crowd. They keep coming. As they shuffle in, they seem to carry the very dust of the past. Spiegel was among them, to the final game they played in Baltimore, back in December 1983: a quarter century, practically to the hour, after that '58 game. Spiegel sells insurance for a living, but he's playing hooky this morning.

"You see these people," he says, "and it's your childhood walking in front of you. It's our whole childhood, right here. I got up this morning and said, 'What's more important, going to work or reliving my entire youth?' "

"But what's the hold these guys have on us after all this time?" I ask.

"I don't know," says Spiegel. "The ones today, they live in a different world. You can't get close to them. Years ago, when the Colts trained up in Westminster, you could just walk into the trainer's room. I walked in one day, and there was Jerry Logan sitting on the trainer's table." Logan was a tough, wiry defensive back. "He took one look at me and said, 'Hey, kid, got a cigarette?' "

I send Spiegel over to Jim DeWald for another round of the Colts' fight song. I'm trying to keep some emotional distance, and it's not working. I need to write a column for tomorrow morning's *Baltimore Sun* newspaper, most of whose reporters weren't even born back in '58. But now the mind fills with another newspaper, and another era. The brilliant sunshine dims and becomes a bare light bulb hanging from a ceiling. The funeral crowd disappears, and the outside of the

Colts' majorettes Marge Schmidt and Doris Snyder lead the parade of cheerleaders onto the field. The modest outfits were a far cry from latter-day costumes where little is left to the imagination. *Courtesy Baltimore News-American Collection, Marylandia and Special Collections, University of Maryland Libraries*

cathedral becomes an unheated empty basement of an old apartment building. The sidewalk becomes a cement floor at five o'clock on a Sunday morning, three days past Christmas of 1958. It's dark and iron cold outside. On that Sunday morning I tumbled out of bed while every other human on the planet continued to sleep, and I walked through the pre-dawn streets to this Seton Apartments complex, several hundred housing units spread across a huge hilly swath of northwest Baltimore. It's the day the Colts will meet the Giants. I've hauled in several bundles of newspapers, the *Baltimore News-Post* and Sunday *American*, that were dropped on a nearby street corner. And now I'm crouched on the floor with the paper spread in front of me.

Down in that basement I'm thirteen years old. It's my job to stuff all these sections of the paper together and then deliver them throughout the apartment development and the surrounding neighborhoods. The *News-Post* costs five cents on weekdays, and it's twenty cents for the Sunday *American*. I am paid fourteen dollars every two weeks if

I make all my collections from customers, some of whom repeatedly dodge me for the fifty cents a week.

Now on this dark Sunday morning of the championship game, in the dim glow of the basement light bulb, I scan the front page. The lead story runs under an eight-column headline stripped across the top: "Railroad Policeman Shot, Woman Arrested Here; Quarreled over 'Other Men.' " Wonderful. The country wrestles with a cold war and a hot nuclear arms race, with the remains of McCarthy hysteria and Little Rock school segregation, with the Middle East and a dangerously divided Berlin. But, in the newspapers of William Randolph Hearst, love triangles still warrant the banner headlines on page 1. "Cuba Opens Big Drive on Rebels," says a story below. It's the beginning of half a century's troubles with Castro. Then there's the city section. It says Tommy D'Alesandro II is gearing up for a fourth campaign as mayor of Baltimore. D'Alesandro's an old Roosevelt New Dealer who rides through the city's Little Italy, his home precinct, every election day. Once, he hears the bells of St. Leo's Roman Catholic Church tolling. Someone is being laid to rest. D'Alesandro turns instinctively to his driver, John Pica. "Don't worry," Pica says of the dearly departed, "he'll vote."

Now I start arranging the sections of the paper on the basement floor. I take the Entertainment section and stuff it inside the Real Estate section. Here we find apartment rentals advertised by skin tone. "Apartment, colored," the ads say. "$15 weekly." In the Entertainment section, the Hollywood columnist Louella Parsons reports Rock Hudson separating from his wife. This is a sly wink to carry a nation through its narrow perceptions of sexuality. The movie listings say the Forest Theater, at Liberty Heights Avenue and Garrison Boulevard, is showing *The Brain Eaters*, which my friends and I stood on line to see yesterday because the other neighborhood theater, the Ambassador, is showing Brigitte Bardot in *La Parisienne*, and our parents would sooner have us watch the digestion of a brain than the devouring of La Bardot's upper anatomy. Girls in the neighborhood are encouraged to see Troy Donahue and Sandra Dee movies, where romantic scenes end with waves crashing on a beach, and everyone behaves as though Bishop Sheen might be lurking nearby. (Or the Maryland State Board of Censors. It meets once a week, in a small Calvert Street room painted black, to view first-run movies and decide which parts are suitable for public consumption. "They're doing things up on that screen," declares Mary Avara, the board president, "that I wouldn't do in my bedroom.") On our television screens, married people such as that nice Ozzie and Harriet sleep in separate beds, and Gene Autry sings all love songs to his horse Champion. Meanwhile, Rita Hayworth's marrying her fifth husband, and Mickey Rooney's divorcing his fifth wife. "Ho-hum," Walter Winchell declares. "Kim Novak's latest romance should endure for several headlines." It's the year Eddie Fisher will dump that adorable Debbie Reynolds for that hussie Elizabeth Taylor. It's also the year Jerry Lee Lewis will marry his thirteen-year-old cousin. When the country finds this objectionable, the thirteen-year-old cousin sniffs, "They're just jealous."

There is a clamped-up energy in the country. Part of it's political restlessness, but there's something more: an earthiness, an indelicateness. It's been contained too long. We've been lulled through the Eisenhower years, and we've had enough. We've embraced pastoral baseball, but it's starting to feel a little slow. We're moving from Perry Como to Presley, from good girls like Debbie Reynolds to bad boys like James Dean. We're starting to figure out that Pat Boone's an embarrassment every time he does a white-boy cover version of Little Richard's furious "Whop-bop-aloo-bop-alop-bam-boom." We go to public schools with kids reminded of their skin color every time they pick up a newspaper. "Holdup Man, Negro, Arrested," says the headline. "Apartment, Colored, $15 weekly." So much of the culture seems ready to burst out of its pores. When we slow-dance to Tommy Edwards singing "It's All in the Game," we focus our feet on the rigid box step. What we really want to do is press our hungry bodies against each other. Our mothers spend their days straightening the house and their evenings oil painting famous works of art by the numbers. It's an entire country that's been trained to keep clean and stay between the lines of things, to paper over the racial and sexual fissures beneath the surface. We've endured movie romance where they never quite get to the good stuff, and newspaper gossip where Rock Hudson passes as a ladies' man. The whole country's got the vague beginnings of a nervous twitch.

Though, on this December morning, none of this occurs even slightly to me. There is only one thought in my mind, one indispensable story in this entire newspaper spread across the cold basement floor: "It's the Payoff, and Colts Are Rarin' to Go," says the headline. My stomach plunges eighteen floors and plunges once again as I sit in the Periodicals Room of Baltimore's Enoch Pratt Free Library and examine the same Sunday *American* newspaper on faded microfilm when we're all half a century older.

I've come back to 1958 as a kind of coroner, sifting through the remains of that game and that era, looking not only for Unitas and the Colts but for all those people from Baltimore howling happily on trains and buses to New York, and flooding the tarmac that night at Friendship Airport, and Reds and Gattus leading cheers through it all.

OUTSIDE THE CATHEDRAL OF MARY OUR QUEEN NOW, the sound of Reds' voice slices through the morning crowd and changes the dim basement light bulb to sunlight again. He and Gattus are talking to a couple from Crisfield, Dianna and Bunky Ford. They've come here all the way from Maryland's Eastern Shore. They boarded a bus at 4:30 in the morning to get to Baltimore on time for the funeral. They approach Reds and Gattus with sweet, open, childlike affection, old friends who've never exactly met.

For fourteen seasons, the two guys marched happily around the football field. They orchestrated love calls from the Colts' faithful. They were working-class guys off on a swell lark that became the defining activity of their lives. In that era before pro football swelled with self-importance, cloaking itself in all manner of smug patriotic images each Super Bowl and dolling up its cheerleaders to look like energized Playboy Bunnies, the guys asked the Colts' bosses if they could march along the sidelines and get the crowds worked up (as if they needed it). The Colts gave them one instruction: Stay out of trouble. So Reds and Gattus became poster boys of an era, of passionate, loopy, off-the-wall grownups giving vent to every emotion they kept stored up the rest of the week.

There they were, regular as Sunday services, in beat-up football helmets and blue and white jackets with Colts horseshoes, carrying a banner and leading the faithful. It sounded like the tide coming in. It sounded, in the great line uttered by a visiting coach, like the world's largest outdoor insane asylum. They came out of the city's east side, an area so passionate about the Colts that the ballplayers regularly hung out at some of the neighborhood bars. Gussie's Downbeat, for example, an Eastern Avenue night spot fashionably located directly beneath a Chinese laundry. Gussie's is where all the bookmakers arrived on Monday nights to settle up on Sunday's ball games. Robert "Fifi" London would be there, and Julius Salsbury, a cab driver who bought a bar on The Block and became known as "Lord." Everybody wondered how he got the nickname. He gave it to himself.

Gussie's had a nice crowd. There was Al Isella, who ran the place and booked sports bets there and once had an affair with Ava Gardner. There was Pete "Bananas" Prevas. Isella told everybody that Bananas had class. What did he mean? "He won't wear stolen clothing to church," Isella explained. There was the ironworker Mimi DiPietro, who looked like a Renaissance painting of Cupid. Mimi booked bets and did a little loan-sharking and later became a Baltimore city councilman. He was a third-grade dropout who always had a little trouble with the language. He liked an east-side luncheonette for its coffee and told everybody, "They got them coffee urinals going day and night." He said he sang in the church quarry. He meant the choir. Years later when Jimmy Carter was president, he had lunch at Chiapparelli's Restaurant, in Baltimore's Little Italy. The mayor was there, and Maryland's two U.S. senators, and Councilman DiPietro, by this time representing the city's east side. He spent lunch informing the leader of the free world, "You gotta do something about them pot holes in East Baltimore." Carter later invited DiPietro to the White House to meet Pope John Paul II. Mimi called him "Mr. Pope." When he was introduced to the president's wife, Rosalynn Carter, the councilman naturally tried to say the gallant thing, to mark himself as a man of class and refinement.

"I'd kiss you on the mouth," said Mimi to the first lady, "but I don't know who you been with."

Mimi would hang with the craps shooter Bobo Sudano, who stored his winnings under his toupee in case of a police raid and learned the most valuable life lesson when he was ten years old. Bobo had gone shoplifting with some pals. The pals got caught and turned Bobo in. When the news reached Bobo's old man, a proud immigrant from Italy, he slapped Bobo across the face.

"Let this be a lesson to you," the old man said.

"What lesson, Pop?" cried the wounded Bobo.

"Always," declared the father, "steal by yourself."

You walked into Gussie's, and a band called The Tilters played in a little alcove with a tiny dance floor. The Tilters had a black singer named Nicky Fields. He married a Polish girl from the neighborhood, and half of east Baltimore fainted. Guys just out of jail would show up, and so would boxers, local club fighters like Irish Johnny Gilden and German Billy Metzger. They wore their ethnicity like a badge; it automatically gave them a following.

A bunch of the old Colts would show up at Gussie's, too. The story was that Gino Marchetti would appear the night before a game, get a load on, and go out and play his best ball the next day. Or Artie Donovan. He came home from the Downbeat at four o'clock one morning.

"Where were you?" said his wife, Dorothy, more than slightly miffed.

"I went out for an early haircut," Donovan explained. "There was a line."

Why did they haunt such places? "Because we were connected at the hip with these people," explained the ferocious linebacker Mike Curtis, who arrived a few years later, when the romance was still hot. "It felt like we were attached to this town at our very core. You understand what I'm saying? It felt like we were attached at our souls."

Curtis started clenching and unclenching his jaw. "You know what I used to do after games?" he said. "I used to drive down to east Baltimore and find a bar and sit there with all those guys from Highlandtown and Middle River. They were our people, see? They were hardworking guys like us, and they loved us. I don't know if you can have that any more. These guys move around so much now, and they're making all that money. It's two different worlds, isn't it? It's like royalty. What we had was different."

The east-side folks were among the earliest Colts zealots. They embraced football because it was as direct as a shot in the mouth. It was about our guys being tougher than your guys, that's all. It hearkened back to schoolyard memories when everybody still imagined possibilities beyond numbing factory jobs. (For the white-collar professional, it was a rejoinder, too. He'd survived the madness on Guam only to come home and put on a gray flannel suit and sell out to the corporate boss. But football gave him back a few hours of his manhood every week.)

These east-side folks were the ones who left their row houses every morning and took the municipal buses to work the blast furnaces out at Sparrows Point's steel mills and stood on assembly lines at the Broening Highway GM plant. They were ship fitters and dock workers, and they punched the time clocks at canning houses and paint factories. They spent their nights at those neighborhood bars that were mainstays on every street corner, where photos of the honored dead from World War II still covered the walls. Bars and churches, that's what you found everywhere on the east side. Over at Our Lady of Pompei, Father Lou Esposito always joked, "We don't know whether the bars came in first and the people started feeling guilty and they built churches, or the churches came in first and the people started feeling guilty and went to the bars."

Or they were down in Fells Point, which everybody still called the Foot of Broadway, where Saturday nights meant the St. Stanislaus Church Hall, with pork and sauerkraut dinners and pitchers of beer and most of the crowd got up and danced the polka while the old men played cards and then, in the morning, everybody went to mass at St. Stan's, or St. Casimir's, or Holy Rosary.

They were the ones who spoke with the Bawlamer accents the wags referred to as Upper Chesapeake Adenoidal. They ate *lemoran pah.* This meant lemon meringue. They *axed* you a question and stood there on the sidewalk *payment* until you answered. They hung magazine *pixtures* of Elvis in their living rooms and slurped raw *urshters* at the Broadway Market where Eastern European immigrants shouted across food stalls in half a dozen different languages. When they went duckpin bowling, they exclaimed, in the Bawlamer patois, "Oh, ma Gawd, did chew see dat? He got de sem-ten split." These were the bowlers who made Elizabeth "Toots" Barger and Min Weisenborn municipal heroes. Toots, because she knocked down more duckpins than any woman in history, and Min, with her bulging biceps, because she stood at the foul line like a Russian shotputter, tossing the ball into the air and catching it before heaving it hell-bent down the alley. You saw Toots and Min every year when the famous Sunpapers bowling tournament was broadcast on local television. In Baltimore, this was considered major league stuff for a very long time.

And then came the Baltimore Colts, and a connection that held for so long that even the team's kidnapping to Indianapolis one snowy night in March 1984 couldn't dim the memory. What the vanished Dodgers of baseball were to Brooklyn, these football Colts were to Baltimore. How Walter O'Malley famously plunged the dagger into Brooklyn's heart, so Robert Irsay did it to Baltimore's. But the Colts' sudden-death win—that's the one that changed the country.

"We were America's Team," said Tom Matte as he walked past Reds and Gattus to Unitas's farewell rituals. Matte played halfback for the Colts for a decade. "All those people who said Dallas was America's Team? That's just bull. The Baltimore Colts were America's Team. And Unitas was the one who put us there."

Matte waved hello to Reds and Gattus, but they were a little preoccupied. For now, outside the big cathedral, the two old cheerleaders stood there as Dianna and Bunky Ford of Maryland's Eastern Shore finally got to them, and Dianna Ford said, "Hey, hon, can I get a picture of my husband and you holding this up?"

She pointed to the Unitas banner. This is their validation, which they will pass on to their children: *Remember, kids, how we told you about a time and a place, when Mom and Dad were young? You see these two men? They were friends of ours, sort of.* Reds and Gattus puffed out their chests, and Bunky Ford of Crisfield stood with them and their banner while a picture was taken, and then the Fords rushed to get inside the crowded church.

"Every time I see somebody, the tears start welling up," Reds said.

"Oh, I cried like a baby when I heard the news about John," Gattus agreed. He glanced up as a shadow passed overhead, and he saw the small plane carrying the banner: "Unitas We Stand."

"Look at this," said Gattus. "I got goose bumps."

"All them Sundays," said Reds, turning away. "All them Sundays."

I went into the church and found a seat in the last row with Joe DiBlasi. His boyish features looked stricken. DiBlasi was like me, an impressionable teenager just starting to come of age when the Colts were everything. He grew up to become vice president of a bank and then spent a dozen years as a city councilman out of south Baltimore.

"Do you believe this?" he whispered. "Unitas wasn't supposed to die. He was never supposed to die." His voice carried a tone of insistent disbelief. "He was too tough to die."

"Everybody dies," I said.

"Did you ever think the Colts would die?"

Well, they didn't die so much as get themselves killed. That's the other shadow hanging over Unitas's funeral: his death follows, by eighteen years, the removal of his football team. On that snowy night in 1984, owner Robert Irsay, a drunk air-conditioning magnate out of Chicago, hired a fleet of Mayflower moving vans to kidnap the Colts to Indianapolis. This was another turning point for pro football, nearly as profound in its murderous way as the '58 title game was a life force.

In removing the Colts, Irsay did two things: first, he froze Baltimore football in time. Other cities got on with their histories. Each new autumn brought new faces, new games, new memories to put into storage before fresh ones pushed them aside. Baltimore was left to consider its past. We nurtured our memories; we paused to give detail to things that might have slipped away with the years. The affection deepened. The names, and the stories, took root. The men who might have slipped from memory became the saintly figures who never deserted us. And the '58 sudden-death game became the heart of it.

But the other thing Irsay did, unconscionably, was to help legitimize a posture of bullying in professional sports. He destroyed all myth of the two-way love affair between a community and a team. Give me what I want, or I leave, all Irsay imitators thereafter declared. He cemented the role of blackmail in the life of professional sports. You want a ball club now, you pay the Irsay price. All the years of fan support count for nothing since he kidnapped the Colts. Ask those in St. Louis or Oakland or Los Angeles or Houston. Or Cleveland. A new stadium, the ball club's owner says. We can't afford a new stadium, the leaders of the struggling city reply, not with our public schools, not with our exhausted cops, not with underpaid teachers and firefighters and mottled highways and decayed houses.

A new stadium, the ball club's owner says again, appearing not to hear the plaintive litany, and it's got to have luxury boxes and personal seat licenses and ticket prices to match the size of a bloated ego.

"Or else?" the city leaders ask.

"Or else," says the owner, "I pull an Irsay."

"I hope his ghost is here today," I told DiBlasi, "so it can see how many people turned out for Unitas."

"And I hope nobody showed up for Irsay's funeral," said DiBlasi.

On the city council, DiBlasi represented a south Baltimore that had been rabid for the Colts. Working class back in '58, newly discovered by a young professional crowd now. Row houses that went for five grand back in the winter of '58 were now heading toward fifty times that price. The Procter & Gamble plant that put generations of south Baltimore people to work was being converted to office space. Back in '58, when you drove down the neighborhood's Fort Avenue from Federal Hill into Locust Point, you found yourself among trucks rumbling back and forth from all the local factories. The neighborhood women had mixed emotions about this. They couldn't hang their laundry out to dry. There was all this black soot shooting into the air, spreading from factory smokestacks down the block; and grain elevators spread red chaff like rain across people's homes, and there was some kind of smelly, burning material hanging in the air on damp or foggy or windless days.

"Yeah," the locals would say, "but it's good, see? It means the plants are open. Everybody's working."

Those plants were now high-tech offices. And those old row houses were going for breath-taking prices, and nobody worried any more about grain elevators shooting chaff across people's laundry. Just across the city's inner harbor, the scruffy old working waterfront had been converted to Harborplace, the tourist mecca that helped draw eleven million visitors a year to the town. Nearby were the modern ballparks for the Orioles and the football Ravens. The area was learning to go upscale. South Baltimoreans who previously did not know how to pronounce *quiche* were now actually eating it.

Joe DiBlasi was fifty-five now and silver-haired. In his youth, his family lived near Fort McHenry, where Francis Scott Key looked across the Patapsco River in 1814 and found inspiration to write "The Star-Spangled Banner." A hundred and forty-four years later, this was still the city's great claim to American history (the unmarked grave of John Wilkes Booth notwithstanding).

"You know what this is all about?" DiBlasi whispered.

"Yeah. If a guy as tough as Unitas goes, the rest of us have no shot."

"Yeah, but it's remembering our youth," DiBlasi said. "Back then, it was all about running down to the park after school, and throwing the football around, and one guy saying, 'I'm Unitas,' and the other saying, 'I'm Raymond Berry.' That's how everybody in this town grew up. That's why we're here. Johnny Unitas was our youth. You ran down the park, and you were Johnny U."

The DiBlasis' house was straight up from Fort McHenry and the shipping slips next door. At the start of the twentieth century, only New York's Ellis Island had embraced more immigrants arriving on America's shores. They climbed out of steerage in south Baltimore and found busy piers. They found packing houses and railroad lines and waterfront markets. All this meant jobs. They found smoking factories and steamships, and they rented rooms in stifling little row houses and found work in shipbuilding and steel making. Almost nobody coming out of these little row houses each morning was ever seen wearing a coat and tie to work—not when the nineteenth century turned into the twentieth, and not half a century later.

It was like Reds Hubbe's east side of town: working-class people living in economic ghettos. For a long time, everybody here seemed to stay in one place. The suburban counties hadn't started to explode yet. A big move was kids getting out of school and finding a place to live down on the other end of the block. Barbara Mikulski, the future U.S. senator, was a young social worker out of east Baltimore back then. She threw her entire neighborhood into a tizzy when she moved out of her family's house. "There were only three reasons for a single girl to move out of her parents' home in those old ethnic neighborhoods," Mikulski recalled years later. "You marry, you enter a convent, or you die." Or it was like Father Lou Esposito's story, from Our Lady of Pompei: "I had a baptism. Five generations were present. I had the girl, the mother, the grandmother, the great-grandmother, and the great-great-grandmother. They all lived within a block of each other." That was white working-class Baltimore in the middle of the twentieth century.

Before they moved to Fort Avenue, DiBlasi's family lived on south Baltimore's Poultney Street. DiBlasi, five years old, looked through his bedroom window one night and saw the Cross Street Market burn down. His pals played tackle football on the asphalt lot across the street from his house. When his folks made a big jump in status and moved all the way to Fort Avenue, it was a ten-minute walk, door to door. Joe's father did shift work for the Amoco Oil Company, in nearby Curtis Bay. When DiBlasi graduated from Southern High, he went to night school at the University of Baltimore and worked at Maryland National Bank. Some of the neighbors wondered, "Where does this boy think he's going?" Their kids didn't go to college. They went to the factories, or they went into the army. If they dreamed real big, maybe they got a numbers business going on the side.

Race or ethnic background divided neighborhoods when work didn't. It was that way all over town. The Italians had Little Italy. The Poles, the Greeks, the Germans, and the Slovaks divided up the east side. The Jews were out in the northwest and the blacks on the west side. It wasn't antagonism exactly; it was just sticking with your own because that's the way it had always been. That's what white people told themselves, anyway. Whites didn't live with blacks. And white collars didn't live near blue collars.

The Colts were everybody's piece of common ground.

They drew together the threads of Reds Hubbe's east Baltimore and Joe DiBlasi's south Baltimore, and my neighborhood out in northwest Baltimore, too, where the Jews and the gentiles had tacitly marked out their little areas of community life and watched their kids mingle in the public schools while both wondered about the arrival of black people.

Inside the big cathedral now, DiBlasi pointed a finger. There was Lenny Moore, closely followed up the aisle by Jim Parker. Two African Americans. In the '50s, in a time when the city needed role models across the racial divide, the tough, triumphant Colts offered it. Nobody made speeches about it. But you watched them on Sundays, and words were unnecessary.

It was Unitas dropping into the pocket, protected by Parker. It was Unitas throwing to Moore, who then ran away from everybody. So what if they lived in worlds separated by race when they weren't playing ball? What an entire city population witnessed with their own eyes was men working across color lines and then embracing each other in victory. You saw them with their arms around each other in the locker room, in all the Monday sports pages. For adults, it was an implicit lesson that such things could happen without the world ending; for their children, attending the public schools integrated by the late '50s, it validated the routine thing happening in their lives: in classrooms and on playgrounds, everybody hung out for six hours a day, and it was no big deal, and life went on.

MY FAMILY ARRIVED in Baltimore in the late 1940s, postwar refugees from the Bronx. My grandmother stood on the front steps of her apartment building on the Grand Concourse, eight blocks from Yankee Stadium, and waved good-bye as though we were heading for Neptune. Uncles and aunts lived a few blocks away. They were the offspring of turn-of-the-century European immigrants who had educated themselves and become schoolteachers and government employees and sales people. Now they were watching us leave and asking, "How can you walk away from all this? For Bal-tee-more?"

For four years, we lived in the Latrobe Housing Projects on Baltimore's east side while my father finished up schooling interrupted by the war and carefully parceled out the $120 a month in GI Bill money on which we lived. The rent was $29 a month. The projects were crowded, hilly, and cluttered with activity. Icemen still made regular home-delivery rounds, and so did uniformed fellows in Bond Bread and Cloverland Milk trucks. Coal chutes were wedged into basement window openings and their contents shoveled into furnaces. Paperboys hopped onto buses at red lights and sold newspapers for a nickel apiece and jumped off before the light turned green on them. Parents sent their kids up to the corner grocery store to buy snowballs, crushed ice with flavoring, for a nickel. Crabcakes cost twenty cents and Saturday afternoon movies a quarter.

After four years, we moved out to northwest Baltimore, where my father, feigning solvency, handed over the down payment on a brand new twelve-thousand-dollar house. Many of the neighborhood homes were still under construction, and the people moving in were the postwar families just starting to crawl onto stable financial ground. We lived on Crawford Avenue, a mix of bungalows and semidetached homes. (Across the street lived the Hyatts, who moved in when Dave

Hyatt spotted a For Sale sign on the development's model home. "I'll need the down payment today," the real estate agent said. "I only have five bucks on me," said Hyatt. "I'll take it," said the agent, sealing the deal.)

"So how are things in Bal-tee-more?" the relatives would tease through the years, each time we drove the two hundred miles to see them in New York. The exaggerated pronunciation was their little poke at what they imagined to be pure Hicksville.

"We have Broadway theaters," my Aunt Edith would say, as if her life were a constant round of Manhattan hot spots. She lived out in Queens. "Have you heard of *My Fair Lady?*"

"We have the Forest Theater on Garrison Boulevard," I muttered back, as if hoping to do better one day. "Have you heard of *The Brain Eaters?*"

That was the best we could do. New York had sophisticated Broadway, and we had the Forest Theater. New York had Yankee Stadium, where Mickey Mantle hit tape measure home runs, and Madison Square Garden, where Sugar Ray Robinson turned a killer sport into an art form. We had an architectural ruin on Monroe Street laughingly called the Coliseum, which seated three thousand people and hosted professional wrestling matches between the likes of the Zebra Kid and Rocco the Acrobatic Italian. New York was the heart of the blossoming world of network television; Baltimore TV was Toots Barger throwing duckpin bowling balls, or the preschoolers on *Romper Room* every morning, or the teenage kids on *The Buddy Deane Show* doing the cha-cha every afternoon. New York had Times Square, where crowds gathered on New Year's Eve after they emerged from the elegant *My Fair Lady*. Baltimore had Ford's Theater, where black patrons had to sit in the second balcony. New York had the Latin Quarter and Birdland and the Stork Club. Baltimore had Blaze Starr undressing at the 2 O'Clock Club on The Block. New York had Lindy's, where Damon Runyon's characters hung out. Baltimore had the Hilltop Diner on Reisterstown Road, a few blocks from our house when we reached northwest Baltimore in 1953. Big deal, you got french fries with gravy there for half a buck. Who knew Barry Levinson was keeping track of things all those nights?

"We have Frank Gifford and Sam Huff on the Giants," my Uncle Solly reminded me from his apartment in the glamorous Bronx, as the '58 title game neared. "You know, we won it in '56."

"That was two years ago."

"We're even better now," said Uncle Solly, who seemed to know.

The Colts had arrived in Baltimore in 1953 and the Orioles a year later. Each was hapless for several years thereafter. But, by '58, when my relatives in New York brought up the Yankees and the Giants, I could finally return a boast of my own: "We have Unitas and the Colts."

And, after that championship game, it stifled all further municipal comparisons for about the next fifteen years.

But now it was four decades later, and the Colts had been gone a long time, and Unitas's death was closing the era for good. DiBlasi and I, in the back row of the cathedral, spotted Mike Gibbons as he walked in and motioned for him to sit with us.

Gibbons headed the Babe Ruth Birthplace and Museum, on the west side's Emery Street. He was in his fifties, like DiBlasi and me. He had sandy hair and sad eyes over a lean athletic frame. Years earlier, when the Babe's old row house was slated for demolition, Gibbons had convinced city hall to hold off the wrecking ball. He turned the place into a shrine to the Babe. Now, nearly two decades later, it was on its way to becoming much more: a sports museum housing Ruthian memorabilia—and all of the old Colts and Baltimore Orioles history.

"You know what's in here?" he said. He smiled gently and held up a dark blue satchel, placed it on the seat between us, and unzipped it. Inside was a football helmet with a horseshoe on the sides.

"Unitas's," Gibbons said softly.

"His helmet?" said DiBlasi, his voice rising with incredulity. "That's what this is?"

"Shhh."

Unitas had donated all of his memorabilia to the museum six months earlier. DiBlasi reached down and tenderly ran his hands over the helmet.

"Did you ever think you'd touch that?" he said. He was fifty-five years old and had a history in banking and in politics, but he had a little boy's awe in his voice now, as though finding the mythical sword

Excalibur. Or maybe he was back at crowded Memorial Stadium on Sunday afternoons a long time ago or pretending to be Unitas as he lofted passes after school let out.

"Leakin Park," said Gibbons, who'd grown up in west Baltimore's Dickeyville. "That's where we played."

"You go long," said DiBlasi, imagining Riverside Park.

I was on Crawford Avenue, in northwest Baltimore, playing in the street where three complete passes made a first down. Everybody wore high-top Keds and beat-up pants, and you huddled up and told your guys, "You go down to the manhole cover and button-hook. You duck behind Mr. Nusenko's Chevy. Everybody else go long." Or you played tackle over at the Seton Apartments or down at the Grove Park Elementary School after the little kids went home for the day. So much of it was coming back now. When the weather was too cold, you went bowling at Toots Barger's place over at Gwynn Oak Junction, or the Hilltop Lanes near the diner where Barry Levinson's crowd hung out. Or you stood in line to watch *The Brain Eaters* at the Forest. In summers, before air-conditioning, you walked past houses and heard songs coming out of people's living room radios and parents hollering at their kids, "Turn down that music." Top Forty stuff, where Perry Como was giving ground to Presley, and Sinatra to Chuck Berry. Disc jockeys like Joe Knight, "your knight of the spinning round table." And Fat Daddy and long, lean Larry Dean, and Hot Rod and Rockin' Robin, the first generation of black disc jockeys teaching white boys how to be cool. And you lived for the weekends, when you could play ball all day Saturday and then, two o'clock on Sundays, when you heard Chuck Thompson's voice on the radio saying, "Welcome to Memorial Stadium, where the Baltimore Colts today meet . . . ," and everything else in the whole world ceased to matter.

"Whoever thought you'd touch this?" DiBlasi said, reaching over to run his hands over the old football helmet. Then he sat back in his seat and cocked his right arm a little, as though setting to throw long.

"I'll be Unitas," he said, "and you can be Berry."

"Gibbons gets to be Unitas," I said. "He's got the helmet."

THE PRIEST'S EULOGY eluded me. It was mostly about religion and not so much about the life of John Unitas or his football team or the ballpark where they once played. They were all gone now. Memorial Stadium was leveled a few years earlier. An out-of-town owner, the famous attorney Edward Bennett Williams, pulled an Irsay. Build me a new ballpark for my Orioles, he said, or else. So a city still traumatized by the loss of the Colts pushed aside its mountain of financial liabilities and built him a new ballpark for about $200 million.

So long, Memorial Stadium. So long, world's largest outdoor insane asylum. Several weeks before they started tearing it down, about thirty of us walked through the place one final time. It was a drizzly day. Mike Gibbons was there, and Reds Hubbe and Bill Gattus, and the old Baltimore sportscaster Vince Bagli. He remembered the earliest days of the Colts, when they held daily practices over at Herring Run Park and the whole neighborhood could hang around and watch. In the team's earliest incarnation, he got three dollars a game as an usher. Now, at the end, the Memorial Stadium playing field was overgrown with weeds and wet gravel. It resembled an unkempt graveyard.

"Come here," Gibbons called out. He stood by a tunnel near the first-base dugout. The Orioles and Colts had shared the nearby locker rooms for three decades. "Just stand here for a second."

He gestured to the big empty stands all around. "Imagine Sunday afternoons around two o'clock, and Unitas is standing here in the dark waiting for his name to be called, and sixty thousand people are out there roaring. Imagine what that moment felt like."

"Like getting swallowed in sound."

Then our imagining stopped. Over in the old end-zone area, Reds and Gattus started leading Colts' cheers. "Gimme a C," they cried. Then a couple of members of the Baltimore Ravens band struck up the old Colts song: "Let's go you Baltimore Colts / And put that ball across the line . . . "

"God," said Vince Bagli, "this is more poignant than the last game the Orioles played here."

That was nine years earlier. The Orioles had their new ballpark downtown. Now Gibbons motioned some of us to another area, where home plate used to be. He pointed toward the outfield fence. As boys, we imagined sending baseballs over it. As middle-aged men, some of us wiped the day's mist from our eyeglasses and peered through the scattery raindrops.

"To me, standing down here, it seems so much bigger now," Gibbons said. "Could you hit a ball that far?"

"I couldn't carry a ball that far," I said. "I can't even see that far."

But now I can see half a century ago. It's right here in the church, as John Unitas takes a generation with him. It's the winter of '58, in the lost city of Baltimore. Joe DiBlasi's throwing schoolboy passes in a park instead of running his hands over Unitas's old helmet. Reds and Gattus are leading cheers down on 33rd Street. We're all so young back there, and so safe. Nobody worries about terrorists. Only the Russians, and they're half a world away. Everybody leaves their windows open, and their doors, too. The folks have a few bucks in their pockets for the first time in their lives, and the mortgage payment's under a hundred a month. You race out of the house and naturally find your friends getting up a game at the schoolyard. "Choose up," somebody says, and two guys buck up for sides. We'll play ball until the last of the day's sunlight disappears. We'll talk about the Colts incessantly. They meet the Giants tomorrow for the championship of the whole world. We'll walk home in the dark, and we'll fall asleep dreaming about Unitas throwing passes to Raymond Berry and never imagine how the vision will cling to us for the rest of our lives.

"JUST LOOK AT THOSE AWFUL PEOPLE"

ON THE MORNING OF January 6, 1958, John F. Steadman arrived at the Pratt Street offices of the *Baltimore News-Post* and Sunday *American* to write his first sports column. The place was a wreck. Scraps of copy paper and telephone books and old newspapers were scattered atop metal desks that seemed to retain all original dust. Newspaper people of the era, believing themselves to be lovable rogues, considered this part of the charm of the business. Wire service machines clacked away, and telephones rang incessantly. A noisy conveyor belt shot through a hole in the ceiling and carried copy paper up one floor to a composing room where a linotype operator known as Mike the Cuban and several colleagues ran a semiprofitable bookmaking operation to make up for their weekly paychecks, which were an affront to humanity.

These were the days before the newspaper industry wallowed in confusion and self-doubt. When people around the country needed news, they turned to their daily papers. When Baltimoreans wanted news, they turned to the *Sun* or its afternoon sister, the *Evening Sun*. Or they got the *News-Post*. Newspaper people weren't worrying about television yet. Rolf Hertsgaard was just getting his feet wet over at Channel 11. At Channel 13, they were running the 7:23 news with

Keith McBee: seven whole minutes every evening to tell you everything they knew about the whole world. At Channel 2, when they
wanted something visual besides their anchor's face, they ran a snap-
shot lifted right out of the *Sun*.

Between the three daily papers, they reached more than half a million homes a day. The *Sun* had bureaus in half a dozen places around
the world, though they tended to cover the important matters out of
South Africa and miss every nuance of south Baltimore. The *Evening
Sun*'s writing was less stuffy than the *Sun*'s. Occasionally it displayed
a sense of humor. When the morning *Sun* attempted laughter, dust
came out of its mouth. The *News-Post* had the Baltimore Colts.

All three papers covered them, but the *News-Post* got there first
and then ran with it when reporters discovered something astonishing. The more they wrote about the team, the more their readers loved
it. On Mondays, the day after a football game, the paper's circulation
mushroomed. The *Sun*'s sports editor, Jesse Linthicum, cared more
about thoroughbred horse racing than Colts; the *Evening Sun* sports
editor, Paul Menton, cared mainly about college sports. The *Sunpapers* didn't jump in with both feet until they realized the thing happening right before their eyes. But, by then, the *News-Post* had branded
itself as the true voice of the city's pro football team.

On his first day on the new job Steadman wore a blue blazer and
striped tie of no recent vintage. He did this every day. He was tall and
wavy haired and had the bushy eyebrows of an evangelical preacher.
He would write six columns a week for the paper for the next three
decades, until that bleak afternoon when its parent, the Hearst Cor-
poration, had heart failure and closed the newspaper's doors forever.
He also helped invent that quasi-religious phenomenon the Baltimore
Colts.

At thirty, Steadman was now the youngest sports editor of any big-
city paper in the country. His first column ran on page 1 and concerned
the outgoing sports editor, Rodger Pippen, who was retiring after a
long and rancorous run. Steadman wrote a respectful column about
Pippen, but he knew in his heart he was faking it.

Pippen's great boast in life was that he once played a game of organized hardball with a kid named George Herman Ruth Jr. The Babe's
parents stuck him in a reform school called St. Mary's, later to be

It was Chuck Thompson's golden voice bringing listeners the play-by-play of the Colts, and it was National Bohemian Beer, the team's sponsor, taking delight whenever the Colts scored and Thompson exulted, "Ain't the beer cold!" *Courtesy Enoch Pratt Free Library*

romanticized as the place where Ruth learned at least a modicum of discipline and refinement. But Baltimore lifers never saw it that way. Generations of angry parents told unruly sons, "Shut up, or you're going to St. Mary's." The unruly sons instantly turned ruly.

Pippen loved dogs but regarded all humanity with scorn. Once, at an Orioles Christmas party, a club official told a joke about dogs. Pippen punched the guy in the jaw. Another time, he wrote about a dog falling out of the upper deck at Memorial Stadium. The dog landed atop some innocent woman sitting in the grandstand below. Pippen devoted the next day's column to a tender account of the poor animal and gave profuse thanks that the dog was going to be all right. The woman on whom the mongrel landed got no mention at all.

Pippen was known for getting into fist fights with golfing partners, with police, and with readers who called to complain about his writing. He told callers, "Go shit in your hat," and then he hung up on them. He screamed at some callers, "Listen, you bleep-bleeper, I just bleeped your wife and caught the gonorrhea from her." Steadman mentioned none of this in his first day's column but did allow that Pippen "can be difficult, as when he's on the phone with people who disagree with him. 'You can hate Joe McCarthy if you want. I love him. . . . You commie, you might have to knock me down for what you believe, but you better not be around when I get up.' "

So right away there was a contrast. Steadman brought civility and a kindly heart to the place. He also had a sense of the changing nature of sports coverage. This was a time when sports writers were no longer describing athletes as gods descended from Mount Olympus, the way Grantland Rice had created the famous Four Horsemen of Notre Dame. ("Outlined against a blue-grey sky, the Four Horsemen . . . " A new generation of readers asked: How could Rice see them outlined against the sky? Was he flat on his back?) Such language was overblown; it was windy. Anyway, television was now offering grainy looks at the real people. Cameras could follow action on the field better than any writer could describe it. So newspaper reporters needed something more. They were reduced to following the athletes into the locker room, where they waited for these young men clad in their jock straps to grunt a syllable or two.

"Was that a curve ball you hit?"

"Looked like a freakin' curve, didn't it?"

Such witty colloquy was perceived as bringing great flavor and insight into the next day's stories. A few years down the road, these scribes would change altogether. They would write about the athletes emerging from their accountants' offices instead of Olympus. Steadman tried to focus on the human beings behind the box scores. He also tended to identify with all underdogs. In Baltimore there were plenty. Steadman went to high school at Baltimore City College, where he displayed an academic indifference but an ability to play ball and to write about it. He covered sports for the school newspaper, the *Collegian,* and he played for the baseball team, well enough that the Pittsburgh Pirates drafted him to catch for their minor league York White Roses. He hit a pathetic .125 for the White Roses. "But it was a hard .125," he joked for years afterward.

The baseball career ended after one season. Steadman, still only seventeen, went looking for work back in Baltimore, where he presented himself to the sports editor of the *News-Post,* the volcanic Pippen.

"There aren't any jobs here," Pippen said.

"Sir, could you send me to a lower paper?" Steadman replied. He thought newspapers were like baseball, a business whose youngsters could be sent to the minors to polish their skills.

"Mister Hearst," said Pippen, biting off each syllable, "only has big papers."

But Steadman had a pal at the *News-Post,* Frank Cashen, who wrote sports during the day and went to law school at night. He later helped guide the Baltimore Orioles and the New York Mets to World Series victories. Cashen put in a good word. The paper hired John, at fourteen dollars a week, to keep track of horse race results and baseball scores and cover an occasional high school game. Two years later, when a reporter named Tommy Dukehart left the paper, Steadman took his full-time spot. His pay jumped all the way to twenty-seven dollars a week. It felt like the big time. He could help out his widowed mother. In 1952, he scooped every reporter in the country with the story that Baltimore was about to get a professional football team. The story got him a twenty-five-dollar bonus, which he spent on a crab feast for everybody in the sports office. The football team would be known as the Colts.

Steadman wrote about them in their stumbling early years, and then he went to work for the Colts as their public relations man as they started to blossom. He got to know them intimately. Then he came back to newspapering again to write about them at the very hour they captured the whole country's imagination.

He watched those early teams lose by scores that read like misprints: 70 to 27, and 56 to 0, and 45 to 2. They were embarrassed in every possible way. But John spotted something beyond wins and losses: Baltimore loved the team instinctively, in ways the town never quite loved the baseball Orioles. In those early years the Orioles fans seemed to watch the game with a self-imposed decorum, as though cheering too loudly was unbecoming. The Colts' fans, in love with the quick pace of the game and the rough-house hitting, seemed to explode. In the 1950s, football looked like a safe throwback to a war half recalled with sentimental romance. Even some of the phraseology sounded the same: the bomb, the blitz. But everybody was up in the stands now; they weren't out there in the mud, getting their asses blown off.

And Steadman, across the club's entire history, would never miss a game: not regular season, not preseason, not postseason. He helped create the team—or, at least, helped create the passionate love affair the Colts had with Baltimore—and then he helped bury them.

While Steadman led the chorus in print, the broadcast voice of the Colts was Chuck Thompson. He did the Orioles each summer and the Colts each fall, but there was a difference. In baseball you heard, "Ball, outside," and then the room went numb while announcers made small talk until the next pitch. This happened about two hundred times a night. In football, the action never stopped; nor did Thompson's enthusiasm. When Baltimore scored a touchdown, it sounded like the Hallelujah Chorus.

"Go to war, Miss Agnes!" he cried. The line became a Baltimore catchphrase. "Ain't the beer cold!" he cried. That became another, not exactly displeasing the Colts' broadcast sponsor, National Bohemian Beer.

"The voice of God in Baltimore," sportscaster Ted Patterson called Thompson.

"On Sunday afternoons," said the sportscaster Fred Manfra, who grew up on the city's crowded east side, "you could look out your window, and there was never a soul on the street. If they didn't have a ticket to the Colts, they were listening to Chuck on the radio."

Thompson grew up in East Reading, Pennsylvania, not exactly brimming with self-confidence. He thought he looked like a collection of spare parts. But the voice was golden. He'd sit in his room and read the newspaper aloud, trying to get his delivery right. Then he stumbled into a part-time job at a 250-watt station in Reading. It had all the power of a shout out a window. But it was a start.

Back from World War II, he hooked on with Philadelphia's WIBG radio as a studio announcer. At Shibe Park one afternoon, he was asked to broadcast a pre-game ceremony honoring two of the Phillies' play-by-play announcers. Then the two sportscasters were to return to the press box and announce the day's game. But the elevator to the press box was hand operated, and nobody could find the operator. Thompson had to start the game himself. He did it well enough that he was soon added to the broadcast lineup.

He came down to Baltimore to broadcast the 1948 Navy-Missouri football game over the Mutual radio network. Thompson's job was to handle brief pre-game chatter with the veteran Connie Desmond and then hand things over to Desmond, who would do all the play-by-play. But Desmond got sick.

"Now for the play-by-play," he said, "here's Chuck Thompson."

Then he put on his hat and coat and walked out of the press box. Thompson was left sitting there with no lineups, no numerical charts, no spotters' boards. And people listening in over two hundred stations around the country.

When the Colts arrived in 1953 and the Orioles a year later, he was a natural to handle their radio broadcasts.

These were the years when the NFL wasn't allowing television for home broadcasts. So, over the radio, it was left to people like Thompson to do what sports announcers are supposed to do: he gave an honest accounting. He created a ballpark inside people's heads. And he did it in the present tense. For most radio announcers, football is brutal. It's twenty-two men in organized chaos. The announcers are lucky if they can catch a ball carrier's name and a yard line. Then they search their memory and try to re-create the play from the nearby TV monitor.

They were the four horsemen of the Colts' backfield before the arrival of John Unitas: *(left to right)* fullback Alan "the Horse" Ameche, halfback Lenny Moore, quarterback George Shaw, and halfback L. G. "Long Gone" Dupre. *Courtesy Baltimore News-American Collection, Marylandia and Special Collections, University of Maryland Libraries*

Thompson brought everybody the news as it was happening. The night before every game, he stayed up late memorizing both teams' numbers. So he had the ball carrier, the blocker, the yard line, the tackler without having to think twice. Fifty years later, when the mood is right, you can still hear the echo of his voice: "Unitas pitches to Moore. Now here's Lenny, moving laterally along the thirty-five. He's got Parker in front of him. Moore slips away from Nitschke at the forty. He ducks Adderly at the forty-five. He's got Mutscheller knocking people down at midfield. Here's Lenny moving into Packer territory, throwing a hip, bobbing and weaving . . . "

And this, too, created the great depth of feeling for the Colts: we didn't always see them, but we could imagine them to our heart's content.

Over their first several seasons, there were many times when the Colts were better left unseen.

They won three games out of twelve in 1953 and three out of twelve in 1954. They were comically bad. In 1955 they prepared for the annual draft of college players in the usual way: they leafed through a Street & Smith preseason football magazine. And they got an assistant coach in each major college conference to hand over a list of top prospects. For this, the coach would be paid fifty dollars.

But, in 1955, they needed none of this to know about Alan "the Horse" Ameche. He was college football's Heisman Trophy winner. The town couldn't believe it. A Heisman Trophy winner, and he was coming to Baltimore? It felt like a mistake. Ameche turned out to be a terrific ballplayer and a gentle spirit. He loved opera. He went to church every Sunday and studied the architecture and the organ music. When friends in his old home town, Kenosha, Wisconsin, threw him a party, he forgot to show up. He was hanging out in the back of a shoemaker shop, talking to an old cobbler.

When he joined the Colts, he got pretty tight with the veterans Marchetti and Donovan. Ameche invited them to church one Sunday when they all roomed out at Western Maryland College's training camp.

"Let's fool with the Horse," Marchetti said.

When Ameche knocked on their door, Donovan hollered, "Come in."

Ameche walked in to find Marchetti and Donovan taking a bath together.

"I thought they'd gone the other way," Ameche said.

"I thought I'd have a heart attack laughing," Donovan said.

The two of them remembered the moment three decades after it happened. It was 1986 now. Raymond Berry had coached the New England Patriots to the Super Bowl, and Ameche was in Baltimore to watch the game with Donovan. I was along as an added starter.

"The toughest guy I ever had to tackle," Donovan said, "was the Horse. Every time we scrimmaged."

"Are you kidding?" Ameche said, pointing to Donovan. "This guy would hurt me."

But from the moment he arrived in Baltimore, it was Ameche doing the hurting. He had powerful shoulders and legs, and hips nearly as wide as his shoulders. Even the biggest tacklers found it difficult to wrap their arms around him.

With his arrival, in a single instant on opening day, everything begins to change. On the first play from scrimmage, Ameche takes a handoff and bolts seventy-nine yards for a touchdown against the Chicago Bears. All miracles suddenly seem possible. Give the ball to Ameche, maybe he'll break a long one. On sandlots all over town where schoolboys play games of tackle, ninety-pound junior high school boys imagine themselves fully grown fullbacks. Ameche leads the league in rushing. The ball club starts the season with three straight wins. When they get on the bus after the third win, Marchetti and Donovan sit next to each other.

"Hey, Fats," says Marchetti, "how good do you think we are?"

"I don't know," says Donovan, "but I hope the bubble doesn't burst."

It does. The Colts win only two games of their last nine.

The next year, they draft halfback Lenny Moore out of Penn State. Moore astonishes everyone. He comes out of Reading, Pennsylvania, one of twelve children in a house with no electricity and no indoor plumbing. Moore walks out the back door, and he's standing atop railroad tracks. With a football in his hands he makes his own tracks. He's there, and then he isn't. He gives a hip and takes it away, and he does this in a blur. Against Green Bay, he scores one touchdown on a 72-yard run, another on a 79-yard run. In thirteen carries that day, he gains 185 yards.

That was the week after John Unitas started his first game. Until then, nobody's even learned to pronounce his name. The Colts' starter is George Shaw, an accurate short passer and pretty good runner. The club is constructing a future out of this young backfield, and Shaw seems the heart of it. But the Chicago Bears wreck his knee, and in comes this Unitas, who will begin to create history.

The Colts got him because nobody else wanted him. He spent the '55 season with the Bloomfield Rams of the Greater Pittsburgh League. This is no place for a grown man. The pay is six dollars a game, the locker room showers are cold, and the field is littered with oil slicks and broken glass. When Unitas plays well, the team owner gives him a bonus for the final two games of the season: fifteen bucks. The NFL this is not.

But the Colts hear about Unitas, and the general manager, Don Kellett, places an eighty-cent phone call inviting him down to Baltimore.

Unlike the Steelers, the Colts give Unitas a shot. On the first day of training camp Coach Wilbur "Weeb" Ewbank takes Raymond Berry aside. When his teammates look at Berry, they wonder what in the world he's doing on a professional football team.

"I want you to work with this Unitas," Ewbank says. Berry nods his head but says nothing. The way he sees it, he's half a step from getting cut himself. But he also knows Weeb appreciates his work ethic and his toughness. That's what Berry and Unitas have in common. At Southern Methodist, Berry caught thirty-three passes in three years. The Colts drafted him on the twentieth round. He weighed 180 and played outside linebacker—what they called defensive end in SMU's setup—and Weeb regarded him as a fighter.

So the two afterthoughts, Unitas and Berry, start pitching and catching together. When everybody else finishes practice, they stick around. This will go on through the years, Berry running his routes, Unitas throwing to a spot, and Berry arriving at the perfect instant to pull it in. Sometimes Ewbank has to make them stop.

"That's enough practice," he says.

"Tell him," says Unitas.

"Just a couple more I want to work on," says Berry.

Around Baltimore, such stories appeal to everybody's work ethic. It's like the guys on the assembly lines: they grind it out. They produce steel and build cars and load ships. They're not like these Manhattan dilettantes who work on Madison Avenue producing thirty-second commercials and calling it a profession. Baltimoreans earn their paychecks. So do Unitas and Berry.

Off the field, Raymond will wander down to John's training camp dormitory room. Neither is particularly social. They'll talk football. When Unitas gets into a couple of exhibition games that first summer, he looks good enough to back up Shaw.

But Unitas, remembering his Pittsburgh experience, takes nothing for granted. One day he's approached by the club's public relations guy, a fellow he barely knows. It's Steadman. John left the *News-Post* when the Colts offered him more than the thirty-six dollars he was making at the paper. He stays with the team from 1953 to '57. Now, in the midst of the '56 preseason schedule, they've got an exhibition game set in Louisville, where Unitas played college ball.

"How about recording a radio spot?" Steadman asks. "People in Louisville know your name. Maybe it'll help the gate."

"Okay," says Unitas. "But, do you really think I'll be around when we get there?" That's the mind-set of the man who will transform the game of football.

He sticks around, but he's mostly invisible until Shaw goes down four games into the season. Ewbank turns to him because he's got nobody else. Unitas, hunched over, scrawny, running in a manner the football writers will describe as a crablike scuttle, enters the game. His first pass throws an entire town into depression: it's intercepted and returned for a touchdown before Shaw's even been carried out of the ballpark. The Colts lose, 58 to 27.

Who is this Unitas? In the beginning, the public address people can't even get his name right. They call him YOU-knit-as. He wears a crew cut and high-topped football shoes that look like holdovers from the cardboard helmet era. Clem Kadiddlehopper, one of his teammates calls him. Not bad, he carries himself like one of Red Skelton's creations. He has pasty white skin that looks like it's never seen the light of day, massive hands, and arms that seem to hang to his knees, like Lincoln's. Then there are whispers. The wise guys say he's not too bright. That's why the Steelers cut him, didn't you know? They figured him out real fast. The poor kid had to hitchhike home and go to work on a construction crew. If Pittsburgh cut him, how good can he be?

After that first pass in Chicago, though, he wasn't too bad. In fact, even the first pass gives a hint of his toughness. There goes the Bears' J. C. Caroline, running the interception back for a touchdown. And there's Unitas, doggedly chasing after him the whole way. The kid had heart. When everybody's on the team bus after the game, Jim Mutscheller overhears Unitas talking to Walter Taylor, the *Evening Sun* beat reporter. He's not down at all. He's analyzing what happened, and he's as cool as could be. Mutscheller's pretty impressed; maybe this kid will work out, after all.

But, Unitas or Shaw, when the season's done, it's the same old story: five wins, all over again.

And yet the town finds them enormously lovable. Every year the attendance goes up, thirty, forty, fifty thousand a game. It takes the Orioles a whole week to draw forty thousand people. And not only do

these lunatic fans fill the ballpark every Sunday, but they start form-
ing clubs all around town. The clubs are called Colts Corrals. Their
members seem to build their lives around the team, holding meetings, bringing in team members for speeches, riding chartered buses
together to the ballpark. Eventually, even the state penitentiary's got
its own corral. They do their rooting behind bars. But it connects them,
the same way everybody else is getting connected.

And out of the woodwork come all these Baltimore characters. Fellow named William Andrews was one of the first. He was dubbed Willie the Rooter. He circled the field and led cheers every game, carrying
signs he'd made when he was supposed to be painting cars for a living.
Then, disdaining all warnings from his family, he ignored his car pay-
ments so he could travel to road games with the Colts. At a Christmas
party the night before he died in 1957, when others started singing
"The Twelve Days of Christmas," Willie led choruses of "Let's Go,
You Baltimore Colts."

But his death, at thirty-nine, reinforced the obvious: a bond was
being forged. Willie's pallbearers included some of the Colts. The ball
club gave Willie's family lifetime season tickets and started a drive to
raise money for them. When Steadman went back to the *News-Post*
two weeks after Willie's death, he wrote columns imploring people to
contribute, declaring that Willie's love of the team "typified the quest
for identity that lurks within all of us." Thousands of dollars poured
in. So did replacement characters.

When the '58 season opened, it was Reds Hubbe and Bill Gattus
moving into Willie the Rooter's old spot almost as if by legacy. Others would follow, such as Hurst "Loudy" Loudenslager and Len "Big
Wheel" Burrier. Outsiders look at these grownup men leading ballpark
cheers, awaiting cold late-night flights at the airport after road games,
and say: Get a life. But these outsiders miss the point. For individuals
such as Reds and Gattus and Loudy, this has become the very heart of
their lives.

On that first Sunday of the '58 season, Reds and Gattus bumped
into each other at Memorial Stadium. It felt like Mr. Laurel meeting
Mr. Hardy. Gattus's outfit was a railroad porter's jacket with a match-
ing Colts helmet. Reds and a pal, Buddy Janowicz, carried a Colts banner. They figured they'd work as a team.

Reds and Gattus were a goofy smile in a town that not only tolerated characters but cultivated them. Reds was a diminutive fellow with a shock of red hair who'd had a distinguished peacetime military career. It lasted nine days before the army decided it wasn't working out for anybody. Then he was a mailman who usually remembered to deliver the mail, but not always. Once, it slipped his mind for a few days, so Reds stored all the envelopes in the back of his car. When the post office found it there, it removed him faster than the army had. So Reds landed new work on the waterfront, where he went back to his former sideline profession of booking sports bets.

He sang, too. He sang in bars and restaurants for the hell of it, and he was a well-known crasher of weddings and dances. He'd get dressed up and find somebody to wave to, such as the groom, so everybody thought he belonged there.

The singing matched his partner Gattus's own musical bent. Bill played the saxophone, mostly in the little bar he ran on North Point Road, over on the east side. His dad bought it while Gattus was working the waterfront as a young man. Then Bill took it over. The place had a Colts horseshoe on the big sign out front. Half a century later, it still does, and never mind that Irsay took the team to Indianapolis back in 1984.

Some of the Colts would make it a stopping place over the years. Artie Donovan could be found drinking a series of Schlitz beers there, and Bert Rechichar, too. Unitas would stop in, but he wasn't much of a drinker. The big lineman Lou Michaels finally had to be barred from the place because he'd get a few drinks in him and start smashing pool cues.

"There were a hundred places like that," Donovan said one overcast afternoon in 2006. He was eighty-three now. His voice still cracked like a teenager's. He walked across his kitchen by shifting his hips back and forth a couple of inches at a time, thereby shuffling his whole body forward. The body had slowed, but the mind still held on to its sense of awe.

"I don't know what it was," he said. "All I know is, Baltimore treated us like heroes right from the start. We're getting beat every week, and they're still coming out there. We finally win a game, and they're carrying us off the field on their shoulders like we just won the championship. We got invited everywhere. Bull roasts, oyster roasts. If they found out your wife was having a baby, they'd knit you little blue and white hats. Colts colors, yeah. We were like poor orphans. I think everybody felt sorry for us. I tell you, I still have people come up to me and say, 'Remember me? We had a beer together one time in 1956.'"

At Gattus's bar, they'd charter a bus every Sunday the Colts played at home, and all would gather at ten in the morning. This was going on all over Baltimore: people meeting at bars and climbing onto chartered buses to go to the ballpark together. By the time they got there, some were too drunk to get off the bus. Meanwhile, Gattus would be playing his sax. "Let's go, you Baltimore Colts." It felt like a national anthem. Then he and Reds would lead cheers all afternoon as they marched around the field. It made them feel important. It made everybody feel there was more to life than the assembly line.

But Reds and Gattus were just a part of the cheerful panorama. The Colts were the first team in the league with cheerleaders. They were women from around town who wanted to have a few laughs. They were attractive but nobody's particular beauty contestants. They didn't dress like strippers, and their choreography was elementary. They'd turn themselves in a circle, hopping on one foot. Approaching Christmas, they might put toy antlers on their heads. They were a smile, not soft porn. There was also a horse named Dixie, with a young lady riding her, who circled the field at a gallop every time the team scored. And they had this enormous marching band, all decked out in uniforms. The band members were so proud to be a part of this weekly celebration, they stayed together even when the Colts abandoned Baltimore. They became the only pro football band in history that didn't have a team to root for. When they performed in New England and Raymond Berry coached there, Raymond made it a point to approach them on the field. "I'm proud of each and every one of you," he said. It was twenty years since he'd left Baltimore. But he remembered the old ties.

After the games, Reds and Gattus would ride the bus back to North Point Road, and everybody would stick around for a few more hours while Gattus got up on the bar and played the Colts' fight song on his sax. The two of them made so many friends that Reds figured, what the hell, why not try politics? He ran for city council. Strictly in character, he was the only candidate in Baltimore history who managed to get himself arrested on election day. This was 1971. In the ancient local tradition, other politicians handed out walk-around money to ensure everybody voted. But Reds had only seventy-two dollars in his entire campaign treasury. So he parked across the street from the polling place, School No. Six at Ann and Aliceanna streets down in Fells Point, and handed out walk-around Seagram's 7, saying it was the least he could do on a hot day.

The cops closed in on Reds like he was dynamiting a building. They tossed him into a district lockup, where he stayed until a couple of guys from the carpenters' union raised money to bail him out. When Reds emerged from jail, he grandly told reporters, "The only reason I got arrested was I was coming on strong and my opponents needed to stop me." In a field of twenty-eight candidates, he just missed finishing in the top twenty-five. When he campaigned for office a second time, he blithely announced, "I run not to get arrested."

THIS IS, IN OTHER WORDS, the perfect match of town and team.

By 1958 the Colts are on their way to the championship that will forever change American sports. And they do this out of rejection and defeat. They have Unitas, kissed off by Pittsburgh without getting a chance. The linebacker Bill Pellington, cut by Cleveland, hitchhiked all the way to the Colts' camp for a tryout. The giant tackle Gene "Big Daddy" Lipscomb never went to college, and he cringes as the only player in the league introduced before games with a high school next to his name. He was discovered in the U.S. Marine Corps, where a football scout found him lifting a forty-pound piece of a cannon with his fingertips. Raymond Berry is considered a complete fluke, a pass receiver with bad eyes and a short leg. "When I take my eye test," Berry admits, "I can see that big letter E, but I can't see anything below it." An entire population of adolescent boys hears this and figures: If Berry can do it, why can't I? The halfback Lenny Moore comes out of such poverty that the males in his family slept for a time at the Hope Rescue Mission while the females slept at the Salvation Army. The defensive end Gino Marchetti played college ball only because the coach at Modesto Junior College wanted to recruit Gino's brother Angelo, known as Itzy. So Gino tagged along. The defensive back Andy Nelson played his college ball before crowds of three thousand people. Now he gets in the huddle and hears the defensive captain Pellington screaming at everybody. Nelson tells Donovan, "I'm going home. This guy scares me." Donovan tells him, "Relax. He likes you." The linebacker Bert Rechichar's blind in one eye. The defensive back Milt Davis's legs are so skinny his teammates call him "Pops Willoughby." Much of the roster consists of players rejected by previous teams. Jim Mutscheller was considered too small to play tight end. When Mutscheller joins the Colts, they're playing an exhibition game at Pittsburgh's Forbes Field. His mother comes to watch. She is a proper lady from Beaver Falls, Pennsylvania, accustomed to watching her son play for Notre Dame, where everyone wore the required coat and tie. She watches this team of professionals get off the bus and turns with alarm to her son.

"You can't play football for those people," she says. "Just look at those awful people."

"They're our team, Mom," says Mutscheller.

"I think she was lookin' at me when she said that," Donovan says later.

Maybe. There are plenty of options. Maybe she's looking at Don Joyce, the defensive end who wrestles professionally in the off-season to keep him off the streets. One evening years later, Donovan tells the story of the poor burglar who broke into Joyce's room one night when they're on the road.

"The guy figured the room was empty," Donovan says. "Joyce gives him a forearm shiver, and then he grabs the guy by his testicles and yanks down."

"That must have hurt."

"Yeah," says Donovan, nodding agreement. "Poor Joyce almost pulled his shoulder out."

Or maybe Mrs. Mutscheller's looking at the linebacker Pellington. "If there's anybody who played harder than Pellington," says Donovan, "he must have been an out-patient." His teammates whisper that Pellington should be thrown out of every game for playing dirty. And he's on *their* side. Or Marchetti, who showed up for his first day of college football practice on a motorcycle, wearing a black leather jacket and boots like some future Hell's Angel. Or maybe Big Daddy Lipscomb. He wears size fifty-six suits and custom-made jock straps and tends to party with several women at a time. But he's a softie. When he knocks down ball carriers, he helps them back to their feet.

"What the hell are you doing?" Donovan yells at him. "Let 'em get up themselves."

"I don't want them to think I'm mean," Big Daddy replies.

One night during a road trip to California, the Colts had a team dinner at a restaurant with a large fish tank. Chuck Thompson watched Lipscomb reach one of his huge arms into the tank, trying to snare a fish. He didn't come close. Then John Unitas walked past, dipped one arm in, and instantly grabbed a fish."How'd you do that?" Big Daddy asked.

"Easy," said Unitas. "All you have to do is know the pass route."

Or maybe Mrs. Mutscheller notices Bert Rechichar. One day in Detroit, he tackles the Lions' halfback Howard "Hopalong" Cassady. Cassady complains to a referee that Rechichar scratched him.

"Listen, Cassady," says Rechichar, "we don't scratch in the NFL. That's for kids at Ohio State. We just tear your fuckin' eyeballs out."

That little story is related to John Steadman by the referee who overheard Rechichar. The young Steadman, doing his public relations work, is falling in love with this team. They're such an easy sell. He sends them around to the various churches and civic groups, where the crowds adore their new heroes. And Steadman, thinking about the future, is making notes of all kinds. He files these away. He has made a discovery that he will take with him when he returns to the newspaper business in 1958: Forget describing the ballplayers as gods from Olympus, and forget box scores and touchdowns, too. There are only so many ways to describe the flight of a field goal or the arc of a forward pass. The heart of all reporting is the story of human beings. And Steadman has learned firsthand about these characters on the Colts and knows them as no other reporter ever will.

Such as Sisto Averno, who goes back to the beginning of it all. The Colts sign him out of Muhlenberg College, and he shows up at their first training camp. The Colts want him because he plays both ways. It means they can get twice the action for the same price. One summer night in 2006, we sit around for a while remembering when Sisto was young and strong. Now, bent over, hair wispy and white, he shuffles along with the aid of a walker.

"You remember that first camp?"

"You kidding?" he says.

On that first morning, with the heat already baking the little town of Westminster, Maryland, Averno comes out of the locker room at Western Maryland College and stands next to a stocky guy with a high-pitched voice that goes squeaky whenever he gets excited. It's Donovan. He's a defensive tackle, a beefy, ebullient Irish kid who fought with the marines in World War II. Marchetti's around, too. While Donovan was out in the South Pacific, Marchetti was fighting the Battle of the Bulge. He was eighteen. He remembered lying in the dark with a few dozen guys, and the Germans out there across a narrow strip of geography. Somebody would soak a sock in gasoline and put it in a bottle and then light it up just so the guys could see. But Gino kept most of his war inside him. With Donovan, an instinct for the self-deprecating punch line always covered the real war experience.

"Pretty rough war?" I asked him one time. He served on an aircraft carrier that came under heavy nighttime kamikaze attack, then found himself in a machine gun squad on Okinawa and Guam.

"Never thought I'd get past eighteen," Donovan muttered. But, instinctively, he looked to lighten the moment. His voice rose comically. "The way they kept firing at me, I kept thinking, 'What are they doing, I'm a nice guy.' "

"You should have told them."

"I couldn't get close enough," said Donovan, laughing heartily.

After the war, he played ball at Boston College and then knocked around the pros for a couple of years before settling in with the Colts for a decade. His father was the famous boxing referee Arthur Donovan Sr., who was in the ring when Joe Louis knocked out Max Schmeling in the first round for the heavyweight championship. The Donovans lived on 202nd Street in the Bronx. When the younger Donovan told his father he was going to Baltimore to try out for the Colts, the father hollered through the apartment as loud as he could.

"Mary," he cried to his wife, "don't let Arthur go down to that football camp. Those big guys will kill him." Donovan weighed 270.

Now, on this first day of camp, he and Sisto Averno stand there at the top of a hill. As they look down, all they can see are bodies. Too many bodies, the two men agree. Too many bodies, meaning too much competition for not enough jobs.

"Where you from?" says Donovan.

"Jersey," says Averno.

"Let's go," says Donovan. "I got my car, I'll drop you off. I'm going back to New York."

The two of them turn to go. Donovan figures he can become a cop in New York City; Averno could sell cars in Jersey. Then they hear a voice, John Bridgers's. He's an assistant coach.

"Where you going?" Bridgers asks.

"How many guys you got out there?" says Averno.

"A hundred," says Bridgers. "Maybe 120."

"Looks like 150 to me," says Donovan.

"I was a guard at Muhlenberg," says Averno. "How many guards you gonna keep?"

"Three," says Bridgers.

"Jesus Christ."

"But you'd go both ways," says Bridgers. "That's why we signed you. Sixty minutes."

"See you later," says Averno.

"Where you going?"

"Artie's gonna take me to New Jersey."

"Come on," says Bridgers, "we're gonna separate the men from the boys. Think of the money they're paying you for this."

Averno ponders this for a moment. Bridgers has a point. What the hell, they're talking about four thousand dollars a year if he makes the team. Pretty decent pay. He and Donovan look at each other and exchange what-the-hell shrugs. They start walking down the hill. Then Averno notices something important.

"There's not enough equipment to go around," he tells Donovan.

"So?"

"So, don't take any," Sisto says. "They won't know if we're any good or not."

The two of them go without helmets for a week, as coaches weed out the guys in full gear who butt heads and are found wanting. They both make the team. Donovan will go on to a Hall of Fame career.

Averno, the two-way lineman at six feet and 235 pounds, separates his shoulder at midseason.

"Which one?" the coach says.

"The right."

"So block with the left," the coach says.

Averno doesn't miss a game. They earn little money, but they're young, and they make the best of it. Everywhere they go, Donovan carries his clothes in a battered suitcase his father lugged when he went off to World War I. They're on the road one time, and the old thing falls apart. Sisto spots a U.S. post office and tears the rope off a post office bag. He wraps the rope around Donovan's suitcase. When they get to the team hotel, they're turned away. The suitcase insults everyone's delicate sense of taste.

"They told me I'd have to use the back door," says Donovan.

Everyone who hears Donovan tell the story laughs out loud because they can identify. These ballplayers are right out of their ranks. They're working-class people scuffling for the buck. Even the stars make no money. Unitas moonlights at Bethlehem Steel with an acetylene torch in his hand. Marchetti's setting pins at his cousin's bowling alley until he gets a better job down at Sparrows Point as an iron worker. One time, Ameche and Marchetti talk salary with Don Kellett, the general manager. Kellett makes the mistake of walking out of the office for a moment. Gino, who always had quick reflexes, tells Ameche, "Stand by the door."

"What are you doing?" says the Horse.

"I want to check something."

Now Marchetti reaches into Kellett's desk drawer. He finds the team salary chart. "Man," he says, "Lenny's only making this much. Berry's only making this much." Then they hear Kellett coming back. The two huge men are terrified. Ameche slams the door in Kellett's face. Kellett's pushing with everything he has. Ameche's pushing back. Gino's so fascinated, he can't put the salary list down. Ameche, the former Heisman Trophy winner, the 230-pound fullback, is having trouble holding the door closed against the middle-aged Kellett. Finally Gino puts the list back into the desk. Ameche stops pushing, and Kellett falls into the room.

"You guys were in my desk. You guys were in my desk."

"No," says Ameche, "I was just leaning on the door."

They all have stories like this: of trying to make ends meet while simultaneously reaching for the laugh. And it's Donovan who gives everybody a smile. The ball club sends him around to every group it can find. He gives speeches and signs autographs. When he stops in at local bars, which is often, since he's selling booze for the Schenley whiskey company in his off hours, he becomes the good time had by all. He's the cheery public persona of the Colts. Never mind that football is an animal occupation in which forearms are thrown into Adam's apples—these lugs are Baltimore's animals. They're scrapping for a living the same as those guys on the assembly lines down at the steel mill, same as the ones who built airplanes during the war. Life is tough; you do what you have to do, including knocking each other down. And then you share a few laughs about it, and some food and drink.

And sometimes you spread the good stuff around. One year, when Donovan's working part-time for Schenley, he treats the stadium grounds crew to whiskey. He figures they'll take the bottles home for Christmas. Instead, as the ball club runs through its daily drills, the groundskeepers open the stuff and have themselves a little party. Soon it looks like rain. The field has to be covered with heavy tarpaulin, but the grounds crew has disappeared from all sight. The players are given a directive: they will have to put the tarp on the field themselves. The groundskeepers are later found asleep under the stands.

"You know what I loved right away about Baltimore?" Donovan said one night. We were sitting at the bar at the Valley Country Club, the place he and his wife bought nearly half a century ago. "It was like the Bronx. It was all these ethnic neighborhoods. The only difference was, people in Baltimore lived in row houses and we lived in apartment buildings. But it didn't matter; it was a melting pot. You have to realize, if you're Catholic, Protestant or Jewish, if you come from the Bronx, they say where you from, you say, I'm from St. Philip's Parish. Or, I'm from Christ the King. And that's the feeling I got right away in Baltimore. Neighborhoods. And ethnics. And it hit me as soon as I got here."

WHEN THE 1957 SEASON ARRIVED, some imagined the Colts had finally put everything together. When you got past Unitas's sheer gawkiness—the hunched-over physique, the dangling arms, the under-nourished chest—he was starting to look like something special. He had Ameche and Moore out of the backfield, and Moore and Berry and Mutscheller catching everything he threw their way.

And now he had protection he'd never seen. The Colts drafted Jim Parker out of Ohio State, where he was maybe the greatest lineman in the history of Woody Hayes's grinding running teams.

"We got Mr. Parker," Raymond Berry says one afternoon, "and we never heard from Mr. Atkins again." He means Doug Atkins, the Chicago Bears' huge defensive end. He beats everybody in the league. But, with the arrival of Parker, he no longer beats the Colts.

But Parker fit right in off the field, as well. He had Donovan's sly sense of humor, and he could tell stories all day. The old halfback Buddy Young said, "Parker'll call you up at three in the morning just to tell you a story." Some of them were even true.

In the locker room one day, somebody asks Parker about the big difference between college ball at Ohio State and pro ball with the Colts. Parker doesn't hesitate. "I had to take a cut in pay to turn pro," he says.

"Coach Hayes," Parker says, "used to sit us all down in the locker room before the game. He'd say, 'Now, here's the story. You win today, I'm gonna let the alumni in the locker room after the game. You lose, no alumni.' After the game, you'd put your helmet in front of your locker. Then you go take a shower. Take a real long shower. Come back, your helmet's got money in it from all those alumni."

Parker insists the story's absolutely true. "First time it happened," he says, "I saw all that money in my helmet and went right to the trainer. I said, 'I'm gonna need a much bigger helmet.'"

As the top draft choice of 1957, he signs with the Colts for $12,500. At the Belvedere Hotel, he and his wife sit down with Kellett, the general manager, to talk money. Kellett extends his hand, which holds $1,500 in dollar bills.

"Look at this, son," he says. "You sign, it's yours."

The stack of bills seems enormous, but Parker says he's not sure. Under the table, his wife kicks him as hard as she can.

"Take it, fool," she says.

Now, years later, Parker says, "We went upstairs to our room and put all the bills in the bathtub to look at them. I never saw so much money at one time." He made $12,500 for the season.

"Twelve-five," Donovan says when he hears the story. "When I broke in, that's more than the whole team made."

In '57, it was pretty decent middle-class money. But Parker still needed an off-season job. So he sold embalming fluid for a while. Then he sold cemetery plots. "Sold them for $95," he recalled one day. "Now they're going for $1,400. I should have bought the cemetery." Later Donovan connected him with the folks at Schenley. They gave Parker a liquor distribution route in black neighborhoods. He wound up with a package goods store on Liberty Heights Avenue at Garrison Boulevard that became a landmark in northwest Baltimore.

"A guy came into my place one day," Parker recalled one afternoon, "and he says, 'Hey, some white man just took six Schlitzes, let's call the police.' I said, 'Nah, he's a friend of ours.' "

"Yeah," said Donovan, sitting nearby, "I never did pay you for that six-pack I took."

In a neighborhood that was turning rough, the cops loved having Parker around. He'd help them grab troublemakers on the street. One day Parker grabbed a young beat cop named Howard Glasshoff.

"You ever get in any kind of trouble out there," he said, gesturing to the street, "you come in and get me. I'll take care of you."

This is Parker telling the city cop: Don't worry, I'll protect you. And the cop remembering it all these years later.

The Colts immediately loved Parker's playing skills, but they weren't happy with his weight. Like Donovan, he seemed to inhale food. Donovan devoured kosher hot dogs, and then struggled to get rid of the weight. Donovan was so bad, he had a clause in his contract saying he had to play at 270 pounds. So, every Friday, Don Joyce picked him up and the two buffaloes would head for a steam room at Calvert and Saratoga streets. They'd stay until 10:30 in the morning, shower, and then head for the weigh-in.

"I step on the scales," Donovan says one afternoon, "and it says 275. I take off my sweatshirt and drop two pounds. My pants, that's another pound and a half. My underwear, I'm down to 270½. Still too much. So I take out my false teeth. Hey, I got onto that scale just the way I came into the world, no clothes, no teeth, no nothing."

The confession becomes a comic routine, repeated for all listeners across those years. Here's our boy Artie, naked as a jaybird before our very eyes. You want intimacy in sports, you got it right there.

To take the pounds back off, sometimes Donovan put on a rubber suit and hopped into a whirlpool bath. Parker took it a step further. In the heat of training camp, he put on a rubber suit, got into his car, and turned the heat all the way up. Parker drove around this way for an hour.

"That only worked for a while," Donovan said. "After a while, when Jim locked himself in the car, he locked food in with him." He said this fifty years later, as we sat in his kitchen. Then he shuffled across the floor to the refrigerator and opened up the freezer. There, on shelf after shelf, were stacks of kosher hot dogs.

They all fought the same fights. Pellington would sit in his training camp room, leaning over the edge of the bed, repeatedly spitting onto the floor. Joyce would have raw beef stashed in his locker. He'd plunge into it as soon as he passed weigh-in. Big Daddy Lipscomb once had a whole turkey and sweet potato pie waiting in front of his locker when he got off the scale.

"You're gonna eat yourself right out of the league," Weeb Ewbank scolded him. Lipscomb, who weighed 288, started to swing the whole thing at the coach. A couple of guys grabbed him.

"What are you doing?" Ewbank hollered.

"He was hungry," Parker explained.

SO IT WAS A TEAM of characters who came to training camp in 1957. And, like Big Daddy, they were hungry.

That included the owner, Carroll Rosenbloom, and the coach, the fussy Wilbur "Weeb" Ewbank. Week after week, Rosenbloom saw the wunderkind Unitas throwing to Berry and wondered why his ball club kept losing more than it won. He saw Ameche running over tacklers inside and Moore running away from them everywhere else. He saw Donovan and Marchetti tearing apart opposing ball carriers. Yet, going into the final game of 1956, the Colts had won four games out of eleven.

This frustrated Rosenbloom on many levels. He was a highly competitive man and a risk taker. Around Baltimore, rumors of his gambling were rampant. The players heard the talk and tried to put it out of their mind. Ewbank heard it, too. But Weeb was afraid to ask Rosenbloom about it. All he knew for sure was that Rosenbloom had friends who were serious gamblers.

One of them was the east-side bookmaker Constantine "Gussie" Huditean, who claimed Rosenbloom placed bets with him every week. Huditean ran Gussie's Downbeat, the Eastern Avenue night spot beneath the Chinese laundry. Most weeks, the betting would have Huditean winning and Rosenbloom losing. Whenever Ewbank saw Rosenbloom with his pals, all they talked about was point spreads. They kept going the wrong way. By the last week of the year, with the Colts at four wins and seven losses, Rosenbloom decided the fault lay with Ewbank. Thus, Weeb's job was on the line as the Colts played the Washington Redskins to conclude the '56 season two days before Christmas.

It was a raw, rainy, miserable afternoon at Memorial Stadium. Washington was fighting for a second-place Eastern Conference finish, but the Colts were mainly playing out the string. With twenty-five seconds left, they had the ball on their own forty-seven-yard line. They trailed, 17 to 12. Unitas sent everybody long, no different than schoolboys playing in the street. He threw the ball about as far as he could. The Redskins' defensive back Norb Hecker went up, and so did the Colts' Mutscheller. Hecker had better position but never caught the ball. It bounced off his chest and came down in Mutscheller's arms at the five-yard line. Mutscheller had tacklers draped all over him. He carried them into the end zone. Ewbank held on to his job.

When the team reported to Western Maryland College the following summer, it seemed to a lot of observers a different kind of training camp. Ewbank was acting tougher. He knew he'd flirted with professional extinction the previous fall, and it changed him. Shape up, he told his players, or pay the price. Fines were fifty dollars and a hundred dollars, pretty big money in those days. Lights out by eleven. No showing up late for meetings. "I'm doing this for you," he told the players, who grumbled about it but began noticing a change in their lives: they were winning ball games that had once gotten away.

In Ewbank, the Colts had a man they respected and sometimes mocked. Donovan called him a rat bastard and a weasel, depending on his vocabulary of the moment. He didn't like Weeb's discipline.

Later he'd admit, "Weeb's the guy who made us into football players." Berry thought Weeb was practically a genius and loved his attention to detail.

They opened in '57 against Detroit, a team of confident veterans. In two of the last three years, they had won titles. They were led by quarterback Bobby Layne, who was famous for two things: drinking large quantities of whiskey, and then winning big. The Lions tried to block Marchetti with three men. Gino overwhelmed them all. He nailed Layne repeatedly. Once, he ripped Layne's jersey from his back. When Marchetti didn't get him, Donovan did. Late in the fourth quarter, Donovan landed atop Layne. As he got up, the big tackle blanched.

"My God, Layne, you reek," he said. "What did you do, tie one on last night?"

"Hell, no," said Layne. "Halftime."

The Colts win, 34 to 14, as Unitas throws four touchdown passes. Then they win again, beating the Chicago Bears, the defending conference champion, by 21 to 10. The Bears have an explosive running game of Rick Casares and Willie Galimore. Together, they gain twenty-nine yards all day against the bruising Colts' line. They have the great outside receiver Harlon Hill. He gets nothing against the Colts' defensive back Milt Davis.

Meanwhile Unitas throws two more touchdown passes, both on fourth down, both on plays the quarterback calls himself. He seems capable and utterly fearless—not to mention, he's nothing like the lunkhead the Steelers called him when they cut him. This guy understands football. He can read defenses. He knows what every player on the team is supposed to do on every play.

"He'd come up with a play we hadn't used since training camp," Jim Mutscheller will recall years later, "and we're all going, 'My God, what do I do on that play?' But he knew. He always knew."

After two weeks, the Colts are the only undefeated team in their division. After three weeks, it's only better. They beat Green Bay 45 to 17. On the radio, announcer Chuck Thompson casually mentions when the club will arrive home. At Friendship Airport that night, Reds and Gattus show up with a Colts banner. They turn around and discover they are not alone. Five thousand others are there to welcome the team.

Then, for three straight weeks, the bottom falls out.

In Detroit, they fumble five times and blow a 27 to 3 lead in the third quarter. They lose, 31 to 27. Nobody can believe it. As they wait for the team bus to take them to the airport, some of them head for a nearby tavern. Donovan's sitting near Big Daddy Lipscomb when a bunch of Detroit fans come into the place and recognize the ballplayers. They start to taunt them. Lipscomb rises from his seat. He doesn't want to hear any of this. The fans head for the door. Lipscomb heads after them. They start running down the street. Lipscomb chases them until they're out of sight.

It's comic relief, but only briefly. A week later, against Green Bay, they lose in the final minute. Against Pittsburgh, they lose by six. Then, with Ewbank's job once again on the line, he gathers everybody in the locker room before the game.

"Fellas," he tells them, "we're not out of this race yet. But we've gotta win today. Now, before I came up here, Gino asked if he could talk to the team before we take the field." Marchetti, the team leader, looks around. He's standing in the back of the room.

He turns to Ordell Braase and says, "Who in the hell told him that?"

"Everybody out," Ewbank says. "Coaches, equipment managers, everybody out."

Marchetti walks to the front of the room. "Everybody know there's a party at my house after the game?" he says.

"Yeah, Gino," a bunch of voices answer back.

"Well, let's go out and win the damn game, and that way we'll have a lot more fun."

Then they went out and beat Washington. Berry catches twelve passes for an astonishing 224 yards. The next morning's paper says, "Colts Win on Inspirational Talk by Marchetti." The next week they beat Chicago when Donovan nails quarterback Zeke Bratkowski so hard that he fumbles, and Marchetti falls on the ball in the end zone.

In Baltimore, they beat San Francisco on a sandlot play known as a flea-flicker. Unitas tosses a long lateral to Cotton Davidson, who's in the game as a halfback. Davidson laterals back across the field to Unitas, who throws long to Lenny Moore.

In the final home game of the season, they clobber Los Angeles.

With two games left, they hold the conference lead by a game over Detroit and San Francisco. Baltimore cannot believe what is happening. The city has never had a modern ball club—not the Colts, not the Orioles—with a better than .500 record, let alone threatening to win a championship. Its last title of any kind was the turn-of-the-century Orioles of Wee Willie Keeler and John McGraw. Now, if the Colts can beat San Francisco, they assure themselves of nothing worse than a tie. But it feels funny. The air up here is too thin. It feels like something terrible is going to happen, which it does.

Late in the fourth quarter the Colts seem headed for defeat when Unitas teams with Moore. Eighty-two yards and a touchdown. They nurse a 13 to 10 lead into the last two minutes. Then, with the final seconds ticking away, the 49ers' Y. A. Tittle connects with Hugh McElhenny at the Colts' forty-five, and McElhenny eludes tacklers all the way to the fifteen. On third down, an injured Tittle is carried off the field. Rookie John Brodie enters the game. On fourth down, with seconds left on the clock, he hits McElhenny in the end zone. The enraged Colts claim offensive pass interference by McElhenny. They say he pushed off his defender. Primitive TV coverage fails to pick up the contact. San Francisco wins, 17 to 13.

The gods have turned against Baltimore; it is what the town half expected all along.

With one game left, the Colts are now in a three-way tie with San Francisco and Detroit. The next week, they are crushed by Los Angeles, 37 to 21. As they used to say in Brooklyn, Wait 'til next year.

THE HOMELY GIRL

ON FEBRUARY 15, 1958, the snow started falling all over Baltimore. At first it was beautiful to watch as it covered all kinds of things beginning to splinter and decay, such as entire neighborhoods. By evening, there was a milky glow beneath street lamps, and some remarked wistfully that it was a shame the snow was too late for Christmas.

Then, when it refused to stop, the downfall pushed aside all thoughts of gauzy sugar-plum nostalgia. At city hall, municipal road crew administrators assured Mayor Tommy D'Alesandro they would do their best to keep the streets clear. D'Alesandro, a short, dapper, mustachioed man in a dark suit with a bow tie, listened attentively but in his heart knew better.

He had been mayor since 1947 and understood how the game was played. D'Alesandro was helped into office by a political boss named James H. "Jack" Pollack, a former prize fighter and fixer of traffic tickets who liked to recite poetry to show he had some class. Pollack made his money during Prohibition, skirting the law here and there. He put together a pretty strong political organization, the Trenton Democratic Club, with six hundred members eventually operating out of a Park Heights Avenue clubhouse. On election days during the depression,

Pollack would sit with a gun on his desk and hand people five bucks or nylon hose or other goodies to do a few hours' work getting out the vote, in a time when some people weren't making five dollars in a week. This made him a god. It created loyalties across a couple of generations. When he helped Tommy D'Alesandro get elected mayor, Pollack wanted something in return. One day he called city hall.

"I got a couple of guys I want you to put on the city payroll," he said.

"What do they do?" asked D'Alesandro.

"They don't do anything," Pollack said.

"Good," said D'Alesandro, "we won't have to break 'em in."

So now, in the winter of '58, the mayor knew better than to trust these brilliant and accomplished men telling him not to worry about his roads. The cleanup would ultimately rest in the hands of entire squadrons of do-nothings and incompetents. The town's three daily newspapers, rushing their delivery trucks onto the messy streets before snow began accumulating, were already urging everyone to conserve food and fuel "until the crisis is over." So Baltimoreans did what they have always done in snow emergencies. They rushed to the nearest stores to buy what they considered the bare essentials: toilet paper and beer.

When they got to their food stores, they found their neighbors lined up like Russians and the shelves emptying in a frenzy. At Eddie's Supermarket in this winter of '58, potatoes were the usual ten pounds for thirty-nine cents. Customers grabbed with both hands. At the A&P, hot dogs were two pounds for ninety-seven cents. They went flying from shelves. At the Acme Supermarket, five pounds of sugar went for thirty-seven cents. And, most important, at the corner liquor store, a six-pack of the local favorite, National Bohemian Beer, went for ninety-nine cents. This, according to all municipal tradition, disappeared quickest.

The snow fell and it did not stop. It fell on houses where people huddled from the cold, and it fell on impassable streets where cars were soon splayed about and abandoned by the hundreds. It fell on downtown's Stanley Theater, where no one showed up to watch *Ol' Yeller*, the children's tale of a frontier dog, and it fell on the Century Theater, where no one showed up to watch *Peyton Place* despite its overtones of torrid adult sensuality. This was just as well, since the members of the Maryland Censor Board, sitting in their dark little room on Calvert Street with their scissors and their sexual discomfitures, had already snipped out any of the good parts. The newspapers that managed to get out the next day headlined, "Don't Let Kiddies Stay Out Too Long" as the temperature plunged to five degrees and a wet and blustery wind sliced across the frozen landscape.

The streets were clogged and mostly impassable, but after a day or so fathers everywhere got wise. They put on galoshes, bid good-bye to their families, and marched off. There was no completed Baltimore Beltway yet, and no Jones Falls Expressway. It did not matter. The fathers grabbed snow shovels and dug out their cars. Or they climbed onto any bus or streetcar able to move. If they had to walk to work, then they walked. Somehow they managed to get there, while the mothers stayed home with the children. This is what people did in 1958. Soon, as the children remained home from school day upon day, the mother would commence tearing out her hair and envying her husband out there in the snow.

"Put on Miss Nancy," she told the six-year-old who was bored by 9 a.m.

So the six-year-old turned on the television and watched the *Romper Room* program for preschool children. This featured a woman named Nancy Claster, called Miss Nancy, who wore a perpetual smile while hyperkinetic children tugged at her sleeves. She worked in a classroom setting with half a dozen children each day. It was intended to look like a typical Baltimore classroom, though all the TV children, morning after morning in 1958, were white. Miss Nancy was the idyllic female role model for her time, in pearls and neatly pressed dress, a local version of that nice Miss Landers, who taught school on *Leave It to Beaver.*

Miss Nancy was a guiding figure for young mothers, who were overwhelmingly stay-at-home housewives when *Romper Room* opened its doors. (The list of 1958's Ten Most Admired Women offers a clue. Most were famous without actually doing anything, such as Queen Elizabeth and Mamie Eisenhower and Princess Margaret. And Grace Kelly, who had given up movies but managed to marry well.) It was a time of

throwback perceptions that were about to change. America still imagined its children might grow up well mannered and still imagined all
women as desiring nothing more than staying home to raise families,
even during snowstorms when the children did not leave the house for
days at a time.

Miss Nancy never seemed to break a sweat dealing with all these
children who had adrenaline bursting out of their pores.

"Miss Nancy," some child would say.

"Just a minute, please."

The kid was yanking at her sleeve while Miss Nancy gazed into a
camera and tried to charm her way through the middle of this snowfall. Meanwhile, unless the *Romper Room* children were banging on
drums, the kids at home were getting itchy. This is the first generation to grow up with sun-up to postmidnight television. In 1950, there
were 3.1 million TV sets in America. By 1955, it was 32 million. By
1958, the average family's watching six hours of television a day. These
families are the first generation to remember when television began.
Sometimes they turn on the set and see nothing but test patterns.
Sometimes the dreaded vertical flip does not cease. They can watch
Howdy Doody five days a week while eating dinner. Nobody has ever
eaten dinner in front of moving pictures before this. Parents will tell
children, "Don't sit too close, you'll ruin your eyes." It's still too early
to know whether this is true, but why take a chance? By the time
these kids reach adolescence, they will have watched twenty thousand
hours of the tube. They are becoming sensitized to the new pace of the
world, to ninety-second rock and roll songs with Atomic Age beats, to
thirty-second TV commercials with rolls of dancing toilet paper. The
kids understood something that neither Miss Nancy nor the young
mothers at home yet understood: they had no patience. By 1958 the
world was beginning to speed up beyond anyone's expectations, and
this whole generation of kids needed attention, and fast. The pace of
TV would have to be speeded up to hold on to the viewers' narrowing
attention spans, their diminishing thresholds of boredom. And this
was just the beginning of the country's cultural speedup, which was
about to make the game of football seem so timely and the languid
rituals of baseball seem so sleepy and outdated.

By 1958, Little Richard and Elvis were pushing Bing Crosby and Perry Como off the Top 40 charts. In Baltimore, the musical sea change was personified by television's *Buddy Deane Show*, where "the nicest kids in town" jitterbugged six afternoons a week. *Courtesy Baltimore News-American Collection, Marylandia and Special Collections, University of Maryland Libraries*

Now, some time before noon, as the great Baltimore snowfall lay on the ground, the fourteen-year-old in the house emerged from wintry slumber to announce boredom equaling the six-year-old's.

"Read the newspaper," the mother said. She stubbed out the fourth of the day's Winstons while washing the previous night's dishes by hand. "Learn something."

At the kitchen table, the fourteen-year-old picked up the newspaper and learned he was about to expire. The *News-Post* carries Walter Winchell, who writes this week, "The U.S. has stockpiled enough strategic material to see the nation through three years of war. Unfortunately, the next war might last three minutes." Then the fourteen-year-old reads about his state college, the University of Maryland, "once known as the football and panty-raid school," now beginning to crack down academically. This is nearly as tragic as the nuclear war threat. In one semester nearly eight hundred students flunk out.

Worse, the school's football team is beginning to be awful. Everyone says America must get serious about schooling now that the Russians have launched Sputnik into the heavens and will soon be raining bombs down on us from outer space. Then the fourteen-year-old reads that city council members are worried about sexually suggestive movies playing in first-run theaters. He checks the movie listings and sees that *Song of Bernadette* and *South Pacific* are currently playing. He wonders what in the world these uptight grownups are talking about.

And he tosses aside the newspaper and retreats to his bedroom to play music on the radio. It will not be Percy Faith. He turns on WCAO, which is cornering the market among Baltimore teenagers, and hears Little Richard singing, "A-wop-bop-a-loo-bop-a-lop-bam-boom." Cole Porter, not yet dead, spins in his professional grave.

The mother, lighting up another Winston, calls out from the kitchen, "Turn down that music," in a voice that can be heard in Finksburg. The fourteen-year-old, on the telephone by now, does not hear a word of it. Little Richard is followed by Elvis Presley, though this will soon change. The newspapers show photos of Presley and his parents as he readies for induction into the U.S. Army. Presley reportedly spent his last civilian day in bed, "after attending an all-night roller skating party." The first generation of Elvis impersonators will quickly be assembled: Ricky Nelson, Frankie Avalon, Fabian, white boys from nice families who know better than to wiggle their midsections in public.

So the snow lay all over Baltimore, and it paralyzed just about everything.

Only the gambling set seemed oblivious. The city had a sprightly collection of such folks, undeterred by the various laws that equated wagering with high crime. As the veteran vice squad cop George Andrew observed, "People in this town will bet on anything. They'll bet on two raindrops sliding down a window pane. They'll bet on which elevator reaches the lobby first." Andrew once led a raid on the home of a big-time bookmaker. He carried a sixteen-pound maul and used it to smash in the bookie's front door. As the cops charged into the fellow's bedroom, they discovered him in bed with a lady not precisely his wife.

"Lieutenant Andrew," said the gambler. "Am I glad to see you."

"What's that supposed to mean?" said Andrew, reaching for his handcuffs.

"When I heard that door crash open," said the gambler, "I thought it was this lady's husband."

In other words, beyond all else—beyond vice squad raids and beyond snowstorms—the games would go on. Mark Kram, an old Baltimore newspaper guy, wrote a piece about the city for *Sports Illustrated* and called it "A Wink at a Homely Girl." (It was taken from H. L. Mencken's epitaph: "If you've cause to please my ghost, forgive some sinner and wink at a homely girl.") Kram wrote, "Don't knock it as a sports town, say the blue collars who are always in the side-street bars when shadows start climbing up factory walls. They say it next to a draft beer and a sports section opened to the racing page. From which the eyes never veer. Looking for a number, looking for an edge, looking for a chance to make tomorrow different from today, or just looking. By bar light or kitchen light, by neon or track light, with racing form or scratch sheet, with money or with no money."

Life had to be more than the daily tediousness at Sparrows Point's steel mills or the assembly line at Crown Cork and Seal, and people who helped remove such dreariness for a little while were regarded with admiration in their little groups, much like Reds and Gattus leading Colts cheers. They lifted each day a little beyond the ordinary. But this was winter. With the snow falling so heavily, the city couldn't even offer pro wrestling at its dreary little Coliseum or a boxing card at Carlin's Park. This made horse racing the only game around as the first flakes began to descend that February afternoon.

Pimlico Race Course was closed, so roughly five thousand people ventured to the track at Bowie, about an hour from Baltimore in the best of weather in 1958. They arrived by car and by train, including some of Baltimore's known gambling professionals. Among them was the immaculately dressed Philip Silbert, also known as Pacey; his associate, the affable Jesse Bondroff; and Nookie Brown, known to God as Daniel Brozowsky and to bettors as Nookie the Bookie.

In gambling circles, this was still the time of the greased palm. Once, Pacey was seen on an east Baltimore street corner holding a small stack of betting slips when he was approached by a veteran police officer. Instinctively, Pacey reached into his pocket, pulled out a twenty-dollar bill, and dropped it onto the sidewalk.

"Excuse me, officer," said Pacey, looking to pay his way out of this slight pickle in the usual manner. "Did you drop that twenty on the ground?"

"Not me," said the officer. "I dropped a fifty."

Nookie the Bookie, whose regular place of business consisted of a Heyward Avenue telephone booth outside Pimlico Race Course, likewise found himself in a delicate position owing to money. Nookie, five feet five, lived with his sister and parted with money only with great reluctance. As he was lunching at Miller's Delicatessen on Reisterstown Road one day, a fellow placed a small pistol at his head and declared, "Nookie, you got trouble. You owe me three hundred bucks, and you're gonna pay me the money right now, or . . . "

"Or, what?" said Nookie.

"Or get out of town," the guy said menacingly.

Nookie asked him to wait a minute. He started walking from table to table, conferring with friends. He whispered to one guy here, another there. All shook their heads earnestly. Finally he walked back to the guy with the gun.

"How did you make out?" the guy asked.

"Terrible," said Nookie. "Nobody had a suitcase to lend me."

So now, on the day of the great snowstorm, there were Pacey and Nookie, looking to do a little business at Bowie. The snow accumulated, and they did not move. Nor did most of the five thousand in attendance. The snow reached sixteen inches by late afternoon and kept on coming. As daylight faded to dusk, it began to occur to these brilliant horse players: How will we make the trek home to Baltimore? Their cars were now immovable, as were buses and trains. Sympathetic officials at the Pennsylvania Railroad belatedly announced they would dispatch a special train to Bowie but had no idea when it might plow its way through the enormous snowdrifts.

As they waited into the night, with a small supply of sandwiches exhausted, many at the racetrack went to sleep. They curled up on benches and tables. Some slept on the floor. Pacey and Nookie, restless types, got themselves into a game of craps. The game was going fine, suckers lined up everywhere, when the special ten-car train finally reached the little Bowie station by the track. Then someone hollered, "The train's coming," and all began to run for it. A man shooting craps for $120 jumped up and left all his money behind. Pacey and Nookie, always loath to part with the merest dime, astonishingly did the same. They would bemoan "the money on the ground" for years to come. A *Baltimore Sun* account described the horse players swarming out of the clubhouse and grandstand "like extras in a DeMille spectacular," storming the train so ferociously that women were knocked off their feet.

There was room for 840 people in the ten cars, but 1,700 somehow jammed their way in. Many smoked cigarettes, causing at least four women to faint. "There was barely room to carry them out," said one passenger. Some climbed onto baggage racks above seats. Others rode in the small vestibules between cars. Even in the war years, there hadn't been such cramming. A conductor had to push a customer off so he could make room for himself.

As the temperature fell to five degrees, ten people around Baltimore died from exposure, and scores were reported missing. The snow fell on telephone wires that sagged dangerously close to the ground, and it fell on trolley tracks where streetcars breathed their last and collapsed in the middle of Greenmount Avenue and 33rd Street. It fell across downtown's Howard Street, the city's busy shopping hub, where Hutzler's and Hecht's department stores closed their doors early, as did Hoschild-Kohn's and Stewart's and the May Company. As the snow approached twenty inches, authorities termed it the worst storm disaster in state history.

In scores of neighborhoods that week, people stayed under bedcovers because their power failed them and this was the only way to stay warm. The timing was just beautiful. Four weeks earlier, the Baltimore Gas and Electric Company requested a 6½ percent rate hike, thus bringing the average utility bill in 1958 to $108.90—per year.

Some had other worries. When Mrs. Joan Hoffbert awakened at her Wilshire Avenue home at four o'clock on the morning of the second day of snow, she felt her first labor pains. The streets were impassable. Her husband, Howard, tried to get an ambulance and found none available. He called police. They were sorry, but their cars were paralyzed. The Hoffberts put on their clothes. Then they trudged half a mile through snowdrifts up to their waist before they spotted a moving police car, which finally delivered them on time to Mercy Hospital.

Boy Scouts on a camping weekend in Harford County were stranded for three days before army snow trucks rescued them. When a ten-mile traffic backup left thousands stranded on Baltimore's Pulaski Highway, army helicopters from Fort Meade were made available to help stranded motorists. The city still had public baths in 1958, but nobody showed up. A city spokesman declared, "In this weather, I'd stay dirty too, wouldn't you?" Bon Secours Hospital nearly ran out of fuel, and so did St. Agnes Hospital. To save whatever power remained, the heat was turned off late at night in all cell blocks at the Maryland Penitentiary. The newspapers reported several cases of homeless people walking into police stations, where they asked to be locked up. "It's cold out there," said Charlie Duff, thirty-nine, at Northeastern District. Police made him their guest for the night.

And schools across the area remained closed for the week, thus thrilling both students and teachers. The dispirited teachers welcomed any excuse to miss work. Two weeks before the snow, Governor Theodore R. McKeldin vetoed a pay raise that would have given them an extra eight dollars a week. In this time when baby-boom children were sometimes packed nearly forty to a classroom, starting pay for Baltimore teachers was $4,000 a year and topped out at $6,500. Thus, year after year, schoolchildren chuckled knowingly to each other that even the city's garbage collectors earned more than their teachers.

So the snow sits there, and now the fourteen-year-old and the six-year-old emerge once again from their rooms. Between the morning's *Romper Room* and this late afternoon hour, the mother has found time to watch her own television shows. She watches *Quiz Club,* a local game show with Jay Grayson and Brent Gunts. The two men run around like lunatics, while the children wander into the living room to sit with the mother. They are witnessing the future, in which grown-ups will conduct themselves with all the dignity and self-discipline of preschoolers. For here comes a network variation of *Quiz Club,* called *The Price Is Right,* in which grownups scream like banshees— "Freeze! Freeze! Higher! Higher"—over new refrigerators and washing machines, thus enabling the children to learn their first important lessons of blind greed.

But the fourteen-year-old is here for something else. It is the Buddy Deane dance program, shown live six afternoons a week from Television Hill, just off west Baltimore's Druid Hill Park. Deane plays "Skinny

Minnie," by Bill Haley and the Comets. The mother gets up from the living room couch. She thinks, What is happening to these children? Deane plays "Breathless," by Jerry Lee Lewis. The mother thinks, "Why can't they listen to Patti Page?" as she heads for the kitchen to find her pack of Winstons. Patti Page is marketed as the Singing Rage. Her hit song is called "How Much Is That Doggie in the Window." In 1958 grownup music, this is what passes for a singing rage.

The parents are upset. With new postwar spending power, teens are now buying 70 percent of all records, in a market previously dominated by more sensible twenty-somethings. The music will follow the money. Not only is rock and roll beginning to take over, but so is a youth-oriented culture that threatens the very foundation of "normalcy" and "family togetherness," as personified by the parents' generation and their marvelous role models. For example, if rock and roll takes over, what will happen to that fine, upstanding Bing Crosby, who plays reverent priests in the movies and sings "White Christmas" and has a twenty-three-year-old son named Dennis?

Oops, bad example.

In May 1958, the son Dennis marries a showgirl who previously dated an older man. The older man she dated? Why, Papa Bing himself. Two days later, the story gets a little more complex when Dennis, on his honeymoon, receives news of a paternity suit that's been filed against him by a young switchboard operator.

All right, the parents tell their children, here's a better morality lesson: those terrible youth movies today. (The first-run Hippodrome's showing *High School Confidential*. The newspaper ads declare, "Behind these 'nice' school walls—a teacher's nightmare . . . a teenage jungle.") If such films are allowed to corner the market, what will happen to such upstanding stars as Lana Turner, whose movies and lifestyle set such a fine example for all America?

Oops, bad example.

In April 1958 the headlines read, "Lana Turner's Daughter Kills Mother's Boy Friend." The boyfriend is a mobster named Johnny Stompanato. "Stabs Hoodlum to Death in Star's Pink Bedroom," the headlines cry.

All right, then, what about such fine Hollywood examples as Rhonda

Fleming (filing for divorce) and Deborah Kerr (filing for divorce) and Rita Hayworth (marrying for fifth time) and Mickey Rooney (divorcing for fourth time) and Jack "Dragnet" Webb (marrying for third time) and that nice Debbie Reynolds and Eddie Fisher (splitting so Eddie can run off with that not-so-nice Elizabeth Taylor)?

Well, never mind all that, say the parents. Why can't you listen to more serious music than rock and roll? Broadway show tunes, for example. There's a story in the evening paper that spring about Queen Elizabeth herself joining the crowds to see *My Fair Lady*.

Oops.

"Did Queen Blush at 'My Fair Lady'?" asks the newspaper headline. The story says, "She blushed a shade of royal pink" as the play's Eliza Doolittle, attending the posh Ascot horse race, breaks all decorum to yell, "Come on, Dover, move your bloomin' arse!"

The kids read this and think, This is what upsets the adults? This piffle? They turn away from their parents' music and their parents' movies. Also, their parents' television shows. Even *Hit Parade*, for years the weekly barometer of pop music, has been taken off the air, the victim of too many embarrassing attempts by the show's old-shoe regulars to sing "Hound Dog" or "Tutti Frutti" without looking like idiots. The adults are left with Dinah Shore, who blows them a kiss and asks them to see the USA in their Chevrolet. Or Arthur Godfrey, offering them Julius LaRosa. Or Ed Sullivan giving them the ventriloquist Señor Wences talking to his hand.

So the kids watch Buddy Deane. All over Baltimore, teenage girls force their younger brothers to jitterbug with them in the living room. If there are no little brothers, the teenage girls dance with other teenage girls, or with brooms or bedposts, or with refrigerator doors that they swing back and forth.

And their parents' fear of the new music spreads like a virus. In the spring of '58, rock and roll shows will be banned in Boston and New Haven. The famous disc jockey Alan Freed declares, "It looks like the police in Boston don't want you kids to have any fun." The cops say rock and roll produces fights.

Then the *Baltimore Sun* sounds its own alarm. The newspaper is normally one of the nation's most serious. It prides itself on its

Washington bureau, its overseas bureaus, its sense of sobriety when covering the most important business of the whole world.

But now, it runs a series of articles on the great threat rock and roll presents to the Republic. In adult minds, the music represents the sum of all fears. In the minds of their children who chance to read the newspaper, it is a great hilarity. Here is how the newspaper series opens:

"Ooo . . . eee . . . ooo . . . ah . . . ah . . . ting . . . tang . . . walla . . . walla . . . bing . . . bang . . ."

The sounds come out of a song called "Witch Doctor." The *Sun* writer is attempting to capture the threat of rock and roll and the decay into which popular lyrics have sunk. The newspaper declares that the song has "bludgeoned" its way to the top of Baltimore's Top Forty charts. It is "a raucous ditty with a jungle beat." (In a racially sensitive time, such words are not chosen lightly. In fact, however, the song has a light, almost Tin Pan Alley beat.) It does not occur to the great thinkers at the *Sun* that "Witch Doctor" is intended to be a good-natured comic trifle, suitable for laughter instead of threat, and has reached the top of the charts mainly because eleven-year-olds find it a hoot.

"A survey of local radio stations," the *Sun* declares ominously, "shows the music seeker finds 'rock and roll' or heavy-beat, country-style rhythm virtually supreme at various peak listening hours. For years, WFBR screened out 'rock and roll' and other guitar-twanging rhythm tunes regarded as hillbilly or junk but a few months ago lowered the bar and put them on the air."

The reason is simple: this is the music that is now selling. The newspaper quotes Alan Drake, the popular WCAO disc jockey. He says he "tried to play some Benny Goodman, Artie Shaw and Glenn Miller" on his nighttime show. Immediately, he says, a teenage girl called him on the studio phone.

"Hey, Drake," she piped, "are you ill?"

"Other disc jockeys," the paper reports, "bear him out. Many of these disc jockeys play at 'record hops,' meaning they spin records at some high school or auditorium." The newspaper delivers these findings in quotation marks so as to distance itself from any prior knowledge of the term. It's as though it has uncovered some alien culture and not the thing happening in the homes of its own reporters and editors. The paper reports that WCAO's ratings jumped into first place just eight weeks after switching to its rock and roll format. It now has more listeners, according to Nielsen ratings, than any other two stations combined and more teenagers than any other two stations combined.

Here is the future at the editors' doorstep, and they are looking down their collective noses at it. Later they will wonder why they are losing a generation of readers. In 1958 the adults are listening to Perry Como sing "Catch a Falling Star" and wondering why their kids are falling asleep. Meanwhile the kids are listening to the Everly Brothers sing "All I Have to Do Is Dream." The Silhouettes are singing "Get a Job." Danny and the Juniors are doing "At the Hop." The kids are laughing and dancing, and their parents are cringing in fear.

John Waters, who will make movies a few years later that will further terrify adults, is a junior high school kid in Baltimore in '58. He's watching Buddy Deane every day. He's also playing the radio, mostly the black stations, to listen to disc jockeys named Fat Daddy and Rockin' Robin and Hot Rod and long, lean Larry Dean.

"It was such a peculiar time," Waters remembers half a century later. "All the white kids were discovering black music. And you've got these black musicians coming on *The Buddy Deane Show*, and thirteen-year-old white girls standing around and clapping for them. That was okay. But nobody could dance together."

It was enough for adults to deal with the music, much less the racial issues tangled into it. In '58 advertisements in national magazines urge adults to buy the new high-fidelity record players "for your college students—so they can play Brahms, Tchaikovsky, Lester Lanin and his orchestra, Strauss," as though their college kids have never heard of rock and roll. Or perhaps the adults consider it a mere phase the youngsters are passing through on the way to enlightenment. Later everyone will call this a generation gap and wonder how such a thing could have happened.

So the fourteen-year-old settled in front of the TV set to watch *The Buddy Deane Show*. It was the most popular local TV show in Baltimore and had higher ratings than any locally produced program anywhere in America. It would run from 1957 to 1964, when its racial segregation became too big an embarrassment. While the rest of the country watched Dick Clark's *American Bandstand*, out of Philadelphia, Baltimore had Buddy instead. He stood there at the historic junction where Eddie Fisher and Teresa Brewer gave way to Chuck Berry and Elvis. It was also the slow ending of that time when kids wanted to look and act like their parents and the start of the other way around. The kids wanted Presley, not Perry Como. They wanted James Dean, not Clark Gable. They were about to want John Unitas, not Joe DiMaggio. It was all part of the general bursting-out that Winston J. "Buddy" Deane discovered and rode as hard as he could.

Deane, out of Pine Bluff, Arkansas, arrived in Baltimore for a disc jockey job at WITH radio. He had a slightly gravel voice and a knack for the smooth, inoffensive adult radio patter of the era. But he had no distinctive flair. In Baltimore, the largest number of teenage listeners turned to WCAO for its Top Forty music and its clear signal. The station's star jock, Johnny Dark, controlled nearly half of the Baltimore-area radio audience, while the hippest young people turned to the black stations, where they heard such fast-talkers as Paul "Fat Daddy" Johnson. He spoke like a man squeezed into a jumpsuit three sizes too small and was given to spontaneous rhyming on the air.

Compared to this, Buddy Deane was strictly mayonnaise. But he could count. Deane spent his weekends hosting teenage record hops, playing the standard hit records of the day. But he noticed the kids weren't asking for Eddie Fisher, who sang "Oh, My Papa." They wanted Bill Haley and the Comets, who sang "Rock around the Clock."

It was primitive rock and roll climbing onto dry land, and Deane initially listened to it with indifference. He was a child of the '40s. Give him Glenn Miller, give him Artie Shaw. But music was a business. If his listeners wanted this other music, he would play the agreeable father figure and give it to them.

"Buddy was a real smart guy," Royal Pollokoff recalled years later. Pollokoff spent forty-three years on Baltimore TV under the name Royal Parker. He arrived at WJZ-TV in 1951, when it was still known as WAAM. Sometimes he'd pinch-hit for Deane, and sometimes he'd handle his record hops. A lot of the time he did commercials for plastic slip covers during the show. He'd yell, "Hey, you kids, get off that sofa." For the rest of his life he couldn't walk down the street in Baltimore without somebody spotting him and hollering, "Hey, you kids . . ." People remembered him from all those years on the Deane show. "Buddy," he said, "was a guy who understood he had a product to sell. He'd sit back in his office reading Bertrand Russell, that's how smart he was. The music guys would come in to hustle records, and he'd humor them. 'How do you like this one?' 'Crazy. Cool.' Like he cared. Guys from all over the country would call for an audience with him—that's how much it meant if he pushed a song."

Pollokoff's career was going fine. He did a daily children's character called Mister Poplolly, but he was also pinch-hitting everywhere. Hosting a bowling show, hosting afternoon movies. Sometimes he'd jump out of the Mister Poplolly costume, and half an hour later he's the Esso news reporter. But he could only sit back and admire the thing happening with Deane's career.

"The record hops," Pollokoff said. "He's running 'em all over the state, that's how big he was. He couldn't handle all of 'em, so he'd have me fill in for him. He'd tell me, 'Royal, take these kids down to Ocean City, we got a hop we're doing down there. Buy 'em a burger and a shake. Hell, they'll run the show themselves.' He was getting seventy-five dollars against 60 percent of the gate. That was good money then."

Deane was smart enough not to buck the commercial tide and slick enough to make the change from radio to live television. The kids themselves weren't hard to find. He'd scout CYO dances, or the Famous Ballroom on Charles Street, or the Dixie Ballroom at Gwynn Oak Park. These kids found other kids. By 1958 *The Buddy Deane Show* was an afternoon tribal ritual where the latest dance steps were performed in the latest teen fashions. All over the metro area, adolescents scrambled home from school to watch the program six afternoons a week. Sometimes it went for two hours, sometimes three. Some regulars on the show—called Committee members—would cut school early to get to the studio for the 2:30 starting time. Kids watching at home carefully studied the Committee members on their TV sets. There were lots of opportunities. For Deane had discovered what Miss Nancy had figured out on *Romper Room*: kids love to look at other kids. An entire generation was solidifying its tribal instincts and learning to preen.

On *The Buddy Deane Show*, the teens became such enduring legends that, decades later, people still remembered their names. There was Mary Lou Raines, who was getting a hundred letters a week, sometimes more. There was Helen Crist, who took three buses each afternoon to reach Television Hill and three to get home in the dark. There was Evanne Robinson, voted the prettiest girl by an entire army base. In their blooming high school years these girls seemed working-class goddesses in their black eyeliner and their cathedrals of hair teased to within an inch of its life. They wore cardigan sweaters buttoned up the back and cha-cha heels and straight skirts that barely reached the knees. Their parents found the length stunningly short and waged high-decibel fights over it. Then the parents gave in. When Committee members modeled strapless outfits from east Baltimore's Etta Gowns for commercial spots during the show, a Catholic priest protested their naked shoulders. Rampant public sexuality, the priest said. The kids' reaction was: Get over it. But it was only 1958, and nervous TV station executives, not wishing to take on the church, decreed all bare shoulders would thereafter be covered with a piece of net.

In fact, most of the country's sexual culture was veiled. Teens seeking even hints of the erotic in 1958 had to rely on the covers of paperback novels (Erskine Caldwell's *God's Little Acre* or any of the Mickey Spillane books) or the movie ads in the newspapers (Elizabeth Taylor in nothing but a full-length slip as *Cat on a Hot Tin Roof* played all summer at the Century). If you were truly desperate to see the female form, you checked out the brassiere ads in the Sunday *New York Times Magazine* or Daisy Mae's form in "Li'l Abner." You were afraid to buy *Playboy* lest somebody call out the vice squad. Maybe you saw the newspaper ads for *High School Confidential*, with Mamie Van Doren and Jerry Lee Lewis, at the Hippdrome, or *Too Much, Too Soon*, whose ads asked, "When did her 'strip act' go too far? What did a messenger boy see in a darkened apartment?" We didn't know, dammit. And teenagers in the first flowering of their sexual anxiety didn't dare look around without the grownups lurking just behind them. If you lived in northwest Baltimore, you considered yourself lucky if you discovered the small men's room at the rear of the Hilltop Shopping Center Barber Shop. There were pinups back there, and you could see Marilyn Monroe's breasts, big as life. ("Mom, I need money for a haircut." "You just got a haircut yesterday." "I want another one.") The Boy Scouts were still passing out handbooks condemning masturbation and declaring sex was harmful to athletes. Even the Baltimore Colts had that problem. Weeb Ewbank had a rule: No sex after midweek during the season. They had to be fresh for Sundays.

In '58 the country still had the last lingering vestiges of Emily Post, of girdles, of virgin brides as the national standard. People didn't live together without marriage papers; if they did, it was called a common-law marriage. The accent was on the word *common*. The grownups seemed as sexually confused as their kids. That June, Mayor D'Alesandro roared his disapproval at the depiction of a nude woman. Pornographic, he said. The mayor chanced upon the depiction in a classic painting at the city's Peale Museum. D'Alesandro wasn't alone. A week later, a group of U.S. senators visiting the American exhibit at the Brussels World's Fair objected to an etching of a woman "nude to the waist." President Eisenhower, quickly alerted, ordered an immediate investigation. A week later, Ike's personal envoy assured him the nude was all right—it was just an Indian maiden reclining on a hammock. The country heaved a sigh of relief, or a guffaw.

Sex was so confusing in 1958. In the *New Yorker* that spring the TV critic John Lardner mentioned a *Maverick* episode where "a father follows his highly nubile daughter secretly on her dates, and occasionally shoots at her lovers from an ambush." It seemed a metaphor for teenage girls everywhere. Marriage manuals of the era presented eroticism as a kind of sex-by-the-numbers, like those oil paintings so many mothers worked on in the evenings: this goes here, that goes there. A European critic called Americans "huddled masses yearning to breathe heavily." That was the winter everybody read Grace Metalious's *Peyton Place*, or tried to. If you managed to steal a glance at it while the drugstore manager was looking elsewhere, you read, "Here? And here? And here?" "Yes. Oh, yes. Yes." But where, exactly, was *here*? In '58, nobody seemed to know. At Baltimore's Seton High School, Sister Rosa kindly explained to her senior class that they would now be studying Renaissance art. There would be nude cherubs displayed. Any young ladies wishing to leave the room ahead of time could do so. Nobody left. In '58, the restlessness needed any avenue it could find to express itself.

It was a tricky time in matters of sex and morality. The week of

Baltimore's big snow, a *News-Post* headline declared, "Welfare Boss Spanked over Baby Pamphlet." Some state legislators were upset by a pamphlet offering help and guidance to unwed mothers. The pamphlet showed a young woman embracing an infant and said, "If you are a pregnant girl or mother, not married to the father of the child, and do not know where to turn with your problems, qualified agencies in Maryland stand ready to help you." In the legislature, this was considered a bad idea. State senator Joseph Bertorelli, out of Baltimore, charged that the pamphlet was being distributed out of state and "practically invites girls in trouble to come to Maryland and have their babies. A pamphlet like this," said Bertorelli, "tends for moral degeneracy."

With the same kind of morality arguments leveled at his TV show, Buddy Deane and others at the station knew the delicate balancing act they were performing on music, dance, and fashion (though it was barely beginning to dawn on them that race would eventually offer an even bigger challenge).

To parents, the Deane kids were an unnerving peek into a dangerous future. The boys with their slicked-back, jet-stream hair, like Elvis, and the girls with their heavy makeup and knee-length skirts—they had to be brewing some kind of trouble up there with that crazy music. In Baltimore, the Catholic schools were warning students that going to an Elvis Presley movie was a mortal sin.

"When I went to Calvert Hall," John Waters remembered years later, "we had one Buddy Deaner there. He got beat up by one of the teachers. They could do that back then. The teachers hated you if you were on Buddy Deane. Of course, that's what I loved about it. The boy at Calvert Hall, he had a D.A. haircut, and he was a fashion rebel. That was his crime. But parents and teachers were terribly threatened by anything connected with the show."

Waters made his reputation as a bad boy of filmmaking, but that's a put-on. He is the most civil of men. But, in his early movies, he insisted on putting himself far ahead of the country's Puritan curve and insisted on telling his comic tales without the slightest subtlety. When they put *Hairspray*—his fairy tale version of *The Buddy Deane Show*—into musical form and looked at the show from a safe distance of five decades, it suddenly became the stuff for middle-class audiences to appreciate.

"I watched the show all the time," Waters remembered, "because I lived in Lutherville." He laughed aloud at the memory. "My parents thought the Buddy Deane kids were the opposite of what they wanted for me. The boys on Buddy Deane were wearing those pegged pants from Lee's of Broadway. That was the Saks Fifth Avenue of the Deaners. It seemed like racy stuff. My parents wanted me in Bermuda shorts and crew cuts. I wanted to go downtown and be a beatnik."

The kids on the show just wanted to dance, just wanted to break away from the old, even if they had no idea where it was all heading. Even if it meant taking three buses all the way across town. Even if it meant cutting school early. Even if it meant trudging through two feet of snow that bleak winter of '58.

One week after the snow started, Baltimoreans awoke to the first harbinger of spring: a front-page newspaper photo out of Scottsdale, Arizona, where three young Orioles prospects trotted across a baseball field, signaling the first day of major league spring training. "Can Spring Be Far Away?" the caption asked.

Well, yes, it could.

THE CITY WAS BEGINNING its wintry descent into years of troubles, which no amount of snow and no playing of ball games—and no amount of wishful thinking—could completely disguise. One month before the February snowstorm, the Baltimore Planning Council issued a report declaring "a bigger, brighter Baltimore in terms of population, business, industry and jobs." The planning council thus officially declared itself a collection of ignoramuses who were cut off from the life of their own city. The *News-Post*, which should have known better, ran the report big on page 1, under the headline, "Baltimore Boom Is Forecast."

This was sheer delusion. White people were already beginning to flee by the tens of thousands to the suburbs, later followed by tens of thousands of middle-class black people. Some of it was mindless prejudice, and some of it was simply fear: of being left behind, of being the last to bail out of a deteriorating neighborhood. And some of the fear was fed by the daily papers, and some of it by local TV news, which was just getting started. For the first time there were human beings on television talking about things, and in 1958 nobody yet imagined a human being on TV shading the truth in any way.

In the winter of '58, the governor of Maryland was Theodore McKeldin. He commuted the death sentence of Alvin Herbert Braxton for killing a police patrolman named John R. Phelan. Braxton, eighteen, roamed the streets as a kid, and there were questions about his sanity. He grabbed Phelan's gun during a botched liquor store holdup. The papers described Braxton as a "Negro who fought like an animal" as he tried to escape. People saw such stories, and saw the equation of black people with animals, and then they turned to the real estate classified ads.

They moved to suburbia, and so did the institutions they supported. Downtown's big department stores, Hecht's and Stewart's and all the others, closed one by one until they were all gone and left vacant. They reopened in suburban shopping malls where people would spend weekend afternoons congregating in food courts, trying to convince themselves that this was the good life. The former throbbing heart of downtown would cease completely.

At city hall, Mayor D'Alesandro looked into the future and glimpsed not only his own troubles but his city's. In nearly a dozen years in office, he had accomplished plenty and been beaten up plenty. He was a New Deal Democrat by way of the Hofferbert-D'Alesandro political organization that held on to power in southeast Baltimore for a quarter century. (Years later, when D'Alesandro's daughter, Nancy Pelosi, became the first woman Speaker of the U.S. House of Representatives, the opposition tried to brand her a "San Francisco liberal." When old-timers in Baltimore heard this, they snorted, "San Francisco liberal? Don't they get it? This woman's the daughter of a machine politician.")

In his years at city hall, D'Alesandro built dozens of new schools and recreation centers. There were fourteen hundred new miles of streets and highways, including a vast new beltway nearing completion, and a new Jones Falls Expressway through the city and new hospitals and firehouses and library branches. The city finally had major league baseball and professional football. He'd presided over a period of blue-collar prosperity that nobody had ever seen. The shipyards were humming in south Baltimore. In east Baltimore's Canton thousands were employed at places like Crown Cork and Seal. Western Electric employed thousands more, and Sparrows Point was still pumping out steel.

But, as 1958 arrived, history was turning against the city irrevocably. A new major office building hadn't been built downtown in thirty years. The wartime industries had slowed down, and unemployment was up. The city still had a solid public school system, but within a decade many of the schools would be dangerous and academically deficient. It had the marvelous Enoch Pratt Free Library system, with branches spread across town, but down the road it would have to close some branches and cut the hours of others. Perhaps sensing the future, the city felt beaten up, exhausted, unsure of itself.

One day D'Alesandro was asked why the city of Pittsburgh, once a symbol of urban smoke and grime, was now doing much better while Baltimore had no massive renewal projects in the works.

"You gotta remember," D'Alesandro said, "Pittsburgh's got all those Mellons. All we got is watermelons."

At the *News-Post* a gentle, white-haired man, associate editor Ralph Sybert, wrote a front-page column headlined "City's Life Is in Your Hands," capturing some of the decay. "I've lived here, man and boy, fifty-five years," he wrote. "I arrived before the 1904 fire and gazed in youthful awe at the rubble of fifteen hundred smoking downtown buildings covering one hundred forty acres. I saw the indomitable courage with which the people of Baltimore built on the ashes." Many improvements followed, "but in the last decade or so . . . a sickening turn downward. Pride has turned into apprehension. Many of the buildings built after the Great Fire are obsolete. Shifts in population have brought the era of profiteering professional block-busters and a mass exodus of city dwellers to the suburban counties. Thousands of dwellings are shabby, crowded tenements. The tentacles of blight have extended outward in many directions."

This followed years of great prosperity and great promise.

World War II brought 1940s jobs to Baltimore, but peace eliminated many of them. In the late '50s, nearly half of Baltimore's workforce was employed in manufacturing. The figure was especially high in white working-class neighborhoods, since the trade unions were reluctant to accept blacks even during the desperate war years. But the war made Baltimore an economic boomtown beyond previous imagining. Glenn L. Martin Aircraft had a workforce of 3,500 in 1939, and four years later it was 53,000. They built more than 8,000 planes for the war. Bethlehem Steel established its Fairfield Shipyard and built more than 500 Liberty Ships that helped turn the tide of war in the Atlantic. The shipyard opened in Brooklyn, a few miles south of downtown Baltimore, with 350 workers in 1941. A year after Pearl Harbor, it employed 10,000. A year later, 47,000.

One of the Glenn L. Martin workers was John Goodspeed. Later he joined Baltimore's *Evening Sun* and wrote the popular "Mister Peep's Diary" column. But across the war years he was thrilled to find work as a tool inspector, making thirty-five dollars a week for a fifty-eight-hour workweek.

"War workers toiled in shifts around the clock," Goodspeed wrote years later in *Baltimore* magazine. "An endless stream of streetcars ran to and from the Fairfield Shipyard and the Sparrows Point steel mill, but most Martin workers commuted to Middle River on buses or in car pools. 'Hitler rides in the empty seats,' the slogan went. . . . The buses were ramshackle, packed, and stinking, especially in hot weather. The car pools usually included mountaineers who drank corn whiskey before breakfast, bores who talked incessantly about their automobiles, and sports who crowed constantly about their prowess at fornication. . . .

"I remember one period of twelve-hour shifts, seven days a week in 1942–43 when I didn't see the sun all winter. 'Get 'em flying!' the posters read on the walls of the vast Martin shops—and we did that. The floors were soaked with grease and crawling with lice. The assembly lines were cold and drafty in winter. The tall, dangerous seaplane hull fixtures were hot as hell in summer. Foremen patrolled the rest rooms and allowed you five minutes for a bowel action—no more: 'Do you want me to come in and wipe you!' one of them was fond of yelling."

And this was considered the city's triumphant era.

"You could live it up on $35 a week in Baltimore at the start of the war," Goodspeed wrote. "You could still buy a steak dinner for less than $1 at Welsh's Black Bottle, crab cakes for twenty-five cents, beer for ten cents a glass, a great meal including biscuits and baked beans for less than 75 cents at Horn & Horn, a Harris tweed suit for $22.50, imported Irish shoes for $12."

At night, downtown streets were filled. Old-timers' descriptions of the Baltimore war years sound like a tipsy party on the last night of the world. At Cy Bloom's Club Charles, Sophie Tucker belted out songs, and then Kate Smith did a week and sang "God Bless America" every night to kids in uniform and weepy middle-aged parents who were sending them off to battle. Milton Berle told jokes, and so did Georgie Jessel. The Club Charles had staircases from a balcony and chorus girls descending to the sound of Cole Porter songs. The chorus girls would scrounge for a living and save pennies by renting four to a room at Herman's Rooming House, St. Paul and Preston streets, and look for fellows with a few bucks in their pocket to show them a decent time.

There were plenty of places: piano bars on Charles Street, dances atop the Southern Hotel, plays at Ford's Theater, vaudeville at the Hippodrome, plus all the risqué nightclubs on The Block. And every place jumped from the pulse of the wartime crowds.

In neighborhoods located near bus and trolley lines, wartime living space was so scarce that property owners subdivided their homes and businesses into apartments, which they rented to people thrilled to find work after the long depression. In one case, reported the *South Baltimore Enterprise,* thirty men employed at the Fairfield Shipyard slept in four rooms, in shifts, and shared one toilet. The first newcomers established "home base." Then friends and relatives joined them, and migrant enclaves sprung up.

Then, one glorious moment in the summer of 1945, the war ended, and so much disappeared.

The boom economy began to slip away. People who'd once turned downtown nightlife into an endless wartime whoop disappeared. Milton Berle wasn't telling jokes at the Club Charles any more, and Kate Smith wasn't singing "God Bless America" to platoons of departing GIs. Nobody danced atop the Southern Hotel. In the 1950s people stayed home to watch *Gunsmoke* and Ed Sullivan instead of venturing into the night. Milton Berle and Kate Smith were now on television, which was free. Downtown after dark was empty in most of the places where it had swung lively during the war.

By 1958 the median Baltimore household income was $5,659. There was still work, but the job numbers were dropping ominously. In January, the *News-Post* ran a front-page open letter to President Eisenhower, plaintively asking why the U.S. Maritime Administration turned down Bethlehem Steel's bid to build four freighters, even though the company had the lowest bid by $3 million. Bethlehem Steel was the city's biggest employer, with 28,000 people, and billed itself as "the greatest steel mill in the world." The freighter deal would mean the loss of 5 million man-hours of work and considerable spending power. It felt like part of a pattern during a difficult recession. The city still had considerable manufacturing jobs: steel and spacecraft, power tools and paper industries, metal cans and containers, car and truck bodies, hydraulic pumps. And there was the great port of Baltimore, second only to New York, with 40,000 workers handling 22 million tons of imports and exports each year.

But insecurity was widespread. Sometimes hundreds of factory workers lost jobs on the same day. Who knew where they could find new ones? Especially with black people popping up as they never had before. And here, in the postwar years, was the heart of all change.

In 1958, barely 30 percent of the city's population was African American. In just over a decade that percentage would double. In '58, enough pressure was applied that Bethlehem Steel, Western Electric, and Kenicott Refining finally agreed to hire more than a relative handful of blacks. But there were remarkable stipulations: union jobs, and jobs with training programs, were to be kept all-white.

Before the war, blacks grabbed housing wherever they could. Many lived in alley houses—ramshackle little dwellings in grubby alleys— while others moved into shabby row houses vacated by whites. In the war years, more than thirty thousand blacks arrived in Baltimore. Existing housing, already rundown, deteriorated even further. By the time the war ended, blacks were finding their collective voice and announcing they wanted jobs and decent housing. Thus commenced the great changes—none greater than the U.S. Supreme Court ordering the integration of America's public schools in 1954.

Everybody talked about this, and in white neighborhoods they worried about it. The city didn't get violent. But there was a lot of anxiety, and sometimes there was overt anger. In southwest Baltimore's

Pigtown, a dozen black kindergarten children entered the neighborhood elementary school that September. Residents appealed to the city's school superintendent, Dr. John Fischer, to keep the school all white. Fischer, unsympathetic, refused to see them. So about two dozen of them picketed the school. When they continued for several days, the demonstrating spread.

In south Baltimore, 39 black students were enrolled at Southern High, which had about 800 students. Hundreds of pickets gathered outside, parents and children. The crowd swelled to about 2,000, and suddenly little pockets of fist fights broke out. A police squad car was overturned. The principal at Southern was a fellow named John Schwatka. He went on television and said, "Look into your hearts. . . . Prevent another day of fear in our community."

Slowly, things calmed down. Students remained in class. City leaders rallied behind the school board, which urged compliance with the Supreme Court ruling. The small, scattered incidents actually helped crystallize a positive stand on integration. A philosophical stand, anyway. Yes, yes, many said, integration is good. They said this as the moving vans pulled up to their front doors. Good luck with your integration, former friends and neighbors, see you in some other lifetime.

Quietly, over time, city residents—even those with good intentions on race—packed their bags and put their homes up for sale. They felt a shadow crossing the land, and it didn't matter that it symbolized the very stuff that the country allegedly stood for. People talked a good game in the schools and the houses of worship, and then they made tracks.

"When my father was mayor," said Tommy D'Alesandro III, who became mayor a decade after his father left city hall, "the city was strictly broken up by ethnic groups. Each neighborhood was cemented by religion, by language, by ethnic background, by race. Racially, there was no movement between the two. And it was based on ignorance. Survival was the first order of business, that's all. This was a generation that came through the depression and the war. It was still about jobs and putting food in front of your family. They looked on other groups as rivals for jobs. What finally happened was, as ethnic groups got stronger, their leaders began to mesh with other leaders."

But by then, the great suburban migration had begun. Families nurtured along the city's marble stoops and trolley lines were now exploring grassy developments in Glen Burnie and Towson and Pikesville. They became first-name pals with real estate agents, some of whom worked on people's fears of the coming black hordes. As the schools integrated in the autumn of 1954, two hundred residential subdivisions were being built all around Baltimore County. Every day, fifty new families were moving to those neighborhoods. Two years later, 86 percent of Baltimore-area housing was being built in the suburbs.

The city began to shrink in size and psychology. Flush with wartime jobs, Baltimore was the nation's sixth-biggest city at midcentury. It would fall out of the top twenty by century's end. Its 1950 population was more than 900,000. By century's end, it was roughly 650,000. In 1958, when the Baltimore Colts would create history in New York, it was a city hungry for something to hold it together.

"WAY YOU CHUCK 'EM IN, HON"

SIX MONTHS BEFORE his last heart attack blind-sided him, John Unitas donated all of his football memorabilia to the Babe Ruth Birthplace and Museum, the converted west Baltimore row house where young George Herman Ruth Jr. first discovered his natural gift for all things delinquent.

The donation was no big deal to Unitas. The family ritual was simple: John would toss a pair of his battered high-top football cleats into the trash can, and his second wife, Sandy, quite appalled, would bolt across the room and fetch them back out.

"How can you throw these away?" Sandy would ask.

"I've tried throwing them out five times now," John would say. "They're worn out. I only wear 'em to cut the grass now."

"They do not belong to you any more," Sandy would say. "They belong to everyone."

"Then everybody must be crazy."

He felt the same way about trophies and plaques. They were OK, if that's what people liked. They reflected his pride as a football player. But he was too modest to put much value in them. And so when his alma mater, the University of Louisville, asked for his memorabilia,

Unitas had the stuff crated and ready for shipping. Then John Ziemann heard about it. Ziemann had been friends with Unitas since he'd
joined the Baltimore Colts band as a drummer forty years earlier. The
band members and the ballplayers got to know each other a little bit
through the years. In 1962, when Unitas heard the fifteen-year-old Ziemann was hospitalized with a burst appendix and pleurisy, he showed
up at St. Joseph's Hospital.

"Johnny Unitas is coming up the hall to see you," Ziemann's nurse
told him.

"Yeah," said Ziemann, "and so's the queen of England."

A moment later, Unitas was standing in the doorway with the game
ball from the previous day's win over Los Angeles. Ziemann was so
weak he couldn't sit up. Unitas spent two hours talking to him, then
left the room around four o'clock. Eight o'clock that night, another
nurse walked into his room.

"You know," she said, "Mr. Unitas is still here. He's been going
room to room, seeing all the critical children."

Ziemann's another piece of work. Grew up in east Baltimore, gradu-
ated from Patterson High, and eventually took over leadership of the
Colts band. After the ball club fled Baltimore that snowy night in '84,
Ziemann gathered his troupe together and asked, "Why do *we* have
to stop playing?" He kept the band together all those years until the
Ravens showed up, playing at halftime in ballparks around the league,
playing at local gatherings of Colts fans, the only pro football band in
America without a team to call its own.

Now, late in 2000, when he heard Unitas was sending all his old stuff
to Louisville, Ziemann telephoned him. By this time, Ziemann was
working for the Babe Ruth Birthplace and Museum, which was com-
pleting plans to build its Sports Legends at Camden Yards Museum.

"What are you doing?" he said.

"Shipping this crap outa here," said Unitas.

"Don't move," said Ziemann. He raced over to Unitas's house and
spent three hours changing John's mind. Baltimore, he insisted. That's
where you made your mark, it's where your fans are, it's where you
leave your legacy.

"Okay," said Unitas, "but get it out of here by eight o'clock tomorrow. Eight-oh-five, I'm throwing it in the trash."

So here he was, six months before the fatal heart attack. A pretty nice crowd, maybe a hundred people, jammed into the biggest room at the museum and saw a couple of tables filled with some of his stuff. Included was the helmet that Mike Gibbons would bring to church the day that John was buried.

I sidled over to Unitas while somebody gave a brief speech calling John the Babe Ruth of football. Now, it was said, the museum would have the two greatest icons of the two great American pastimes. John seemed to listen only sporadically.

"Nice trophy," I whispered. It was the Most Valuable Player award he'd won in high school.

"I was so well known," he whispered back, "that they spelled my name wrong."

"How about that one?" I said. It was the 1970 NFL Man of the Year trophy.

Unitas shrugged. "Sometimes," he said, "they give you trophies just for showing up."

He glanced at a TV monitor high on a wall on the far side of the room, like a quarterback spotting a secondary receiver way downfield. Always, the great peripheral vision. The trophies and plaques were a yard or two in front of him, but Unitas kept looking deep to the monitor, where it showed a grainy black-and-white film he hadn't seen in many years.

It was John in his youth, at St. Justin's High School in Pittsburgh. There was Unitas, ducking a linebacker. Along the sidelines, a coach named Max Carey hollered from the sidelines. Linemen named Tom Boyle and Rich Keeling tried to throw protective blocks, and Unitas recited their names as he watched them.

He still remembered them and still remembered his world back then: the father who died when Unitas was five, and the mother who ran their small coal delivery business during the day and scrubbed office floors from ten at night until six in the morning for twelve bucks a week. It was half a century since he'd scrambled out of that miserable Pittsburgh youth and forty-six years since the famous eighty-cent telephone call that brought Unitas to Baltimore. He gave the city its identity. Maybe we were just row houses and marble steps and assembly lines, but we also had this guy throwing footballs across the horizon and doing it in our name. Maybe we weren't much—but nobody thought Unitas was much, either, when they first saw him. Even his own teammates.

"Unitas? No, never could have figured he'd turn out the way he did," Lenny Moore was saying one day. We were sitting in his suburban home, decades after he'd retired from the game. His Pro Football Hall of Fame bust rested on a pedestal in a hallway. Unitas always called Moore "Sput," short for Sputnik, the nickname for his out-of-this-world speed.

"That's the genius of watching the guy grow," Moore said. "Always steady. Kept it all inside. He never was a guy to talk a lot. He never was with any group. Even when we were out of town, guys go into the airport bar, he'd have one or two but you could never identify him with any group. He was just around. And in the huddle, he was on target. He knew what he wanted to do, and which guys could do it. He'd say, 'What you got, Sput?' I'd say, 'I can do so-and-so.' Raymond would say, 'I can do so-and-so.' He wouldn't call it. But later he'd say, 'You still got it?' 'Yeah, it's still there.' Whenever he was ready to call it, but not until then."

"It had to be when he was ready."

"Right. There were times," said Moore, chuckling slightly, "he'd call my number and I'd tell him I was tired. He'd say, 'Shut up, I'm calling the plays.' Oh, yeah. To anybody. If you can't handle it, then get the hell out of here, we'll get somebody in here that can. He ran that huddle. Don't tell him you didn't have anything left, or you couldn't do nothing. Then get out, we'll get somebody else in here."

It was the exact opposite of the defensive team's huddles.

"In our huddles," Artie Donovan said one afternoon, "everybody talked. I'm screaming, Joyce is screaming, Pellington's screaming. I got so mad at Pellington one time during a time-out, I threw a whole bucket of water at him."

Jim Mutscheller remembered the defensive huddles from his first year on the team. He was a backup on both offense and defense. "Everybody cussing at everybody else," he said. "Pellington's yelling. Marchetti's yelling. I'm thinking, 'I don't think this is for me. My pursuit should be offense.' Those defensive huddles, it was all screaming."

"Yeah," Moore said, "our huddles were Johnny U's huddles. I

remember one time in Detroit, Alex Sandusky coming to the huddle, saying he couldn't handle the Detroit tackle. He said, 'He's giving me a fit.' John said, 'You can't handle it, we'll get somebody in who can.' There was no yipping and yapping in those huddles. That's *his* huddle. We admired that. He knew what everybody was supposed to do at any given time. One time I ran the wrong pattern, and it didn't open up enough for Mutscheller. He said, 'Sput, you gotta get down there and tie him up. Don't slow down on me, man. That opens it up for Mutsch.' I said, 'OK, man.' He's got all this stuff going on, but he knows what I'm not doing. And he was right."

He mulled that over for a moment. "But the toughness," Moore said. "That's the thing nobody will ever understand."

He came back to it another time. He was sitting with Berry and Mutscheller one afternoon, and Bruce Laird was there, too. Laird was a defensive back with the Colts in the '70s. A real good one. It was the fiftieth anniversary of Unitas's entrance into the game, and Tom Callahan's book, *Johnny U,* had just come out so they were talking about that era.

"Was the play dirtier in your day?" somebody asked.

"Oh, my," Moore said. "They could beat on you till the whistle blew. Come here, Brucie."

Laird and Moore got up from their chairs. Moore was past seventy. Laird, twenty years younger. Moore feinted his way left and right.

"I still can't cover you," Laird said.

"In our era," said Moore, "I'm fighting off these blows." He gestured, lifting Laird's arm as though a defender was throwing a forearm at his throat. "See, they can't do that now."

"Darn it," said Laird, "that must have been a good time."

"But they'd really pound the hell out of the quarterbacks," Moore said. "The referees would let 'em—it was just the way the game was played. And they all came looking for Johnny U. They used to time their hits, just as he released the ball, and try to drive right through him."

They all had stories like that about Unitas. These were tough men, standout professionals, and they all talked about him with a kind of awe. And now, as Unitas stood there donating his memorabilia to the Sports Legends Museum six months before he died, it occurred to everyone that three decades had slipped past since he'd retired from pro football.

It was a moment for sentimental reflection on one of the great rags-to-riches sagas of the century. Just as Babe Ruth had done more than anyone to make baseball part of the American psyche, it was Unitas more than anyone who'd made pro football part of that same athletic devotional. Gazing at the old film clip from Unitas's high school days, I found myself getting nostalgic by proxy, since I knew John wouldn't allow himself to feel it.

"What are you thinking?" I asked.

"Boy, I was slow," he laughed. That's all.

"You were never a sentimental type," I said. "Does this stuff . . . ?"

"No, I'm not," Unitas said. "I'm just not that kind of guy. Unless it's children or dogs."

A man who loses his father at age five does not give in easily to emotions; a man who recalls his mother scrubbing office floors all night long to feed her family knows, even in the fury of a championship game, that there are more important things in life than football.

Unitas shifted his weight awkwardly. He looked every bit his age. He still had all his hair, but his body was a mess. He'd been through one heart attack, and he'd survived every physical blow imaginable on the playing field. He'd lost track of the number of times he'd gone through surgery. But the old Unitas stoop was now far more pronounced, and when he walked, his shoulders shifted noticeably from side to side and his arms swung loosely. He'd already told a close friend, "I expect to be in a wheelchair, if I live long enough."

He and Moore and Jim Parker went regularly to Kernan Hospital for physical therapy. Parker seemed to be in the worst shape. Years earlier, he was the big guy protecting Unitas and Moore; now, the two smaller men were holding Parker up as they walked into the hospital.

I remembered the first time I'd met Unitas, when John Steadman hired me as a sports writer at the *News American*. This was 1968. I went up to the old Western Maryland College and drifted into the locker room one afternoon during summer training camp. The place seemed empty, and I was ready to walk back outside when I ran into Unitas as he stepped out of a shower.

He was without modesty. After more than a decade of standing naked in front of sports writers from coast to coast, what was the big deal? I muttered something about Steadman sending me over to do a feature.

"Is this a bad time?" I asked.

"Nah, what do you need?" Unitas asked.

"I was wondering about injuries," I said. It was in all the papers; the Golden Arm was wearing out. Sure enough, Unitas was out of action much of the upcoming year as Earl Morrall led the club to the Super Bowl and that ignominious loss to the Joe Namath Jets.

"What injuries?" said Unitas. "Never had any."

"Huh?"

He smiled slyly. "Except, you know," he said, "a punctured lung, three broken ribs, a broken . . . "

He chuckled his way through an endless assortment of punishments, which I scribbled dutifully but distractedly. So this was the great Unitas, I thought: his body was so pale as to be albino, his chest hairless and lacking any noticeable musculature, his legs bony and bent like a wishbone. But he had long arms and enormous hands with bent fingers darting this way and that.

The interview went fine, and then I didn't see Unitas much the rest of that year. Morrall led the Colts to an easy conference title. Then, on a freezing afternoon in Baltimore, they beat the Minnesota Vikings to advance to the championship game against the Cleveland Browns. When I went into the Colts' locker room afterward, I got a glimpse of Unitas at his locker, dressing quietly, content to let Morrall get his moment of glory.

A week later, with a ferocious wind whipping off Lake Erie into Cleveland's old Municipal Stadium, the Colts clobbered the Browns, 34 to 0. We flew back to Baltimore right after the game. A bumpy ride, bad enough that receiver Preston Pearson, sitting across the aisle from me, prayed aloud. I wasn't nervous; God wasn't going to take down a plane with the fabulous Baltimore Colts aboard.

At the old Friendship Airport, a pretty good crowd awaited the club's arrival. It was a nice moment in a difficult time: December 1968, the war in Vietnam going badly, the country deeply divided, people sneering at each other over matters as trifling as the length of a haircut. The Colts were still the great common denominator.

As we moved toward the door of the plane, I stood near the back of the line with Unitas and a TV camera man. Outside, the crowd cheered loudly. There weren't thirty thousand, the way there were ten years earlier, but as we peered through the doorway, we could see they were thrilled. Unitas glanced at the camera man, whose hair fell slightly below his ears. He was not pleased at what he saw.

"Why don't you get a haircut?" Unitas said. He seemed oblivious to the noise of the crowd just outside. The camera man looked back at Unitas, his expression a mix of confusion and hurt.

"There's only two kinds of guys wear their hair that long," Unitas said. "Guys that play the gee-tar, and . . . " He mentioned a sexual activity best left unsaid here. It wasn't his hour at all. It wasn't December 1958, and it wasn't his championship this time, and the years were beginning to get away from him. He was feeling a little old and maybe a little surly. He was never one for hiding what he felt.

When the Colts drafted John Mackey, in 1963, owner Carroll Rosenbloom took the new tight end around the team's training camp locker room. When he reached Unitas, Rosenbloom thought he'd have a little fun.

"John," he said to Mackey, "this is Mr. Unitas. You know, he doesn't like colored guys."

Unitas wasn't amused. He fixed Rosenbloom with a hard stare and said, "Jews, either."

He could give the needle as well as take one.

And there was also this Unitas: a week before he died, the Babe Ruth Museum arranged a small lunch at the Camden Club, inside the warehouse at Oriole Park. Julia Ruth Stevens, Babe Ruth's stepdaughter, was in town and wanted to meet Unitas. He and Ziemann decided to walk the half mile or so from the Birthplace to the lunch.

When they reached downtown Baltimore's busy Russell Street, the light turned green against them. But no traffic moved. People on both sides of the thoroughfare, which leads directly to and from the Baltimore-Washington Parkway, honked their horns at Unitas. Some rolled down their windows and shouted at him from their cars. Others opened their doors and got out, waving their arms back and forth.

"John! Hey, Johnny U."

"Hey, man," Unitas told Ziemann, "you better wave. They're all waving at you."

When they finally navigated their way across the street, Ziemann spotted a homeless man walking toward them. He was the full catastrophe: the missing teeth, the matted clothes, the awful smell. Ziemann reached into his wallet and pulled out a ten-dollar bill. The homeless guy looked right past him.

"You're Johnny Unitas," the guy said.

"Yes, sir," said Unitas.

The homeless guy wiped his right hand on his overcoat to clean it off. Unitas pulled the hand away and shook it warmly. Ziemann stood there for the next fifteen minutes while Unitas and the guy chatted away. He kept holding out the ten bucks, but the guy never took his eyes off Unitas. When they parted, Unitas told him, "Come on, man, take care of yourself, get yourself back in action."

"Yes, sir."

And the fellow wandered off, never thinking to take the ten dollars Ziemann was still holding out.

"That was nice of you to talk to him," he told Unitas.

"I don't know," Unitas muttered. "Maybe that's why God put me on this earth, to make people happy."

He was coming to the end of the line and finally starting to put some meaning to his life and admit to himself the profound effect he had had on so many people for so many years.

WHEN UNITAS AND THE COLTS began to change the American sporting culture, baseball was still perceived as the personification of the nation's great obsession with games.

By March 1958, as Baltimore dug its way out of its second major snowstorm that frigid winter, the Orioles were enjoying tropical spring training sunshine. The town's three daily newspapers all sent reporters south to file reams of daily copy, much of it no edgier than a publicity handout.

The ballplayers were young men said to be making perfectly fine money. The papers reported that veteran first baseman Bob Boyd, after hitting a splendid .318 in 1957—fourth best in the American

League—had agreed to a new salary of $12,000 a year. In the four years since Baltimore had returned to major league ball, Boyd, nicknamed El Ropo for the "frozen rope" line drives he hit, was one of only a handful of black ballplayers the Orioles had ever suited up. He was the only one who had played regularly. The ball club made his salary sound like the money of millionaires; later, such money would lead a generation of athletes to revolt against owners who suckered them across decades, and they would all take home money to make sultans envious. But, in 1958, the Orioles signed a "bonus baby" by the name of Dave Nicholson to a contract that no one could believe, so large were the numbers.

"Young Dave," wrote John Steadman, "will never have to carry a lunch bucket, punch a time clock or work for a living. He has it made. Nicholson became independently wealthy last night when the Baltimore Orioles handed over a contract . . . that is the greatest gamble in Baltimore sports history."

The contract was for $80,000, and the money would be paid out over three years. Though manager Paul Richards, widely regarded as a genius, said the deal "could mean the pennant," Nicholson discovered that all this money could not buy him a base hit. Across his first summer, he dropped from one minor league team to another and hit .222. He would never in his life be a major league regular.

The rest of the news about the Orioles was not exactly marvelous. The previous season, the club finished twenty games worse than the New York Yankees, who won the pennant as usual. The Yankees had Mickey Mantle and Yogi Berra and Whitey Ford in their glory years. The Orioles had a promising young third baseman, twenty-year-old Brooks Robinson, and not much more. Their top power hitter, Gus Triandos, hit nineteen home runs in 1957. Their most promising young pitcher, Billy O'Dell, won four games while losing ten.

Now, with these spring training reports arriving each day, the weather in Baltimore began to change. The sun came out, and the first warm breezes of spring slipped into town without warning, and the streets were cleared of all lingering snow. Soon the days were so unexpectedly balmy that schoolboys burst out of their homes with baseball gloves on their hands, preparing to holler, "Way you chuck 'em in, hon."

In 1958 they still did this by instinct, and by the multitudes. Though

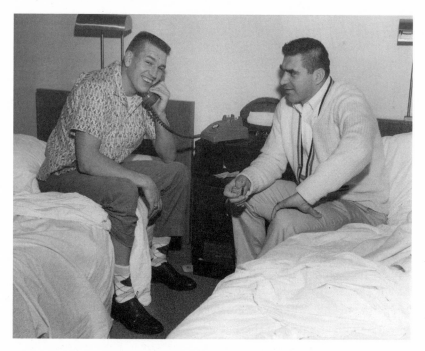

The kid with the flat-top haircut and checkered socks, John Unitas, will eventually hang up the phone and learn a few lessons about life in the National Football League from the veteran Bert Rechichar, who believed in "tearing out the eyeballs" of opposing ball carriers. *Courtesy Baltimore News-American Collection, Marylandia and Special Collections, University of Maryland Libraries*

TV and rock and roll were beginning to speed up the culture, ancient baseball still clung to the national consciousness. In every neighborhood games were played with baseballs and softballs, and spongeballs and pinkies, and whiffle balls, too. They were played in schoolyards and backyards and on neighborhood streets where the traffic would allow it.

In south Baltimore's Swann Park each spring, the great Leone's amateur baseball team held practices. Leone's would produce a bunch of major leaguers, such as the Mets' Ron Swoboda and the Orioles' Tom Phoebus. One day a kid named Reggie Jackson showed up for a tryout. He was spending the summer in Baltimore, where his father lived. Jackson's only problem was his color. Leone's had never had a black player. Jackson wore a muscle shirt and kept hitting balls over the right field fence, down a distant slope, which were last seen headed toward the Patapsco River. Nobody had ever seen such cannon shots, including Walter Youse, the team manager, who stood gawking behind a metal backstop.

"What about the colored kid?" somebody said.

"He's getting whiter every time he swings," said Youse.

In southeast Baltimore, Patterson Park was cluttered with boys hitting fungoes. There were soccer players there, too, but they were regarded as European sentimentalists; baseball was the American game. In the city's Little Italy, boys carved out a diamond on the empty lot near the city's sewage pumping station. On Sundays the neighborhood's grownups took it over: the married men played the bachelors. In Druid Hill Park, ball games were played alongside the Baltimore Zoo's Reptile House. In schoolyards all over town, boys bucked up for sides, odds against evens. Or they chucked up on Louisville Sluggers, squeezing fingers for the top spot on the handle.

On Crawford Avenue, in my neighborhood in northwest Baltimore not far from the Arlington Cemetery, if you played in the street, you learned to hit the ball up the middle so you didn't shatter somebody's window. Second base was always a manhole cover. First and third were lamp posts or the bumpers of parked cars. When the cover of the baseball wore out from scraping the cement, somebody always found black electrician's tape to keep the ball from unraveling. Fifty years later, try finding such a sight. The other choice was to walk a few blocks to the nearby Grove Park Elementary School, where there were variations of baseball if you didn't have enough bodies for a full game: stickball and throwball and punchball. If you really lacked players, there was curb ball or stepball or running bases. Now such games are mostly the stuff of memory.

These were still the great American pastimes in 1958. The best ballplayer in my neighborhood was Rob Meyer. He was five feet five, and his nickname was Dynamite. He was apparently made of burnished steel. He starred as a running back and middle linebacker for Forest Park High School's football team. When he walked home from practice every day, at least one girl would be waiting for him around Gwynn Oak Junction to help poor Rob carry his football gear home. In his first year on the varsity baseball team, he hit well over .400. He was so good that his father bought him a real Mickey Mantle glove. Everybody told him, You can't use that in a game; you'll get it dirty. A glove with Mantle's autograph wasn't a glove; it was a religious artifact. The

Boston Red Sox scouted Rob until he hurt his arm throwing serious tennis ball curves in neighborhood stickball games. But everybody envied him because at least he got to dream for a while.

From our neighborhood, those of us in our early teens would walk to Gwynn Oak Junction, at Liberty Heights Avenue and Gwynn Oak Road, to catch the Number 22 bus across town to Memorial Stadium. The junction was one of the bustling marketplaces of northwest Baltimore. Read's drugstore was there, in an era when Read's blanketed the Baltimore area. (The wise guys would call the store's tobacco section and ask, "Do you have Prince Albert in a can? You do? Well, let him out—he's smothering.") The Ben Franklin 5 & 10 was there, downstairs from a fly-by-night pool hall. Across the street was the Ambassador Theater, where the crowds lined up along Liberty Heights past the Ellsworth Armacost Funeral Home the weekend Elvis Presley opened in *Love Me Tender.*

The Number 22 bus took everybody down Liberty Heights to the old Baltimore Junior College, where we would transfer onto the crosstown bus that would take us to Memorial Stadium to watch the Orioles. But the traffic always backed up where University Parkway turned into 33rd Street.

Rob Meyer sat in the back of the bus. As the traffic slowed to a grind approaching 33rd Street, he would bolt out the back door. He was impatient not to miss even a single batting practice pitch. And so he ran, from University where it turned into 33rd, all the way to the park. It was close to a mile. When the rest of us got there, we all got bleacher seats. They cost fifty cents. A wire fence separated the bleachers from General Admission, where the seats were seventy-five cents. Nobody had that kind of money. If we got there early enough, we waited for ushers to turn their back, and then we sneaked over the fence into General Admission, from where we could roam all over the place, since so many seats remained empty.

These were a generation's summer rituals. And in Baltimore that year they were tied to something that was supposed to be special: four years after the Orioles' rebirth, major league baseball scheduled its All-Star Game for Memorial Stadium. This meant the city could puff out its chest for a little bit while the whole country took notice. For a moment, everybody could forget the dreariness of the assembly line,

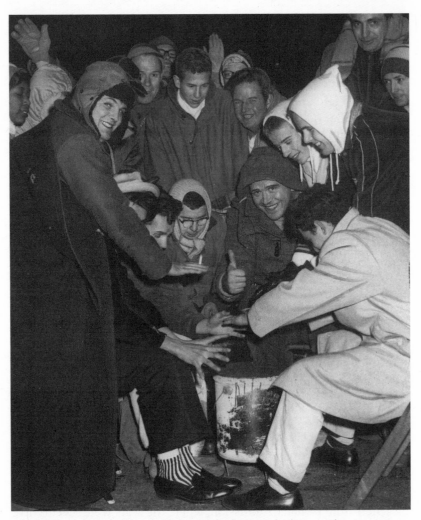

Colts' faithful gather around a fire on an all-night vigil before lining up to buy big-game tickets. In an era when many National Football League teams were still trying to find a fan base, Baltimoreans were filling the ballpark week after week. *Courtesy Baltimore News-American Collection, Marylandia and Special Collections, University of Maryland Libraries*

the beginnings of downtown decay, and the town's traditional feelings of municipal inferiority. The game signaled that we were truly big league, even if we weren't so sure of it ourselves. It meant money and prestige. Also, a certain anxiety.

In May Steadman wrote a piece headlined "All Star Game Puts City on Spot," reflecting the town's bone-deep self-consciousness. "Dream game or nightmare?" he asked. "Baltimore is on the spot as never before in its proud baseball history. . . . Baltimore can look good or it can embarrass itself. Much needs to be done. Time is of the essence. . . . Three managers of leading hotels term the room situation critical. . . . The mayor should declare a holiday. Couldn't the city dress itself up in red-white-and-blue bunting? Couldn't animals march? Couldn't floats roll up Charles Street? Could a Mardi Gras atmosphere be generated?"

When it arrived in July, the All-Star Game was all right. Baltimore looked big league, and nobody got embarrassed. But it would also be the last full measure of attention to baseball before the midsummer arrival of the Colts for summer training camp.

Nobody was quite saying it yet, but baseball was becoming a diversion between football seasons. The Orioles arrived in 1954, and with all kinds of pushes from city hall and grand talk of civic pride and organizations urging their members to attend games, the team managed to draw barely one million people. Across its first decade it would reach this figure only three times. The Orioles were consistent losers, and they were boring. The crowds, such as they were, sat there like Europeans at an opera. Unlike the raucous Colts' fans, they seemed self-conscious about showing any emotions, even on those rare occasions when they had genuine reason to let them loose. The front office shuffled players in and out so quickly that players were gone before anybody could find them lovable.

This at a time when not only were the Colts establishing a generation's worth of familiar names—Unitas and Marchetti and the rest— but their owner, Rosenbloom, was urging them to stay in Baltimore during the off-season. They gave speeches and helped sell tickets. They mixed with people in bars and restaurants. Often Rosenbloom helped them find jobs. They were identified as members of the community in ways the Orioles were not. Their general manager, Don Kellett, would say: Unitas, you're speaking to this Cub Scout troop next week. Ameche, you're going over to Our Lady of Pompei's street carnival. Donovan, you're doing Sunday breakfast with the B'nai B'rith. The whole ball club? You'll head for that new shopping center out York Road. The Colts band will greet you when you step off the bus. The Orioles, meanwhile, had no strategies of such magnitude.

What's more, they were pretty awful.

In their first season back in the majors the Orioles won 54 games and lost 100. So they shook things up. That winter they changed managers and spent money. And they traded. One trade, with the New York Yankees, involved 17 players. The big names were Bob Turley and Don Larsen, who went to New York. In Baltimore, Turley showed great promise but walked nearly 200 batters; in New York, he became a 20-game winner and, in '58, the World Series hero. In Baltimore, Larsen won 3 games while losing 21; in New York, he would pitch the only perfect game in World Series history. The big Orioles' grab in this deal was Gus Triandos, who would set a club record for home runs the following season. He hit 12. With such power, the Orioles did not limit themselves to a mere 54 wins out of 154. Now they managed to win 57.

It caught our enthusiasm for a while. In neighborhoods all across the metropolitan area, the baseball rituals took on new meaning. Schoolboys sprinted across outfields and imagined they could be the Orioles' Chuck Diering, if not Willie Mays. No one had yet imagined the sprints of Lenny Moore. They threw fastballs and thought they might become Bullet Bob Turley. No one had yet heard John Unitas's name. In my neighborhood one of the old men, a Baltimore lifer, saw me dive for a schoolyard grounder one day and come up covered with dirt.

"Look at you," he called out. "You're playing like an old Oriole."

I didn't know what he was talking about. I only knew about the new Orioles, reborn out of the dismal legacy of the St. Louis Browns. But the sound of the old man's voice was clear. He was complimenting me on my hustle and trying to connect me to something.

"You never heard of Wee Willie Keeler?" he said.

I shook my head.

"Hit 'em where they ain't," he said.

I shrugged and went back to fielding grounders. The old Orioles, the championship turn-of-the-century teams of Keeler and Hughie Jennings, of John McGraw and Uncle Wilbert Robinson, seemed impossibly ancient. They went back fifty years, for Pete's sake, to a time that seemed primordial. How could any human being remember back that far?

But, again, a connection had been forged: not only to the Orioles but to the history of a community. Merely by tossing a ball, neighborhood kids were becoming a part of something. When news of the modern Orioles' birth hit the newspapers, the poet Ogden Nash wrote words that stirred the municipal soul:

Wee Willie Keeler
Runs through the town
All along Charles Street
In his nightgown
Bellowing like a hound dog
Gathering the pack:
Hey, Wilbert Robinson
The Orioles are back!
Hey, Hughie Jennings!
Hey, John McGraw!
I got fire in my eye
And tobacco in my jaw!
Hughie, hold my halo,
I'm sick of being a saint;
Got to teach the youngsters
To hit 'em where they ain't.

So we learned the rituals. We stuck wads of bubble gum in our cheeks and pretended it was chewing tobacco, imitating Nellie Fox of Chicago or Billy Gardner of the Orioles. If we threw a knuckleball, we tilted our heads like Hoyt Wilhelm. We stood in the outfield and yelled, "Way you chuck 'em in, hon," the way we were told the big leaguers did it.

When we played little league ball, we opened each season with a parade through the city's streets. We wore our baseball uniforms with high-topped black sneakers or rubber cleats. The parades felt like something sprung to life from *Saturday Evening Post* magazine covers, courtesy of Norman Rockwell, with parents waving from front porches as though welcoming sons home from war. We were conscious of taking part in American rituals. In schoolyards each day we played variations of the game. In backyards we batted grounders to each other and played running bases and filled our summertime hours with stepball and curb ball. When assigned book reports for school, we found a writer named John R. Tunis and a young right fielder named Roy Tucker of the Brooklyn Dodgers in a book called *The Kid from Tompkinsville*. Tucker was not so much older than us. He approached the game with a kid's awe, and when his Dodgers reached the World Series and his teammates talked of bonus money, all young Tucker could think was, "Four thousand! Imagine what that would do on the farm. Gosh, wouldn't Grandma be tickled if . . . "

That was our image of the big league ballplayer: he wasn't playing for the money. Heck, if there was money to be made, he'd make it for his family. Thus, in our minds, was the great game tied to all things good and noble, all things American.

But something else was happening that wasn't tied in to Chuck Diering running through the grass, or Roy Tucker looking out for Grandma, or the guys on Crawford Avenue hitting 'em where they ain't, like Wee Willie Keeler. And it took us a few years to figure it out along with the rest of the country.

By 1958, when the Baltimore Colts and New York Giants seemed to transform the sporting culture before our eyes, baseball was already in trouble.

The baseball Giants and Dodgers fled New York for California, counting their new money every mile of the way. Farewell, sentimental suckers. Farewell to Mays, the Say-Hey Kid who played stickball on the streets of Harlem when he wasn't racing across the Polo Grounds outfield. Now he was seen on the cover of *Life* as his Giants were paraded three thousand miles away through the streets of San Francisco. Farewell, too, to the beloved Bums of Brooklyn, hijacked to Los Angeles by their owner, Walter O'Malley. Later, three of New York's newspaper legends—Jimmy Breslin, Pete Hamill, and Jack Newfield—played a little game. They each made out a secret ballot of the three most evil men in history. Each wrote the same three: Hitler, Stalin, and the Dodgers' O'Malley. (In years to come, Colts' fans would add the name of Irsay.)

So New York was left alone with the mighty Yankees, and what happened? With all of the vast metropolis now perched strictly at their feet, the Bronx Bombers flung open the doors of Yankee Stadium on opening day of 1958 and found precisely 23,463 souls waiting to enter. Meaning, two-thirds of the ballpark was empty.

That was only part of it. Over the previous decade, attendance across all professional baseball had dropped by 50 percent. Half of the game's minor leagues had collapsed. A third of the major league clubs had moved from one town to another. While the Yankees were winning one pennant after another, attendance around the big leagues had plummeted.

A month after the '58 season opened, it was clear the Yankees were marching toward their fourth straight American League pennant, and their ninth in ten years. Former Oriole Turley was en route to a twenty-win season. Figures, everybody in Baltimore said. We trade 'em, and they get good.

When the Orioles opened their season that April, their kid third baseman, Brooks Robinson, dubbed the human vacuum cleaner over twenty-two seasons, led them to victory with three hits and several terrific fielding plays. "Not even the great Pie Traynor could have been more spectacular," the *News-Post's* Hugh Trader wrote. But the opening-day crowd was 34,377, which meant there were about 20,000 empty seats.

By early May, Robinson was hitting .436. His sacrifice fly in the thirteenth inning beat Cleveland. But there were 2,282 people who paid their way into the Baltimore ballpark that day. When the Orioles went to Chicago a few days later and beat the White Sox, 5 to 1, there were 632 fans in attendance. When they returned home to play Washington and lost on a ninth-inning error by shortstop Willie Miranda, attendance was 5,432.

When the 1958 baseball season reached its halfway point, attendance was down more than 100,000 fans from the previous year's mediocre figure. Not coincidentally, the Yankees had opened up their widest July 4 lead in twenty years. The game was over when it had just begun.

In hindsight, some have called the '50s a golden decade for baseball. These are mostly New York writers who have no sense of the world that exists ten minutes beyond the Lincoln Tunnel and no sense of the boredom that was settling in across the country. The Yankees won the World Series consecutively from 1949 through 1953. New York's Giants won it the next year, and then Brooklyn's Dodgers won in '55. The Yanks won again in '56, won the American League pennant in '57, and would win everything again in '58.

Sport, the great monthly sports magazine of that era, tried to defend the game but instead showed most of its weaknesses. In July 1958, in an editorial headlined "A Good Ballgame Is Never Too Long," the magazine opined, "A ballgame is drama, classic in its form and lavish in its ritual . . . the slow, reluctant walk to the mound of the worried manager, the pawing around of the harrassed pitcher, grumbling out of the side of his mouth that he's still got his good stuff and he knows he can get the next guy out; the tense moment when the manager tries to decide; the umpire edging over from third impatiently; then, finally, the hook—and the fans settling in for the next stage of the drama as the manager ceremonially hands the ball to the new pitcher."

And here was the real heart of baseball's problem: not just Yankees dominance but the game itself. While all this ancient, labored ceremonial business was going on, football was running off fourteen plays— delighting both crowds and boys playing the game.

We appreciated baseball's rituals, but playing the game was a little different. We loved being out there like Willie Mays, but it took forever for somebody to hit the ball that far. We wanted to be Roy Tucker and win one for the whole family. But the game could be so paralyzingly slow.

In July, the All-Star Game came to town, and everything worked out fine, except for the actual contest. It was a colossal bore. It was the only All-Star Game in history without a single extra base hit. Willie Mays was there, and Mickey Mantle and Ted Williams and Stan Musial. Hardly anybody hit the ball. The Orioles' Billy O'Dell was named Most Valuable Player because he pitched three shutout innings in relief.

Steadman called it "the city's greatest sports spectacular, surpassing Army-Navy games of 1924 and 1944, and the War Admiral–Seabiscuit race of 1938. For color, ballyhoo, fanfare, pageantry, pomp and ceremony, the All Star show was an overwhelming success. The performance on the field was far less exciting as not one play occurred which brought the crowd to its feet or sent the spectators away on an enthusiastic note."

The All-Star crowd was 48,829.

Four weeks later, the Baltimore Colts staged their annual intrasquad game—a glorified but meaningless scrimmage—at the same Memorial Stadium.

The crowd was 48,309.

FATHER RAYMOND BERRY

TEN O'CLOCK ON A SPRINGTIME NIGHT IN 2007, Raymond Berry walks into the dim Pikesville Hilton Hotel lobby looking as if he could still put a few moves on Harland Svare. Berry is seventy-four years old. In the sudden-death game, he caught a remarkable twelve passes for 178 yards. He caught three in a row in the Colts' frantic drive for a tying field goal when much of Baltimore kneeled in front of their black-and-white television sets muttering hoarse prayers to any deities who might be listening, and then he caught two more passes in the overtime drama to set up the winning touchdown. Mr. Svare of the New York Giants is still trying to locate the elusive Mr. Berry.

He lives in Tennessee but comes to Baltimore for reunions or funerals. Too often now it's a combination package. He arrived for Jim Parker's service two years earlier, and it looked like half the roster showed up at the church. On this balmy May night Berry's in Baltimore for another old teammate. Lenny Moore holds a dinner every year to honor his late son, Leslie, who died of a hideous disease called scleroderma. The event raises scholarship money. It has also become an annual gathering of a generation of Baltimoreans who continue to cling to their memories. More than a thousand of them lined up earlier this evening outside the big Martin's West banquet hall. They were mostly people in their fifties and sixties and older with photographs and footballs they wanted somebody to sign, as though these would validate a connection to their own distant past.

They stood in line telling each other where they were when Ameche lowered his head and plunged into the end zone. They talked in shorthand to each other: "How about when the television went out?" "How about when Gino refused to leave the field?" Fifty years later, nobody needs an explanation; these moments are part of their folklore.

They remembered the boozy Sunday morning train ride to New York, when the Colts band romped through the cars playing the fight song and everybody yelled, "Gimme a C," and they talked about the pandemonium at the airport that night when the Colts came home and it felt like the closest thing in their lives to the joys of V-J Day.

And they remembered Unitas somehow finding Berry again and again in the gathering darkness when it seemed far too late for any miracles.

Berry walked into the Hilton lobby wearing a blue suit and cowboy boots. The fine blond hair, the lean physique, the easy gait—he looked as if he could still run a pretty good sideline pattern. It figured. He was always a man who made up for his shortcomings by force of will. Couldn't see past the E on the eye chart? He was early with contact lenses, and with special goggles if the sun was too strong. (Once, in practice, he lost a lens. Picture this: Berry and thirty-five teammates, Weeb Ewbank and five assistant coaches, two trainers and an equipment man, all on their hands and knees looking for the lens until somebody found it in a tuft of grass.) One leg was a little shorter than the other? He had one of his cleats made longer. He was too slow? He made up for it with slavish preparation, including endless watching and rewatching of game film. When he got married, Chuck Thompson asked Berry if his new wife, Sally, was a football fan. "I don't know," said Raymond, "but she can run a projector." His fingers were a little weak? He spent hours using Silly Putty to strengthen them. In training camp he carried a football with him wherever he went, to keep his fingers supple. The ball club was headed for the West Coast? He lived on West Coast time for a week, changing his mealtimes and his bedtimes, to get ready for the three-hour time difference. He didn't like the way his uniform pants fit? He'd hand-wash them himself, so they wouldn't go to some other guy after the team laundry was done. He needed extra work on tough throws? He'd take Sally into the backyard to throw passes in his vicinity.

"You could throw a football?" she was asked.

"I never touched one before in my life," she said.

Her throws made Raymond dive all over the place, which is what he wanted.

Jim Parker once described a Berry ritual when the Colts played games on the West Coast. He claimed Berry planted dried fruits and nuts in secret parts of the ballparks in Los Angeles and San Francisco "in case there was an earthquake and he needed survival food." Parker told the story to a small gathering one winter afternoon a few years before he died. None of us who heard the story knew whether to laugh or take him seriously, so deeply ingrained were the tales of Berry's idiosyncratic nature and his microscopic attention to every conceivable detail. Art DeCarlo tried throwing him extra passes one afternoon. Berry made him stop after a few tosses. DeCarlo was left-handed. The ball was spinning the wrong way.

He always seemed a little different from his teammates. He was quiet and earnest and studied like an Ivy League gentleman readying for his law boards. He took none of his skills for granted. He didn't make the starting team in high school until his senior year—even though his father was the coach. Once, with the Colts, he got turned away trying to enter a ballpark on game day. A security guard couldn't believe he was one of the ballplayers. When Jim Mutscheller's mother asked, "Who are these awful people," she could not have been looking at Raymond.

The first time I met Berry, in the fall of 2006, I told him, "John Steadman used to say, 'When Raymond Berry was in the room, the other players acted as if a priest had just walked in.'"

"Well then, John didn't know me very well," Berry said.

"He meant it as a compliment."

"Or else," said Berry, "he never heard me after I dropped a pass in practice. It wasn't exactly the king's English, I can tell you that." He said it with a hint of pride in his voice, like a schoolboy saying, Hey, I know some pretty good cuss words, too, don't you worry.

In the sudden-death game, Raymond Berry caught a dozen passes from John Unitas, including three in the final, miraculous minute of regulation time. This is Berry against the Detroit Lions, on opening day at Memorial Stadium, reaching for a patented circus catch. *Courtesy Baltimore News-American Collection, Marylandia and Special Collections, University of Maryland Libraries*

That first meeting we had was at Sabatino's Restaurant, in Baltimore's Little Italy. There was a gathering at the Sports Legends museum that weekend to mark the fiftieth anniversary of John Unitas's first appearance in a pro football game. The museum's director, Mike Gibbons, invited a group of us to dinner. Sally Berry was there. So was Tom Callahan, who had just written his book on Unitas.

That night at the restaurant I remembered the afternoon I'd spent back in 1986 with Alan Ameche and Art Donovan, when they talked about Berry a lot because he'd just coached the New England Patriots to the Super Bowl.

"The only thing wrong with Raymond," said Donovan, "is he won't drink. He had a few beers, till Shinnick got hold of him." Don Shinnick was the one who led team prayers. "Shinnick told Raymond, 'Don't drink that stuff, it's the devil's brew.' "

"Yeah, but I love Raymond," Ameche said.

"Oh, hell, yeah," said Donovan.

"He was the least likely guy to do what he did," Ameche said. "In '55, everybody in camp thought it was a big mistake going with him. He had very limited ability, but he was the hardest-working guy anybody ever saw."

"They used to bring the ends in to block the defensive line in our scrimmages," Donovan said. "Here's skinny Raymond up against us. We'd hit him a shot. He'd say, 'Mmm, let me try that again.' Holding his jaw together. Hah."

"He used to stay after practice and work on impossible catches with Unitas," Ameche said. "He'd flip around. God, over and over. Finally it'd be dark. John would say, 'Come on, Raymond, my arm's getting sore.' We'd go to dinner, and Raymond's sitting there squeezing Silly Putty to strengthen his fingers. But, you know, he and John knew each other like books."

Now, two decades later, I looked across the table at Berry. The restaurant was packed and noisy. One table over, a dozen people sang a loud Happy Birthday to a teenage girl. Then somebody asked Berry about the final moments of regulation play in the sudden-death game. The room suddenly went silent. Even people from nearby tables seemed to strain to listen in.

"We were down to a little more than a minute left to play," Berry said in his soft drawl.

All nine of us at the table knew this, of course. Nearly half a century later, we have memorialized the moment in Baltimore. We can tell you yard lines and time remaining on the Yankee Stadium clock and precisely where we were sitting when Unitas kept throwing the football to Berry. But this is Raymond reliving it now. To hear him talk is to have Moses himself explain the contents of these stone tablets he lugged into the desert end zone.

The Colts trailed by three with about ninety seconds remaining. Unitas had just thrown two incomplete passes, so now it was third and ten from their own fourteen-yard line. Unitas found Lenny Moore for eleven yards. First down.

Now in the Colts' huddle, Unitas tells Berry to run a ten-yard square-in. When they get to the line of scrimmage, there's Harland Svare, the Giants' outside linebacker. He's practically on top of Berry, and he's maybe fifty pounds heavier. If Berry sticks to the play Unitas has called, Svare will flatten him before he can make a move.

In their infinite attention to detail, Unitas and Berry discussed such a situation and decided on a backup move. But they went over it God knows how long ago and haven't talked about it since. The world has turned over many times since then. In the twilight din of Yankee Stadium, with the wind blowing heaps of dirt everywhere and the clock running out, Berry looks silently back to Unitas and wonders if John remembers. Unitas glances back at Berry and hopes Raymond remembers.

And now, all these years later at a table in a crowded restaurant, Berry tells the story, and it feels like living those final seconds all over again.

"TOO MUCH COMMOTION down here," Berry says. "Let's go up to my room."

It's eight months after the dinner in Little Italy, and we're out at the Pikesville Hilton. Berry, still wearing the blue suit with the cowboy boots, sits on the edge of the bed with a small pad of paper in his hands. As he talks, he makes occasional notes to himself. It's as if he's monitoring his thoughts the same way he used to monitor his actions on the playing field.

"That summer when you came back to Baltimore," I say.

I mean the summer of '58. Berry had gone back to Paris, Texas, when the '57 season ended. He was ticked off, like the others. They'd blown it badly. They'd gone into the final two games of the season in first place and gotten nosebleeds from the height and proceeded to lose and lose. This year, everybody agreed, was theirs.

So on the morning of July 26, in the baking heat of Westminster, Maryland, they began arriving on the grounds of the old Western Maryland College for the first day of summer training camp.

Art Donovan was there, regaling everybody with stories. So were Don Joyce and Big Daddy Lipscomb, who'd spent the previous winter as professional wrestlers. Jim Parker was there, after an off-season selling cemetery lots. Jim Mutscheller had sold insurance. They were doing all right; they were making a pretty good middle-class living. This was about money, but it was more than that. They were a little embarrassed. They'd let it all get away the year before, and they knew it. Unitas and Berry spotted each other and quickly got into old pitch-and-catch rhythms.

"We might just go all the way," said general manager Don Kellett.

John Steadman, newly returned to the *News-Post,* agreed but urged caution. He remembered the first Colts camp, when the general manager, Walter Driskill, predicted Baltimore would win the league championship. They went one and eleven that year.

But everybody sensed something special happening here, including the crowds showing up right away at training camp. Many drove up from Baltimore. They maneuvered all the way out cramped Reisterstown Road toward Carroll County and then crawled through Westminster's narrow Main Street to Western Maryland College. The long trip didn't matter.

Baseball was becoming an afterthought. The Orioles, as usual, couldn't get out of their own way. They had Brooks Robinson but not much else. That summer they had weary veterans holding on for a final paycheck, such as the former Yankee Gene Woodling and the former batting champ George Kell and Bob Nieman and Billy Loes, the former Brooklyn Dodger pitcher. There were kids not yet ready for prime time, such as Milt Pappas and Jerry Walker. Also, the flashy shortstop Willie Miranda, once described as the only man who could hit three ways: righty, lefty, and seldom. And there was the lumbering catcher, Gus Triandos. The previous year, the big hit movie was *Around the World in Eighty Days.* Triandos's life story, it was said, would be called "Around the Bases in Eighty Days."

Meanwhile, the ball club was playing before acres of empty seats. It was this way night after night not only in Baltimore but around the league. Attendance was down everywhere as the Yankees once again ran away from all competitors. With the season half over, Baltimore home attendance averaged barely ten thousand a night. By the time the Colts opened their summer camp, the Orioles were fourteen games behind the Yankees. When the team played in the afternoon—which still happened with some regularity in '58—manager Paul Richards invented ways to get himself thrown out of ball games. He wanted to catch the last couple of races at Pimlico.

By the time the Colts staged their annual Police Boys intrasquad game at Memorial Stadium, the Orioles were nine games into an eleven-game losing streak. Bye-bye, baseball; hello, football.

In the crowd that night were half a dozen guys from my neighborhood. We rode the bus across town and took one home later that night. The air was hot and sticky. We were all about thirteen or fourteen years old. When Lenny Moore ran the opening kickoff back ninety-five yards for a touchdown, we felt we were at a circus. Nearly five years of watching Orioles baseball games, and we'd never seen a single play so exciting. As the crowd roared all around us, we sensed we were in on something marvelous, and we wanted more than ever to be connected to it.

"When the Colts appeared," Steadman wrote the next day, "the eruption of applause sounded more like Vesuvius blowing its top than anything human. That 48,309 would turn out for a glorified scrimmage is further evidence that the 'Colt fever' epidemic is with us early this year. It's probably the only time in the history of major league sports that a crowd hit standing-room only proportions for a practice game. . . . It's incongruous. But they were there. It wasn't an illusion."

Raymond Berry hated what happened that night: he dropped a pass. In the hotel room fifty years later, Berry smiled wanly. "You know," he said, "Jimmy Orr once told me, 'I dropped six passes with the Colts.' He wasn't kidding. He remembered each one. I got to thinking, How many did I drop? Some years, I don't think I dropped any. Several years, I dropped one."

But he dropped one in the intrasquad game that night, and nobody could believe it. Maybe a stranger was wearing Berry's uniform number. "Berry will probably take the football to bed with him for a week as a self-imposed reminder that he has no right to lose a reception," Steadman wrote.

When we rode the packed bus back across town that night, the guys in my neighborhood talked about the game the whole way. We couldn't get over it. Unlike Orioles games, where you usually went home deflated, we felt the electricity from this piddly exhibition game still pulsing through us.

When our bus reached Liberty Heights Avenue by the old Baltimore Junior College, it was close to eleven o'clock. We knew the buses were pretty infrequent so late at night. So one of the guys said we should walk home.

Within a few years you wouldn't do such a thing at night on that stretch of Liberty Heights, but in the summer of '58 it didn't occur to anyone to worry. The curtain of fear was not quite descending. We were out late, we were part of something exciting, why not let the night play itself out? So we began the long walk home, bursting from the game, everyone puffed up, full of talk, full of breathless laughter, full of so much energy we ran sprints up the sidewalk against each other, the way Lenny Moore might race Leonard Lyles.

All around us, the world was about to change. Down Liberty Heights Avenue, where it merged with Reisterstown Road, the developer James Rouse had opened the doors to the Mondawmin Shopping Mall. Years later, when cities were said to be dying, Rouse would build Harborplace, which transformed downtown Baltimore and became the centerpiece of the city's rebirth. But in 1958 he was beginning to build those air-conditioned malls that were draining away the crowds of downtown shoppers. The advertising jingle went:

Mondawmin, Mondawmin
A new shopping day is dawnin'
Just park your car
And there you are
In beautiful new Mondawmin.

The place was billed as the area's first enclosed mall. It had a winding staircase and a pool with a shooting spray. To Baltimoreans, it looked glamorous. People tossed coins in the water and made wishes. The owners of Mondawmin should have made their own wish: better timing.

In no time at all, the mall emptied out: first white people fled, then store owners broke their leases and fled. They had anticipated bigger spenders. Directly below Mondawmin, the neighborhoods were all black; to one side, Druid Hill Park loomed; to another, the Ashburton neighborhood where the Jews had lived but into which the blacks were moving.

That summer, as For Sale signs began to dot front yards there, the *Jewish Times* sounded an alarm of equal parts diplomacy and worry. The magazine noted that the Ashburton Area Association, "whose board is composed of both white and Negro residents of this tradition-rich neighborhood, are beginning an all-out campaign to remind home-seekers that it is a highly desirable residential area. Although less than five percent of the residents are colored, Ashburton has earned the reputation of a 'changed' neighborhood. . . . Melvin Sykes, acting chairman, points out that twenty white families have moved into Ashburton within the past few months and that both white and colored residents are anxious to preserve the neighborhood. . . . Panicky home owners are losing tens of thousands of dollars in quick sales of handsome, spacious homes to flee the imaginary 'invading hordes.' "

Not only did the story capture the poignant, panicky, often exasperating mood of the era—it also failed to stem the tide. Within a few years, the neighborhood was completely black. Whites around the city, even those who professed belief in the era's great civil rights movement, had commenced their mass migration to suburbia.

Directly across the street from Mondawmin was the Gwynns Falls Parkway Junior High. When the city schools first integrated in 1954, Gwynns Falls' first black students enrolled. By the next year, the school was 45 percent black. A year later, 77 percent. By 1957, 96 percent.

As the guys from my neighborhood made our way along Liberty Heights Avenue late that night, we were oblivious to much of this. We were talking football. We passed within a block of Garrison Junior High School, which most of us attended. The school had integrated three years earlier. It was now about one-third black. In another five years, it would be two-thirds black. Five years after that, almost all whites would be gone.

We passed Yosemite Avenue. The street was beginning to change. Lenny Moore had just moved in. The same white people who cheered him on the playing field were moving out on the very day he arrived on the block. Moore strolled up to a man with a moving van in front of his house. He was trying to hold on to his composure, but he knew what was happening.

"Hey, man, why are you moving out?" he asked.

"It's nothing," the man said. "It's just that the neighborhood's breaking up."

"Oh," Moore muttered, knowing it was too late for any lectures about the brotherhood of man. "I know what you're saying."

There were other measures of the continuing racial distances. In June, the *Evening Sun* ran photos of area high school graduation classes. Day after day, there they were: City College with 461 graduates, maybe 20 of them black; Polytechnic, 258 grads, all but a handful white; Patterson High, 240 grads, all white; Loyola High, 149, all white; Catonsville High, 310 graduates, all white; Dundalk High, 336, all white.

The town leaders, insisting on ignoring reality, instead rationalized. At least we aren't Little Rock, Arkansas, they told themselves. That spring, more than two hundred police and National Guard troops were called out to keep the peace at graduation ceremonies at Little Rock's Central High School following a year of riots and bomb threats and constant tension over the enrollment of nine black students.

In Baltimore that summer the Gwynn Oak Amusement Park ran big newspaper advertisements: "Heading for Fun! Gwynn Oak Park Open! Rides! Games! Thrills!" But the thrills were only open to white people.

Again, the town leaders rationalized. At least we aren't in Chalfont, Pennsylvania, they told themselves. There, racial fights erupted at the Forest Amusement Park. Fifteen injured, thirty-four arrested. Newspaper reports said weapons included baseball bats, tire irons, bottles, and "small trees."

In June, the Reverend Dr. Martin Luther King told Morgan State College graduates, "Never use second-class methods to become first-class citizens. Those of us who have had to face lynch mobs, to withstand bombs, who are the last hired and the first fired, are tempted to act with bitterness. But somebody must have sense enough to cut the chains of hate, to meet physical force with soul force." King was identified in the *Baltimore Sun* story as "the man who led the Montgomery, Alabama, bus boycott."

At least, local white leaders said, we aren't Montgomery. This was true, and it meant nothing to blacks who were simply biding their time that summer.

It was a time when people knew their place in the worst sense of it. Black people, and women, too. Women stayed home and raised their children. All fulfillment was supposed to come from this. The Sunday *Sun Magazine*'s Curious Camera asked, "Do you think attending classes or lectures would aid the modern housewife?" Mailman Harry Kennedy answered, "Once a person's out of school, I can't see any sense in them attending classes to learn something they should already know." Dental assistant Robert Whitney answered, "The average housewife is too set in her ways to be changed." Housewife Patsy Horsely said, "I've never attended such classes, and I feel as if I've missed nothing." (That was the same Sunday *Sun Magazine* that went through the entire year ignoring black people. The magazine was thick with stories and with dozens of photographs week after week. In October it ran a feature on the football coach at the all-black University of Maryland Eastern Shore. In November, the magazine ran a feature on Lenny Moore and another on singer Sallie Blair. For the entire year, there were no other black people in story or photo.)

It was the summer Ike and Mamie Eisenhower celebrated their forty-second anniversary and Annette Funicello marked her fifteenth birthday. Hula hoops were everywhere. Ed Sullivan introduced the Kingston Trio on television and said they were a nice bunch of boys even though they weren't wearing jackets and ties. James Dean was everybody's idea of a rebel—but, against what? We weren't so sure. He got killed in a car crash before he could tell us. It seemed a cautionary tale to the latent rebel in each of us. (And that other great rebel, Marlon Brando, was no clearer. In *The Wild Ones*, Brando was asked, "What are you rebelling against?" "Whattaya got?" he replied.)

The '50s are seen, in retrospect, as a time of great order and calm. When people turned on their television sets, they saw the perfect middle-class nuclear families on *Father Knows Best* and *Ozzie and Harriet*. But in Baltimore it was beginning to feel like a disconnect. The city was already heavy with families living below the poverty line. Seventy percent of the state's welfare families lived in the city, and so did 80 percent of its dependent children. That summer the FBI called Baltimore a national leader in street crime and took note of a growing narcotics problem. In 1958, there were a reported 60,000 drug addicts across America. Half a century later, there would be 60,000 in the city of Baltimore alone.

The week after the FBI report, city cops grandly announced they'd broken up a pornography ring. They confiscated thousands of photographs "of a nature that cannot be described in print," the newspapers declared. The raid was seen as a big deal. Clergymen all across town applauded, especially when the newspapers ran the names and addresses of all the individuals who were arrested. Then Captain Joseph Carroll, head of the Baltimore Police Narcotics Squad, announced that twenty-four people were arrested on narcotics charges. The newspapers noted that all but two of those nabbed "are Negroes." Captain Carroll said his officers' series of raids would "break the backs of narcotics traffic in Baltimore."

When Baltimoreans needed something else to worry about that year, they worried about their children. Especially the teenagers. The *News-Post* sent reporter Eddie Birrane to a high school fraternity party at Gwynn Oak Park's Dixieland Ballroom. Birrane was shocked at what he found: "flagrant law-breaking . . . drunken boys and girls, not yet 20 . . . whiskey and beer bottles lay openly on tables while 'policemen' assigned as chaperones stood idly by, closing their eyes to everything." That wasn't all. " 'Necking' and 'petting' were very popular," Birrane wrote, "and when the band played a slow number, it played, unheard, to couples passionately embracing on the dance floor." Birrane reported that he left early. "I was disgusted," he wrote.

To anxious parents, the Dixie Ballroom crowd seemed a mirror image of those wild kids on *The Buddy Deane Show*, those Committee members with their pegged pants and their short skirts, and their beehive hair and their crazy jitterbug dances, who seemed the local manifestation of all things rebellious. The irony was, as youngsters of the '50s, the Buddy Deane kids were subjected to rules of behavior far beyond the strictures of most of their friends. They needed a letter of recommendation from their pastor merely to qualify for the show. Future Committee member Carl Parks's pastor was on vacation, so the Arlington Methodist Church secretary, Mrs. Irma Jones, had to suffice. ("Carl is one of our 'Teenage' boys here at the church," she wrote. "He is honest, faithful, trustworthy. He is a fine Christian boy.") The Buddy

Deane Rules of Behavior included a point system. Lose too many points, and you lose your precious Committee membership. No gum chewing and no smoking. You could lose points for "not applauding at the end of each record. For leaving Coke bottles, ice cream cups or candy bars any place improper. For not dancing with guests on the show."

"They used to bring the Powerhouse hamburgers up to the show from Ameche's Drive-In," Parks remembered years later. "They were there for the guests. I got caught eating a pickle one time. Big trouble."

Parks remembers getting free passes to see *Rock around the Clock* at the Hippodrome Theater. The place was filled with Buddy Deane fans. Parks went with two other Committee members, Doug Constantine and Buddy Bell. They sat in the front row in the balcony and leaned over. They were spotted by four girls downstairs. The girls went bananas.

"Come on up," Parks called to them.

"Can't," one of the girls said. She pointed to her friend, a polio victim in a wheelchair.

"No problem," Parks said. He went downstairs, picked up the girl, and brought her upstairs with her friends so they could all watch the movie together.

And these were the kids parents found so frightening in 1958.

WHEN BALTIMOREANS went to the racetrack that year, they saw Silky Sullivan flop at the Preakness before thirty-five thousand people. When they went to the movies, they saw *The Bridge on the River Kwai* and *No Time for Sergeants* and *Gigi*. When they turned on the television, they saw Ed Sullivan and *The Donna Reed Show*. It was all very safe, very middle of the road, very comforting.

When they went to Western Maryland College after the huge intrasquad game, they found their football team's marvelous cast of characters.

They found Don Joyce, who worked in the off-season as a professional wrestler. "Joyce is known as a baby face," John Steadman wrote, "meaning he doesn't go in for hair pulling or eye gouging."

One night at the dump called the Coliseum, Joyce wrestled a fellow named Mad Man Managoff, a lunk out of North Carolina who warmed up by reciting the Bible verbatim and shooting out the locker room lights with a pistol. Joyce fit right in with this kind of behavior. Once, he and the Los Angeles Rams' Les Richter got into it pretty good. Richter needed fifteen stitches to stop the bleeding around his eye.

In the Colts' training camp, Joyce shared wild-man honors with Bert Rechichar. He's the one who threatened to tear the Lions' Hopalong Cassady's eyeballs from his head. Rechichar could be found in his room at training camp smoking cigars and wearing nothing at all. He was the youngest of eleven children and could see out of only one eye. As a kid, he'd worked the mines around Belle Vernon, Pennsylvania. Whenever he heard his name called out, Rechichar was given to roaring, "What the hell do you want?"

He roomed with the halfback Buddy Young, the team's first black star, who was his closest friend on the ball club. One day an old Rechichar teammate from his college days at Tennessee showed up. Young was sleeping in the next bed.

"Is that a nigger over there?" the guy asked.

"Nah, that's Buddy Young. He stayed out in the sun too long today," Rechichar replied.

By '58 Young had retired, but Rechichar was hanging on. Steadman wrote admiringly of him, "He might get beat on a play but he would always tackle hard or jump on the pile. It was his way of teaching a pass catcher that he'd better not take the liberty to come back in his territory again."

When Raymond Berry looked at such characters, he did not see precise mirror images of his own personality. He graduated high school weighing 150 pounds. There was nothing physically intimidating about him until he set foot on the playing field. He played outside linebacker—what SMU called defensive end—though he was puny even in his senior year when his weight finally reached 180.

"But I was a tough, tough defensive player," Berry said the night we met in his hotel room. He nodded his head, as though fending off any doubts. "When Weeb went to draft, he saw a smart and tough and aggressive competitor. I was balls-out. And I was the same way on offense."

"But you had all that stuff the writers used to write about," I said. "The bad eyes, the short leg, all that stuff."

"It was more than that," Berry said. "I didn't know anything about being a pro receiver." In three varsity seasons at SMU, he'd averaged eleven receptions a year. "The only reason I'm there is Weeb saw something in me. Heck, when Unitas arrived, I was number one ready to be replaced. I hadn't done much of anything. But Weeb saw the same stuff in me that he saw in John, I guess. We were hungry, and we were disciplined, and we were pretty tough.

"I mean, I knew how to size myself up. I had a whole lot of things going for me. I had a body that was built to bend and bounce and not break. I could take hits, dive on the ground, fall down. It was great for playing the way I did. Also, I had the mental ability to absolutely tune out the world. I could concentrate. You can't teach that. You're born with it."

He also spent hours studying film. On Mondays, the whole team watched. On Tuesdays, Berry would go to Unitas's locker with a legal pad and say, "This is what I want to run on this guy on Sunday." Whatever the plays were, that's what he and Unitas would work on all week. Berry would say, "What you call is your problem. But this is what I can do."

There's a matter-of-fact quality to Berry's voice. He knew his short-comings but his pluses, as well.

"I had as great a natural pair of hands as anybody ever had," he said. "But early in my career I realized there were passes I wasn't handling. I was getting my hands on them and not catching them. And that upset me. I started studying catching. I took notes and notes. I identified different types of passes, and how you've got to master them. Twelve or thirteen short ones, and six or seven long ones. And then I'd drill. I had the list of drills taped on the top of my thigh pad. In practice, I'd say, 'Throw it low. Throw it high.' I was embarked on a training program, and I didn't even know what a training program was."

Then there was one more adjustment: He'd broken in with George Shaw, but by the middle of '56, the battered Shaw had been replaced by Unitas.

"Shaw," he said, "was a lot easier to catch. He didn't have a real fastball. He threw a soft, perfect spiral, nose up, very easy to catch. Unitas could throw every which way. He had a soft touch when he needed it, but he could also throw a rocket. That's when I started using the Silly Putty. Eddie Block gave it to me. The trainer, yeah. I'd push it side to side with my fingers, because I needed to make them stronger to handle Unitas."

By 1958, they'd had two seasons to get to know each other's physical abilities and thought patterns. Their after-practice sessions became the stuff of legend: the hour growing darker, the cold biting, and Berry asking Unitas to throw him a few more because Berry hadn't worked on every single pattern he thought he might use on Sunday.

In Unitas's training camp room, they studied together, rehearsed game situations, talked, talked, talked. They talked situations. What do we do if this happens? What if this happens? At some point—and Berry can't remember now if it was '57 or '58—he and John talked about the ten-yard square-in. What would they do if a linebacker came up to the line of scrimmage?

"He's out there to knock my head off," Berry said.

He was still sitting on the edge of his bed in the hotel room, the hour approaching midnight, and still wearing his suit and tie, though he'd taken off his cowboy boots.

"Harland Svare," he said. The Giants' outside linebacker. This was the play Berry had talked about that night at Sabatino's, when the noise at all tables seemed to cease as he remembered that paralyzing moment in the sudden-death game.

"Weeb didn't send the play in?" I asked.

"Weeb didn't know anything about this."

Berry praises Ewbank lavishly. But, like the others, he witnessed the coach's shortcomings. Ewbank understood talent, he prepared his teams—but, on game days, he stood on the sidelines and went all aflutter. "On game days," Unitas always claimed, "you could have left Weeb in the closet most of the time. He got too nervous." It was Unitas's game to call and Ewbank's to fret over.

When the Colts took over for that final drive in regulation time, the clock showed just over two minutes remaining. They were eighty-six yards from the Giants' end zone. Then, on third and ten, he hit Moore for eleven yards. First down. But now the clock was ticking toward the one-minute mark. Again Unitas threw, and again it was incomplete.

When they huddled up again, Unitas told Berry to run the ten-yard square-in. But he hadn't imagined the Giants' outside linebacker

Svare, who outweighed Berry by about thirty-five pounds, coming up tight enough to knock Berry off his stride.

Now Berry, in the hotel room with the clock approaching midnight, rose to his bare feet, still wearing the suit and tie. "Now this is Svare," he said. He gestured toward a television set and stood nose to nose against it and leaned in as if trying to hear Unitas call signals.

"The clock's running, we have no time-outs left, so we can't talk about it," Berry said. He turned his head far to the right, as though looking for Unitas somewhere on the other side of the room, which became Yankee Stadium in the dusk. "I'm looking for John, and he's looking at me. And I'm thinking, 'I hope he remembers what we agreed we'd do in this kind of a situation.'"

"Which you had talked about some time back."

"Right."

And, in the hotel room, Berry bolts. Arms swinging, body bent low, he fakes to the outside coming off the line, trying to get the TV set— the imaginary Svare—to lunge for him. And then slants underneath the lunge. Harland Svare had about as much chance as the TV set.

By the time the Giants found Berry, he was at midfield, twenty-five yards closer to the Giants end zone.

Berry sat back on the bed now and jotted a few more notes on his little pad. Maybe something to use if Harland Svare ever shows up again. He took off his suit jacket, but the tie remained. How many times has he run that play, and that game, through his mind? And yet, he says, for all his attention to detail, and all his studying of game film, it took him years to figure out everything that happened on that famous drive that changed everything.

Always, he was a student of game film. He studied himself, and he studied opponents. He looked at the tendencies of defensive backs. He studied other wide receivers, looking for moves he could use himself. Others spent their off-seasons unwinding from the game; Berry, back in Paris, Texas, had coaches send him films. He'd give himself grades for every play of every game.

"What kind of grades?" I asked.

"Effort," he said. "You give the most you can, and only you know how much effort you really put out."

We had begun talking about the other great game that year, the one that clinched the division championship. The sudden-death game has always gotten the big national billing—the Greatest Game Ever Played—but the players usually said it was the San Francisco game, where they trailed at halftime by three touchdowns and came back to win.

"Donovan and Moore," I say, "have always maintained that that game was the greatest. Didn't have the greatest impact on the country, but the greatest come-from-behind."

"Yeah, I think so," Berry says. "I'll tell you this. When I went over the films, it was the highest marks I ever gave myself for effort."

"What did you get?"

"Eighty-seven."

"Wait a minute," I said. "You're the guy everybody said made it because of sheer effort. You're telling me the highest grade you ever gave yourself was an eighty-seven?"

"My standard," he said. His eyes flashed. "You've got to be true to yourself. The rule is, in order to get a plus, from the time the ball's snapped until the time the whistle blows, you've got to put out 100 percent effort. Want to know what I got in the Giants' game?"

"What?"

"Fifty-six."

"What?"

It's inconceivable. It was the greatest game of his life, and he's saying he didn't put out?

Berry let out an audible sigh. There's a guilty moment that's clung to him for half a century, and it could have changed the course of the ball game.

It's the sudden-death overtime period, and the Colts have just risen from the dead again. On third and fourteen, Unitas finds Berry for twenty-one yards to the Giants' forty-two. An exhausted Berry returns to the huddle, where Unitas calls a fifteen-sucker, a trap play with Alan Ameche running the ball when the Giants are likely to be looking for the pass.

"My job," says Berry, "is to get to the safety or the corner and throw a block. But I'm huffing and puffing. I'm thinking, 'We've been running this play for four years, and it hasn't gained more than two yards yet.' So I go through the motions."

"You were exhausted," I say. "It was overtime, you're out there catching all these passes."

"Doesn't matter," says Berry. His eyes flashed intensity once more.

"You were pacing yourself."

Ameche carried for twenty-three yards.

"Jimmy Patton brings him down from behind," said Berry.

At the twenty-one-yard line.

"Patton's the man I was supposed to block. If I make my block, maybe Ameche goes all the way. I don't make it, and he's brought down. What if we don't score? What if the Giants come back and win?"

Fifty years later, he's still asking himself such questions.

"Nobody knew it but me," he says. "And John."

LENNY AND BIG DADDY

THE REST OF THAT SUMMER OF '58, everybody was so awful that the whole town got ready to be depressed all over again.

The Orioles were terrible, which was expected, but so were the Colts. Fifty years later, who cares about a bunch of exhibition games? They're all vanished from memory, and rightfully so. But it's a fact that the Colts lost their first three preseason exhibitions. They were everybody's great hope, and instead they were turning out dreadful. They lost to the Philadelphia Eagles, 30 to 28. Then they lost to the Washington Redskins, 27 to 7, causing Ewbank to blast the whole squad. He figured this would fire them up. So then they went out and lost to the Pittsburgh Steelers, 13 to 10.

This meant the losing was now universal. The Orioles were woeful, and everybody in town stopped caring. By mid-August, the team had drawn barely six hundred thousand fans. Somebody said they were like that year's Kleenex Tissues commercial: "Pops up, one at a time." The Yankees were the only team in the entire American League playing over .500. So deep was Baltimore hatred for the Yankees, and all things connected to New York, that a *Boston Daily Globe* columnist, Harold Kaese, wrote, "Baltimore fans put Casey Stengel in the same class with Hitler, Rasputin and Benedict Arnold." Stengel was managing the Yankees to another world championship; Hitler at least had the solitary grace to lose.

In September, a rare Orioles highlight: the veteran knuckleballer Hoyt Wilhelm pitched a no-hitter against the Yankees and won, 1 to 0, on a Gus Triandos home run. The ballpark was mostly empty. Then the Orioles went back to losing in front of more empty seats.

But there was also an unsettling racial undercurrent to the Orioles' ongoing failure. They did it, year after year, with almost no black players. This was a decade after Jackie Robinson integrated the game. By 1958 the major leagues included Willie Mays, Hank Aaron, Frank Robinson, Ernie Banks. Fifty years later it's hard to imagine a team so racially insensitive, and so stupid, as those Orioles.

But they were. They had a kid named Jehosie Heard who put on the uniform briefly in that first summer of 1954 but didn't get to pitch. Nobody ever heard from him again. They brought up an outfielder, Joe Durham, at the end of that season but didn't call him back again until 1957.

They had one black player, part-timer Dave Pope, on their roster in 1955. Paul Richards, shuffling players in a summer-long frenzy, used fifty-four players that year, ten at third base alone. All fifty-four were white. Over the next two years, the Orioles brought in the first baseman Bob Boyd, who became their best hitter over a couple of seasons, and the veteran Connie Johnson, who was their best pitcher. In 1958, they had a couple of part-time outfielders, Durham and Lenny Green.

And that was it, a handful of African American ballplayers in the course of the first five seasons of Orioles baseball. The newspapers wrote nothing about this curious fact, and the TV and radio people didn't breathe a syllable. But late that summer a group of black businessmen invited Paul Richards to speak to a luncheon gathering on Pennsylvania Avenue. Steadman was with him and forty years later remembered the day vividly.

"A real long, narrow restaurant," he said. "There was an undercurrent in the questioning, that Richards was antiblack. He picked up on it right away. He said, 'If you think I'm not interested in colored ballplayers, you talk to Robert Boyd, Orestes Saturnino Minoso or Cornelius Johnson.' He always gave 'em the full name, you know. 'You ask them what they think of me.'

"Me," Steadman said, "I never heard Richards say a prejudiced word. But the next question was, 'Why do you put 'em all in the outfield?' I never forgot that. Like, to keep 'em away or something."

Bias or not, it was a fact that the Orioles were putting virtually all-white teams on the field every year. The Colts were not. They had only a handful of black players a year, but most were high-profile. The flashy Buddy Young had retired, but by 1958 they had the future Hall of Famers Lenny Moore and Jim Parker, the All-Pro defensive tackle Gene "Big Daddy" Lipscomb, the speedster Leonard Lyles, the defensive back Milt Davis, and the upcoming Johnny Sample and Sherman Plunkett.

Their presence meant something: Look at this bunch of big, tough, brawny guys who come from all backgrounds, and see them working things out right in front of everybody's eyes. Unitas pitching to Moore, who runs for touchdowns. Big Daddy and Donovan burying a halfback. Parker opening up holes for Ameche to run through. Black and white, just like America was supposed to look.

For black fans, who were indifferent to the all-white Orioles, the Colts felt like the dawning of something. Spats turns the corner and blurs past everyone: finally, they can cheer one of their own; finally, they can show white Americans the full athletic capabilities of a black man. Then there's Big Daddy. He's knocking down ball carriers, and some of them are white. And white people are cheering him for this! Such a thing has never happened in the entire history of Baltimore. And his white teammates are congratulating him!

No one made speeches about it, but it set an example for the city, especially in the newly integrated public schools: If these guys could get along on the ballfield, maybe this was a glimpse of everyone's future.

The city needed that kind of model. It was not yet the time of the great civil rights confrontations. Nobody yet imagined Martin Luther King sharing his dream in front of a sunlit Washington throng. Nobody conceived of Selma, or Watts, or John Carlos and Tommie Smith with their Olympian fists thrust in the air. But things were already happening that touched people's lives in intimate and promising but also threatening ways.

In matters of race, Baltimore in the '50s wasn't an explosive city, but it seethed. In 1954, when the Orioles and Colts were both brand new, the U.S. Supreme Court outlawed public school segregation. In Baltimore this was a crossroads moment. Not only were its public schools segregated, but so were its Catholic and private schools. Now these places sheepishly said they would change their policies. As if, until the Supreme Court reminded them, they hadn't noticed that they were in America but somehow had no black students or teachers. The state's teachers colleges were also completely white. So were Goucher College and the Maryland Institute of Art and the Peabody Institute, allegedly progressive schools. They all now promised to change. Likewise the Baltimore state's attorney's office, which was all white. Public housing projects were still divided by race, and the Baltimore Fire Department had finally integrated only a year earlier. And, despite all the major league teams now coming through town, the Baltimore Hotel Association refused rooms to blacks.

Half a century later it is difficult to conceive of such institutionalized bigotry. But that was only part of it. It was 1955 before Read's drugstores, the biggest local chain, opened their lunch counters to blacks. The same was true at the Friendship Airport restaurant. It offered friendship, but only if you were white. Some downtown movie theaters were still segregated. Lenny Moore was turned away at a downtown theater in 1956. A year later, when Jim Parker heard about this, he considered not signing with Baltimore. The city's liquor board had a regulation against serving alcoholic drinks to "mixed clientele." It was a way to keep blacks in certain bars, whites in others.

Not until 1956 did the city integrate its municipal swimming pools. For the first time, blacks were employed as operators by the Baltimore office of the Chesapeake and Potomac Telephone Company. A year later the all-white, all-male members of the Baltimore Bar Association voted by secret ballot to admit women and blacks. The victory margins were not substantial. For the first time, all-black high schools were allowed to participate in the Maryland Scholastic Association's athletic program. And Baltimore's hotels, pressed by all those professional sports teams arriving in town, inched toward integration by

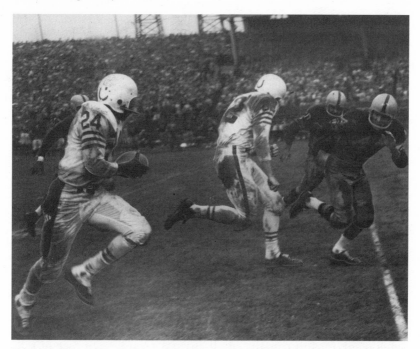

With Raymond Berry running interference, Lenny Moore sprints for big yardage against Green Bay. Moore was nicknamed Spats for taping his ankles on the outside of his football shoes. And nicknamed Sputnik for his out-of-this-world ability to run with the ball. *Courtesy Baltimore News-American Collection, Marylandia and Special Collections, University of Maryland Libraries*

opening their doors—but only to black athletes and to delegates to conventions "in reasonable numbers." It was also the year the city finally removed the last of its "White" and "Colored" signs from public buildings. The last to go? The Lexington Market.

By the summer of '58, the whole country was caught up in such changes. In Little Rock, where hundreds of police and National Guard troops had to baby-sit that spring's graduation ceremonies at the newly integrated Central High School, Governor Orval Faubus ordered all Arkansas schools closed for the fall semester as he sued the federal government. "The greatest civil rights struggle since the Civil War," he called it. In Jacksonville, Florida, southern mayors gathered to talk about the race-related dynamite bombings in scores of their cities. They asked the FBI to investigate. J. Edgar Hoover said his FBI had "no legal basis" for doing so and took a pass. In Norfolk, Virginia, the city school board asked a federal judge to stay his order integrating six schools. This was four years after the Supreme Court ruling. In Morgantown, West Virginia, an elementary–junior high school was dynamited after it was cited as "a model desegregated school."

Around Maryland that year, there were variations of such troubles. In Bladensburg, a junior high school teacher named Alan Goodsand told his students that brutality against blacks in Georgia made him "ashamed to live in America." Goodsand was told to quit or be fired. He said, "I love this country. I have no other. If things happen in this country that are shameful, I think we ought to point them out. We shouldn't be indifferent. We must be vigilant over our democratic liberties." School officials shoved him out the door.

In St. Mary's County, a black man named William Groves, with two teenage children, sued for his children's right to ride the same school bus as white students. This was three years after the Montgomery bus boycott.

There were some voices of sensitivity that year. At their state party convention in early June, Maryland's Republicans called for "a civil rights plank for full equality of all citizens regardless of race or religion." Behind the scenes, it was Governor Theodore McKeldin, Representative Charles Mathias, and state senator Harry Cole wielding the most influence. But when the GOP tried flexing a little muscle, it got nowhere. Mathias said, "About twenty-five Negro delegates and friends have asked where they could eat lunch." He wanted downtown hotels to say, "Eat here." The hotels said no. Then McKeldin told an Ad Club luncheon, "The United States cannot give mere lip service to the doctrine that all men are created equal. . . . There will be no second class citizens." A *Sun* editorial, noting that McKeldin wanted to run for mayor of Baltimore, where the black population was growing, sniffed that he "added up the minorities and discovered that they make a majority." Never mind the moral message. The newspaper, lacking all courage, found it itself caught between some of its editorial board members' liberal sensitivities and the awareness that many of its longtime readers did not share those feelings.

But the most intimate and threatening changes were happening in neighborhoods. Blacks moved in, whites moved out. Blacks were said merely to think about moving in, and whites moved out. It was happening all over the country, but in Baltimore it was so widespread that *U.S. News & World Report* put it into headlines.

"Latest Problem for Cities in North: Blockbusting," the magazine said. "In city after city, white families are likely to wake up some morning to see a Negro family moving in next door. When it happens, chances are a 'blockbuster' has been at work—and before long the whole neighborhood may be Negro."

The entire article focused on Baltimore, but the city's residents didn't need a magazine to explain what was beginning to happen all around them. People talked about race at the dinner table. Neighbors gathered on street corners to assure each other they had no intention of moving and by week's end hired real estate agents to pound For Sale signs on their front lawns.

Blockbusting took a few forms. Sometimes when the first black family moved onto a block, white residents found circulars in their mailboxes, urging them to sell. The circulars promised "confidential" transactions. This meant whites could sell to blacks without their neighbors knowing.

Sometimes real estate agents would telephone home owners. "You know there's a Negro family moving in, don't you? Property values will be dropping. If you want to sell your house while you can still make money, give us a call."

Sometimes so-called panic circulars were distributed to a few thousand homes at a time. These said that blacks were about to "invade" the area. Everybody said this tactic was terrible, panicking people in such a way. But it went on. White families packed their bags and left by the tens of thousands. Even the most racially liberal families feared being the last whites on the block. A drawbridge was beginning to go up, and nobody wanted to be left behind.

In the *News-Post* the veteran columnist Lou Azrael wrote about bumping into an old friend who decided to move to the suburbs. The column was headlined "Who Pays When a Family Moves?"

Azrael spent the whole column talking about the city losing a good citizen with an above-average income, a fellow who kept a good home, went to church on Sundays, paid a lot of taxes. He said poor families would probably move into the dwelling, which would now be split into two apartments. Eventually, he wrote, these new families would leave behind "a poor neighborhood and probably a vacant house."

Never, in the entire column, did Azrael come close to mentioning the issue of race. He didn't have to. Everybody knew.

That October the Greater Baltimore Committee issued a report on the economic impact of blockbusting. The report didn't mean anything to anybody. What became a flood tide had begun, and nobody had the slightest clue about slowing it down.

At the city's peak, in 1950, its population was 950,000. Well into the decade Baltimore was still the seventh-largest city in the country. But by the middle of the 1960s its population was falling fast, and by century's end it barely topped 600,000 as the exodus of whites was followed by that of middle-class blacks.

That atmosphere was just beginning to build when Lenny Moore arrived with the Colts in the summer of 1956. Buddy Young was getting ready to retire, and he took Moore aside for a little advice when he arrived at the Western Maryland training camp.

He had plenty of stories to offer. The first time Young emerged from the Colts' locker room, he came face to face with six people with blackened faces. They did not intend to be a welcoming committee. Young thought, "Either they're gonna do some lynching, or else they want me in a minstrel show." He ran right past them.

When Moore showed up for his first camp, Young pointed directly down the heart of Westminster. "This area up here is very, very segregated," he said. He pointed to a little confectionary store down Main Street. "You can go there," said Young, "but stay out of the restaurants."

Later Moore found a Twin Kiss ice cream place near the college, by a duck pond and some picnic benches. After practice, Moore spent a lot of time there, sometimes alone, sometimes with Jesse Thomas or Big Daddy Lipscomb. The white players went into town, which had a couple of restaurants and bars. Moore stayed out at the duck pond, sometimes into the evening. For Lenny, all of this fed on the sense of isolation he'd known growing up in Reading, where his friendships with white classmates had strict unwritten boundaries, and at Penn State, where Moore was part of a tiny group of black students.

When the Colts broke camp, Moore married and moved into an

apartment on west Baltimore's Brighton Street, just off Poplar Grove, because it was near his mother's cousin. It lessened his sense of isolation. One day he and his wife went downtown to the New Theater. His new wife was fair skinned. Moore asked for two tickets. The woman in the ticket booth said, "She can go in, but you can't." Moore, standing in a line of white people, tried to stifle his humiliation and rage.

On the playing field that first year, he was sensational. He averaged seven and a half yards a carry, nearly twice what a solid professional running back will average. A year later, he gained five yards a carry and caught forty passes for nearly eighteen yards a catch. In 1958 he would average more than seven yards a carry and twenty yards a reception.

But the numbers don't begin to touch the magic. He was there, and then he wasn't. He gave a hip and took it away. He ran under control, and then he bolted. Sometimes he just outran everyone in sight. Once, he scored a touchdown running the last five yards backward. When the New York Giants prepared to meet the Colts, their defensive coach, Tom Landry, said, "Any team that plays Baltimore goes in with a seven-point disadvantage. They don't have Lenny Moore." Art Donovan always called him the best football player he ever saw. Raymond Berry narrowed it to three: Unitas, Jim Brown, and Moore.

In 1958 Moore was phenomenal on the field and dismayed off it. A pattern had developed by this time. The white players went one way, and the black players went another. It was the normal pattern of the era, and of the city. But Moore had expected something closer to their on-field bonding. They were pals out there, warriors in battle who were looking out for each other. And then it ended for the day.

Off the field, he felt they never got to know each other. He hung out mainly with Big Daddy. Each had come up the hard way, though few had come up harder than Lipscomb. Moore, one of twelve children, never knew central heating or indoor plumbing. His mother worked as a domestic for two dollars a day, and his father worked in a steel mill. Their house was located on Reading's Poplar Lane. The address reads better than it was. The front door opened to an alley and the back door onto railroad tracks. They had no electricity until the father wired the house himself. He brought home scraps of leather from the mill to put soles on the children's shoes. "I never saw one hungry day," Moore recalled one afternoon years later. "Saw a lot of one-pot meals, but no, never hungry."

To Big Daddy, all this would have seemed luxurious. His father died when Lipscomb was a toddler, and he and his mother moved from Uniontown, Alabama, to Detroit. Gene was three. Several years later he was awakened by police, telling him his mother had been stabbed to death by one of her boyfriends. She was standing at a bus stop when he attacked her. Gene moved in with his grandfather but had to pay room and board and buy his own clothes. He was eleven. He washed dishes in a café. He loaded trucks. The grandfather beat him when he felt like it. Gene helped out around a junkyard. Anything to make a few bucks. In his teens he worked in a steel mill from midnight until seven and then went home, changed clothes, and went to school. He played ball but struggled in the classroom. His classmates taunted him because he didn't know his lessons and he kept growing out of his clothes. He dropped out of school and joined the marines, where he played football at Camp Pendleton and found at least some semblance of order to his life.

Pete Rozelle, the future NFL commissioner, was scouting for the Los Angeles Rams and spotted him. The Rams loved his potential but worried about his lifestyle. He liked to drink, and he liked women. He married three of them, two of the marriages slightly overlapping. When the Rams put him on their waiver list, thinking his lifestyle too risky, the Colts quickly snatched him up. When the line coach John Bridges, who'd previously coached at the Johns Hopkins University, saw him, he said, "He's bigger than the whole line I had at Hopkins." In Baltimore, Lipscomb found a kindred spirit in Moore, who loved jazz and hated early bedtime.

The two of them cruised the joints on Pennsylvania Avenue, the west-side strip of bars and jazz joints that catered to blacks: The Alhambra, the Casino, the Club Tijuana, the Comedy Club. These were the years when alcohol still fueled the night but heroin was beginning to move in. Moore stayed away from the drugs and imagined Big Daddy did, too. But on a spring morning in 1963, Lipscomb's body would be found with a lethal amount of heroin in his veins.

"I loved him like a brother, but I never really knew what was going on inside him," Moore said long after Lipscomb's death. We were sitting in Lenny's home off Liberty Road, in northwest Baltimore County, where a large picture of Lipscomb dominated a wall.

"Was it the education thing?" I asked. Everybody in Baltimore understood the procedure during pre-game introductions. Each player's name was attached to a college, all except Lipscomb's. "Miller," the public address announcer declared each week. Or else, "Miller High." It came between Marchetti's University of San Francisco and Donovan's Boston College.

"We all made it a point never to talk about college around Daddy," Moore said. "That was a protective thing. He'd say, 'Oh, man, why you guys always talking about that bullshit college?' You know, so we cut it. That was no problem. But I didn't know till our later years that he lost his mother when he was eleven. She was stabbed something like forty times. Never knew his father. He had the grandfather we'd see when we played in Detroit. And that was it.

"He was big and strong, but he had a lot of complexes. We'd be in a cab—this was before we got our cars—and he'd start crying. I'd say, 'Hey, man, what's wrong with you?' He'd say, 'The Daddy don't feel too cool, man.' I'd say, 'What's wrong? You hurting somewhere?' He'd say, 'No, I'm all right, don't worry about it.' And these episodes would happen—all of a sudden he'd just break down and cry. I was rooming with him. His protective covering was to drink. That was his shield. So you didn't get in and see all his weakness and hidden pain and hangups. Just, 'Get out of my face.' And the guys would be saying, 'Don't go near Daddy, man, he's in his act.' And you'd pull back."

Moore shook his head sadly. "So many times," he said, "we'd sit there and I'd say, 'What are you thinking?' And he'd say, 'What are *you* thinking?' You couldn't get into feelings."

That was the year Moore's mother died. The funeral was in York, Pennsylvania. Buddy Young showed up, and Jesse Thomas and Lipscomb. Moore came out of the church and shook their hands. Lipscomb threw his arms around Moore and sobbed louder than anyone.

"Hey, Sput," he said.

"Don't worry, we're together," Lenny told him. Lipscomb stood behind him as the casket was lowered, and the big man's tears did not stop.

"He was reliving the loss of his own mother," Moore said. "He was reliving his life."

In training camp, the Colts roomed in the dormitories at Western Maryland College. Sometimes Lipscomb walked the halls late at night, a man pursued by demons. Sometimes he kept a gun under his pillow and his bed against the door so nobody could get in. When he and Moore roomed on road trips, Lenny would hear Lipscomb cry himself to sleep at night.

But there was also this: as Baltimore Colts, the two of them were marvelous. They brought not only their playing skills but their skin color. To the people watching, in a city that still separated things by race, it was all part of a package. They were a common bond. For hundreds of thousands of people who had never seen blacks and whites in such physical conjunction, they were a revelation.

On the playing field, the two of them were at the top of their game. Even in those ugly preseason exhibitions that summer, when the Colts kept losing, Lenny was spectacular. There was that ninety-five-yard kickoff return in the stadium intrasquad game. Then he had a sixty-two-yard touchdown run, a forty-five-yard run, and a thirty-two-yard touchdown run. When the Colts beat the New York Giants in their last exhibition, Moore ran ninety-one yards for a score.

Lipscomb, too, was becoming one of the great ones. He had Marchetti at one end, chasing quarterbacks all over the lot, and Donovan and Joyce knocking down pass protection. Big Daddy could roam. He pursued wide runs and screen passes. He ran sideline to sideline, crushing people all over the field. Later, other linemen would try to take credit for the line, but it was Weeb Ewbank's originally. Asked about Lipscomb's tackling technique, Weeb said, "Big Daddy just reaches out and grabs a bunch of guys and peels 'em off until he finds the one with the ball. That's the one he keeps."

SO THE BALL CLUB felt pretty good heading into the regular season. By now, the Colts owned the town and its sports pages. The Orioles continued to play before empty ballparks; in Chicago, they drew 734 fans. Across the American League that year, only three teams drew as many as 1 million people. The Red Sox and Tigers reached that figure in the final week. The Yankees, in the final month. The ground was shifting beneath baseball's very feet. On the day the Colts opened their regular season, the Orioles finished theirs—losing a double-header to the Yankees.

Whatever off-the-field angst the Colts had, they were finally winning. They finished up the exhibition season with back-to-back wins over the Giants. These brought back much of the good cheer of the early days in camp. Maybe this really was the year. And the town, asleep through much of the summer's baseball, now seemed to come awake again.

It was the beginning of my own ritual, as well. I delivered the daily *News-Post* and the Sunday *American* that year and brought home the paper each day to devour the sports section. This was the whole world. In 1958 there was no ESPN broadcasting sports all day and night. There was no sports-talk radio. The television showed baseball games here and there (the first games of Sunday double-headers and an occasional weeknight game), and pro football only telecast each team's away games. But that was it. Pro basketball? You'd get the last game of the NBA finals, nothing more. You wanted sports coverage, you read the newspapers.

In the five o'clock darkness of Sunday mornings I walked to the Seton Apartments, where bundles of newspapers, wrapped in brown paper and held together with baling wire, would be waiting at the bottom of Bowers Avenue, near Liberty Heights. I lugged them from there to a nearby basement storage area of the main apartment building, to stuff the sections together before delivering them across the big, hilly complex.

Down in the basement I spread all the sections of the paper on a cement floor. A bare light bulb hung overhead, just bright enough to read Steadman's column before starting my work. Here, long before the rest of the world had awakened, I learned what to expect in the coming afternoon's Colts game.

Now, on the morning of the 1958 opener, Steadman wrote, "Fever-pitched, fanatical enthusiasm doesn't come out of a can. Sure, fans screech and scream at games everywhere. But Baltimore is getting a reputation the nation over as the wildest, zaniest, cheeringest city of all. It's a spirit and love which must be preserved. When that dies, the team will, too. It happened once before. But the Colts came back to life again because the mourners themselves breathed new life into the corpse."

So it was already more than a game; it was a municipal crusade. This was all people talked about as the season opened: the Colts, the Colts. Schoolboys playing pitch-and-catch mimicked the sound of Chuck Thompson: "Here's Unitas, throwing long." If you went to the Hilltop Diner on Reisterstown Road, or Gussie's Downbeat on Eastern Avenue, or almost any bar or restaurant anywhere in town, the talk was all football.

In the '58 opener, the Colts met Bobby Layne and the Detroit Lions. They were the defending division champions, and Layne was their quarterback, their swashbuckling leader, and their late-night drinker.

"And tough," Art Donovan said as the Colts readied for the '58 opener. "Two years ago, I hit Layne with everything I had. But the guy got up laughing at me."

This time, on a balmy late summer afternoon, Detroit got the laugh for the first three quarters. The Colts had a punter named Dick Horn. Once that afternoon, he punted for twenty yards. Another time, for nine yards. Detroit capitalized. Layne hit Hopalong Cassady for a thirty-one-yard touchdown. The Lions led, 15 to 14, in the fourth quarter. Then things got worse.

Unitas tried a slant-in pass to Moore. The Lions' Bob Long stepped in its way and intercepted at the Colts' thirty-three-yard line. Long, six feet four, 230 pounds, headed for a touchdown. The scrawny Unitas took off after him. Long was eight yards from the goal line when Unitas caught him in the open field and knocked him to the ground. The tackle saved a touchdown.

Now the defense stepped up. Halfback Gene Gedman carried for Detroit, and Big Daddy dropped him. The big Memorial Stadium crowd roared. Then Gedman tried a sweep. This time Milt Davis, Raymond Brown, and Don Shinnick nailed him. More roars, more imploring the defense to do the improbable. On third down it was Donovan. He knocked down a desperation pass. There was bedlam inside the ballpark, and even more when Jim Martin tried a field goal and it failed.

"The greatest defensive effort seen in many a year," the *Sun*'s beat writer, Cameron Snyder, said the next morning.

After the goal-line stand, the rest was all Colts. Every time Unitas threw the ball, Berry seemed to catch it: ten receptions for 149 yards. Colts win, 28 to 15. Snyder wrote, "Sometimes it is hard to decide whether Unitas makes Berry a great end or Berry makes Unitas a great passer."

In Monday's *News-Post*, Steadman wrote about the Colts' goal-line stand. He compared it to a war zone.

"One of the greatest goal-line stands in a history that has been similarly highlighted by courage and fortitude near the shadows of the goal post." Whew! One game into the season, and the language was already the sound of a crusade. The next week, it became religious.

THE AUTUMN RITUALS

BY NOW, ALL OVER TOWN, the rituals had begun. It's autumn, so we talk incessantly about the Colts, who mean nothing more than life and death. You wake up on a Sunday morning, and you realize it's game day, and so the nausea hits you and stays. They win, you feel great all week; they lose, and a cloud of depression seems to cover all human existence. They win, and life is grand in the classroom and the workplace for the rest of the week; they lose, and housewives know they'll be dealing with brooding husbands. We were learning to define ourselves by this football team. It was this way in every neighborhood, and it went on week after week, and fifty years later on scruffy little Poultney Street it still touched Joe DiBlasi as he walked through his old neighborhood.

The street's down here in south Baltimore's Federal Hill, just north of the Cross Street Market. The block's not much longer than a football field. On Poultney Street you don't have to search very far to locate your memories.

"That house over there," says DiBlasi, the former city councilman. He points to Number 42. His parents bought the little row house back in the 1930s. The price was eight hundred dollars. DiBlasi mentions this strictly in passing. The real attraction down here is the lot directly across from the house. It's about fifty yards long and twenty yards wide. The surface is asphalt. In this part of crowded, working-class, row-house south Baltimore, this was the neighborhood football field.

"Every day," says DiBlasi, "from the minute school let out. And every Sunday, from the minute the Colts game ended and you turned off the radio. You came out here and imagined you were Unitas throwing to Berry. Or you were Marchetti rushing the quarterback. It didn't matter—you were out here playing ball, and you felt like the Baltimore Colts."

It was happening everywhere back then. The moment the Colts' game finished, boys bolted from their houses. The energy was bursting out of everyone; we were an entire metro area full of young people listening inside our heads for the echoes of the heroics just broadcast into our homes.

So the kids gathered in places like east Baltimore's Patterson Park wearing their sweatshirts and their black high-top sneakers and whatever knockabout "after-school" pants they had. Nobody had Colts jerseys yet; the NFL hadn't learned to merchandise itself so calculatingly. And the kids played on the side streets around west Baltimore's Druid Hill Avenue, where three complete passes naturally meant a first down and street lamps marked the corners of the end zone. Near Little Italy they gathered in the gravel area between the city morgue and the Scarlett Seed Company and played rough-house tackle, where the one kid with a helmet lowered it into tacklers' midsections and got to be Alan Ameche. In northwest Baltimore there were swarms of kids running down to the Grove Park Elementary School, which was still being built, and there were grassy areas all over the place. That was my neighborhood.

"Our games," DiBlasi said, gazing across his old neighborhood field, "were tackle."

"On asphalt?" I said.

"Sure," said DiBlasi. "We didn't know any better. We'd go home every day with skinned elbows and knees. Your pants were ripped every time you went into the house. Nobody had helmets or pads or real uniforms. You had street clothes. And everybody had pants that were torn at the knee."

Precisely.

DiBlasi began to recite names: Lefty Ashenback, who could throw long; Bernie Gruss, who later played for Southern High; Pat Feely and his cousin Bobby Kelly; and Marvin Counselman, who was liked by everyone for the obvious reason that he had the best football in the neighborhood.

DiBlasi remembered Lefty and Bernie and Kelley, and I remembered my own gang. Fifty years later, standing there on the asphalt of Poultney Street, it still felt important. We were all in our sixties now, but maybe it wasn't too late to get up a game. Joel Kruh, who ducked and weaved, could still be Lenny Moore. Henry Leikach, who was five feet four but weighed two hundred pounds, could be Artie Donovan. In the old days Barry Director was the worst tackler in the neighborhood—he faded away from the ball carrier like the bull fighter from the bull—but he was the best at piling on after somebody else made the tackle. Sometimes you ran through the line and Bobby Minnix was waiting to tackle you. But Minnix didn't tackle; he aimed a fist directly at your face. What the hell, he could be Bill Pellington.

It didn't matter. You survived the hits, and it helped define you. You were a little tough. The Colts were tough, so this was a good thing. You wanted to be like them. You went to the games when your father could scrounge tickets, and you sat in the cold, and this made you feel tough, too. In '58 you had to be tough. Only tough people could stand up to the Russians. This was a whole city where the fathers had proved their toughness in the war years and come home to work the grueling jobs in the factories. This made you a man. Football was manhood, too, but it was displayed on the asphalt of Poultney Street in south Baltimore, and Patterson Park on the east side, and Druid Hill Avenue on the west, and down at the schoolyards in northwest Baltimore.

Now DiBlasi pump-faked his arm, the way Unitas always did. He was a kid when Unitas was looking for Berry. Now his hair had turned gray. In his time each neighborhood had its links to the Colts, and so did each generation. The kids wanted to be like Unitas; the older generations had their own connection, and they found these equally thrilling.

IN SOUTHEAST BALTIMORE, the bookmakers and the steelworkers and the assembly line guys gathered at places such as Gussie's Downbeat, famously located beneath the Chinese laundry at Eastern Avenue and Oldham Street. Gussie's was like all the corner bars in this part of town: it was the neighborhood social club, as crucial to the community as the church or the school. This was where politics and crime and sociology got their verbal workouts. In the case of Gussie's, it was also the place where all money that was gambled on football came to settle up.

On the other end of town, out in northwest Baltimore, was the area sometimes called the Golden Ghetto for the nouveau middle-class Jews who made it north of Park Circle in the postwar years. They were the original cast from the east side's Lombard Street area of synagogues and delicatessens, where the city's twentieth-century Jews first congregated. Then, in the great migration northwest, they followed the smell of the hot dog. Now all kibitzers gathered at the Hilltop Diner, on Reisterstown Road across from the Hilltop Shopping Center. In both cases, for fun or profit, at Gussie's or the Diner, one discussion echoed the other: the Colts.

"That was the whole world," Donald Saiontz was saying one sunlit morning in the summer of 2007. He was an attorney known for his legal savvy and the punch line of his TV commercials: "If you've got a phone, you've got a lawyer." He was also part of the late '50s diner crowd where everybody hung out until the early morning hours, and all language consisted of two topics: the Colts and sex.

"And I think the Colts came in first," said Saiontz, "because you didn't have to lie about them."

He looked like Jerry Garcia from the Grateful Dead. But his mind-set was more '50s, when he was part of the adolescent gang Barry Levinson made famous in his movie *Diner*. The comic highlight of the story was the young man who will not marry unless his fiancée can pass a written test about the Colts. Everybody in America thought this quite hilarious. Except people in Baltimore, for whom the premise made perfect sense. Who could marry a woman who didn't love the Colts?

"Eddie Krichinsky," says Saiontz. "He gave his girlfriend the quiz. So did a bunch of guys." Saiontz's expression was absolutely deadpan. "Why would that be unusual?" he said. "I'm not saying guys wouldn't get married if a girl didn't care about the Colts. But how could you hang with a girl who didn't care?"

They cared so much that, if you didn't have a ticket on Sundays, you found a way to get into the ballpark anyway. Guys sat around the diner dreaming up scams to sneak in. One guy knew the stadium guard who let the supply trucks in. For fifteen bucks, he'd let eight or nine guys in with the trucks. Then there was the bull-rush approach. You got in line, and when the ticket taker asked for your ticket, you pushed him and ran.

"What's he gonna do?" Saiontz said. "Chase you? He chases you, he's got three hundred more guys sneaking in behind you. Or you walk in with some guy who's got eight tickets in his hand for his whole family. The ticket taker's counting, and you take off. It wasn't that hard. And you had to be there. The Colts are playing, you had to be there."

He and Levinson still talk about those days. To be a Baltimore Colts fan wasn't just about football. It was about casting off an inferiority complex built in over decades, a sense that the city was perceived by the rest of the country as a nowhere town—and the sense that neighborhoods were isolated little fiefdoms lacking common ground until the Colts drew everyone together.

"Today," said Saiontz, "we talk about the diversity of Baltimore. But back then the blacks were here, the whites were there. The Jews didn't cross Falls Road, they couldn't go into Roland Park. We were out here in northwest Baltimore because we didn't fit anywhere else."

It was an old municipal pattern that took generations to unravel: the Jews were out in northwest Baltimore, the blacks in west Baltimore. As you moved east, you found the little pocket of Little Italy. Farther east, more European ethnics, but even in crowded east Baltimore they divided themselves by unwritten ghettos: the Germans here, the Czechs there, the Poles there, the Greeks there.

"It was a city of neighborhoods," said Saiontz, "but it was all these different neighborhoods in search of a city. We had nothing in common with guys from Patterson Park or Pigtown, or with the blacks from west Baltimore."

It wasn't just the Jews who felt this way; the blacks were way ahead of them. And then there were the European ethnics. At east Baltimore dances, fights would break out if an Italian boy tried to dance with a

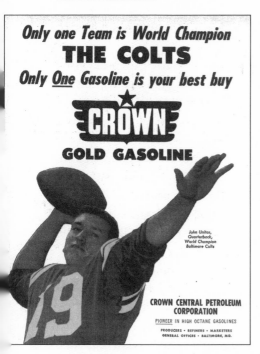

In the glory years, advertisers realized the benefits of linking their business with the Colts. John Unitas backed Crown Gold Gasoline. And (clockwise from top) Alan Ameche, Unitas, Art Donovan, and Raymond Berry signed on with Baltimore Federal Savings and Loan. *Courtesy Enoch Pratt Free Library*

Polish girl. If an Irish girl wed a German, this was considered a mixed marriage. Some Catholic school students were told not to play with public school students. You never knew who might turn out to be Protestant.

"We were enclaves," Saiontz said. "We were fiefdoms without a country. And then, all of a sudden, you got these ballgames where judges are sitting next to steelworkers who are sitting next to cops, and everybody's slapping each other on the back, screaming and yelling."

And they were finally yelling over something triumphant.

"We were so used to getting our asses kicked by New York," Saiontz said. "I mean, the Yankees had Mickey Mantle in center field, and we had Chuck Diering. And, in football they had Sam Huff. They had Frank Gifford. We couldn't believe it when the Colts drafted Alan Ameche. He was a Heisman Trophy winner. We couldn't believe a guy like that was coming to Baltimore. In our heart of hearts, we thought we'd never be any good. We were just Baltimore. And then, all of a sudden, Is this really happening?"

He still talked to Levinson about all of this. Back then Levinson was a seventeen-year-old Forest Park High School kid perfecting the art of hanging out. The Hilltop Diner was filled with such people, including those who would bet on anything. Football, food, whatever. In the movie, the kid Modell's played by Paul Reiser. In real life, Gene Modell bet money one night he could run a mile in less than ten minutes. Twenty guys rode down to the Johns Hopkins University track to see if he could do it. He took off his shirt, his pants. He was down to his Jockey underwear, to cut down on wind resistance. He beat it by two seconds and fell across the finish line to a standing ovation. This was four in the morning.

Then there was Fat Earl Magid, who sat at the diner and ate his way through everything. Fat Earl pulled up to the table at 385 pounds. He claimed never to have lost an eating bet. Who would argue? He ate competitively and bicoastally until he ran out of people who would eat against him. One night Fat Earl ate fifty-two Little Tavern hamburgers. Another time, in Little Italy, he ate five pounds of spaghetti and one hundred meatballs, plus one and a half gallons of wine. He won fourteen hundred dollars for it. But the Hilltop Diner was his pride. There, with witnesses who could testify, he ate the entire breakfast menu. For a joke, Fat Earl explained.

A whole generation of people went to the Hilltop Diner after something else: racetrack types and so-called tin men who'd spent the day hustling aluminum siding, and parents who had just come from PTA meetings. Or people who bowled at the Hilltop Lanes around the corner or gathered at one of Jack Pollack's Trenton Democratic Club meetings, where everybody asked Jack to fix a traffic ticket.

Or they went after the CinemaScope feature at the Crest movie theater directly across the street. The Crest had frosted interior windows and a winding staircase leading to a plush balcony. Patrons came outside afterward, turned right, and a few doors down the little strip mall was the Mandel-Ballow Delicatessen. They could stay there, talking about Unitas and the Colts, or the PTA, or whatever, until two in the morning. If they hadn't run out of all conceivable words by then, they walked across the street to the Hilltop Diner, which never closed.

And the teenage boys would drive past the diner with their Saturday night dates to check whose cars were parked out front. If their buddies had arrived, they had that awful teenage dilemma: Which is better, the potential for a serious make-out session (in 1958: not so likely) or hanging out with a bunch of funny guys?

So, figuring the odds, they dropped off their dates and went back to the diner. They went partly for food, but mainly for the adolescent knock sessions.

"You're Hud."

"No, you are."

Translation: You look as good as the teenage Gary Huddles with his movie star countenance. No, you do. The lines were wrapped in sarcasm as certainly as the diner's hot dogs were wrapped in bologna and its french fries swam in gravy.

The place was owned by George Stamas, then in his mid-thirties, who never seemed to go home. He was fussing in the kitchen one moment and wiping off tables in the next. Some thought he slept there. He was there when people came for lunch, and when they went home at three in the morning, he was still there. Some people got into their cars and drove home, and some walked. Imagine fourteen-year-olds walking through the streets at four in the morning. And nobody thought twice about it.

"I'm not saying we stayed till four in the morning every night," Donald Saiontz said.

"You didn't?"

"Nah. On a slow night, you might go home at three."

Among Barry Levinson's crowd was Leonard "Boogie" Weinglass. Mickey Roarke played him in the movie. Boogie worked his way through high school on the six-year plan, since he was usually too busy to attend at all. He hustled football pools; he hustled blank report cards. He hustled his way into Colts games.

Twenty-five years after the sudden-death game, on the night *Diner* opened at Baltimore's Senator Theatre, Weinglass and Levinson shared a private moment in a little room while a premiere crowd gathered outside. Levinson was becoming a major Hollywood player. Weinglass had a chain of clothing stores called Merry-Go-Round, which made him a millionaire a few hundred times over. He wore his hair in a pony tail.

"I don't want to say Barry was rich," Weinglass said, "but his family had tickets to the Colts games. I had to climb over the fence in back of left field and sneak in through the tunnel back there. I was in high school then."

"High school?" said Levinson. "This is a guy who graduated high school at twenty-one. We figured he was getting his doctorate in high school."

"I'd go in and take tests," said Weinglass, "and I didn't know anything. I wasn't there half the time—I'm outside hustling somewhere. So I'd write the answers on my arm before I went in. And I'd still get six out of ten wrong."

By this time he could laugh about it. But he had a rough time growing up. His parents were poor European immigrants. The father worked as a tailor and ran a grocery store on Park Heights Avenue, but tuberculosis put him in a sanitarium. The family was left on Violet Avenue, in a deteriorating neighborhood off lower Park Heights, where Boogie learned to punch with both hands.

He ran the streets. At Forest Park High School, he played basketball but left under less than ideal circumstances. He spent the next few high school years at Baltimore City College. He hooked in with the guys handling football pools and thus took all serious bets on the Baltimore Colts. Also, he continued playing varsity basketball, where he was a standout. On some days, the guys on the basketball team would get into their uniforms and head out to the floor for pre-game warm-ups. All except Boogie. He slipped outside, in basketball uniform, to the stone wall between City and Eastern High School. This is where he booked his last-minute football bets.

Once, he failed to notice the huge man approaching him from behind. It was George Young, the school football coach, who later worked for the Colts and then became general manager of the New York Giants.

"What do you think you're doing?" Young asked, lifting the teenage Weinglass off his feet.

"Just trying to make a living," said Boogie.

When he wasn't hustling football pools, he was hustling other things, such as blank report cards. How he got them nobody knew. They went for a buck apiece, perfect for fooling your parents into thinking you'd actually paid attention in class. Years later we talked about this.

"The report cards. How did you get them?"

"In those days," said Boogie, "I was getting sent down to Mr. Yost's office every day." Henry Yost was City's principal, a gentle, rheumy-voiced man who wore the last high-collared dress shirts in America. "He got so used to me being in his office, one day he got up and just walked into the hall. I looked down and noticed his desk drawer was open. There's all these report cards inside." So many years later, a look of sheer delight crossed Boogie's face.

"It was a no-brainer," he said. "I only made one mistake."

"What's that?"

"I took all of them."

Sometimes he didn't leave the Hilltop Diner until early in the morning and went straight from there to school. One night he was thrown out of the diner for some transgression long since forgotten. He walked across the street to the Mandel-Ballow Delicatessen. Within minutes, he got into a fight. The owners called the police, and three squad cars quickly pulled into the small parking lot out front.

"They come charging in," Boogie recalled happily, "and I walked right past 'em like I didn't know what was going on. I walked outside, and I noticed one of the squad cars had its motor running. I figured, What the hell? I mean, I didn't have my driver's license or nothing. But I jumped in and drove it around for a while. I went right up the street to Ameche's."

Everybody went to Ameche's, if they didn't go to Gino's. The two football players, Alan Ameche and Gino Marchetti, started their hamburger operations in this time. You went there for the burgers, but also for the atmosphere. It tied you closer to the Colts. Ameche's even had big action photos on one of the walls.

After the second game of the '58 season, the crowds at Ameche's were so big, police had to be summoned for control.

IN GAME 2 THAT YEAR the Colts played the Chicago Bears, whom everyone called the Monsters of the Midway. They came at you with Doug Atkins and Bill George to break your legs and Willie Galimore to run around you. The game was played on Saturday night. If the first game had seemed the opener to a municipal crusade, the second game bordered on religious crusade.

John Steadman wrote: "Through the tunnel and into the dressing room. Outside 52,622 enthralled spectators looked at each other and shook their heads in disbelief. This had been the Baltimore Colts' finest hour. Their greatest game. Their most important victory.

"Thirty-five football players, dirty, scratched, bruised, battered and tired, started to holler and carry on like little boys. Exhausted? Yes. But, oh, so happy. Wives, parents, girlfriends, even children waited to see them. The shower water was hot and starting to steam up the place. But this was a post-victory celebration. Noise? It was bedlam.

"Above all the pandemonium came a voice. It simply said, 'How 'bout the prayer?'

"Like the snap of a finger, like the throwing of a switch—the scene around you became quiet instantly. Thirty-five professional football players dropped to their knees. They were Baltimore Colts. They were in uniform.

"Linebacker Don Shinnick, with No. 66 on his jersey, was the only man speaking. In unison they followed. Some spoke louder than others. But they all knew the words. To some it was The Lord's Prayer. To others it was 'The Our Father.' The words were just slightly different in places, but the prayer of thanksgiving was coming from the depths of the soul and being offered to a Supreme Being, to the Great Scorer above Who cares only how the game of life is played."

Steadman called them "an interdenominational congregation of Baltimore Colts." He said all were "Americans playing a team game where it makes no difference what church you visit or what your bloodline is."

He mentioned, somewhere along the way, that the Colts had beaten the Bears, 51 to 38.

But, two games into the season, it had already become more than a football campaign. Steadman's column felt like something out of myth. You read it, and there was sunlight coming through stained-glass windows. You waited for Bing Crosby to show up in a priest's collar, or Norman Rockwell with a paint brush. In Baltimore we were not just on intimate terms with the Colts; through them, we were all praying to the same God now.

"This was the aftermath of a once-in-a-lifetime performance," Steadman wrote. "This was the picture of a courageous football team, a group of intense, almost ferocious men. They had scored a truly great victory. And what had they done in the privacy of their inner-sanctum? They had dropped to their knees, bowed their heads and prayed. Atheists in fox holes? No. Atheists in locker rooms and on football fields? No, never."

If Steadman's language seems, with the years, breathless and over the top, so did the paper's game story. It was written by N. P. Clark, known as the Swami, perhaps the most acerbic man on the planet. He greeted each brand-new day with the fresh hot breath of cynicism. Now, in front of everyone's eyes, he seemed to be waving pom-poms.

He wrote, "Let's just part the hysterical hair from our eyes and see what goes on here. The Colts are undefeated. Whee! In two weeks the safari has already bagged the biggest game around: a Lion and a Bear. Whee! Everybody's breaking every record in sight. Two whees!"

When the cheerleading ceased and Swami's game story reached actual facts about the previous night's game, it turned out John Unitas had thrown touchdown passes to Raymond Berry and Jim Mutscheller and two to Lenny Moore. And Moore scored twice more on runs. The rookie Leonard Lyles ran a kickoff back 103 yards for a touchdown. Lyles was black. Buddy Young told everybody, "He was running like Faubus and the Faubusites were chasing him through Little Rock." Bill Pellington and the rookie Raymond Brown each intercepted two passes and Andy Nelson another.

In the *Sun*, Jesse Linthicum wrote, "The crowd's roar—old-timers could not recall anything like it at a local sports event." Despite the noise, though, "Ball carriers were hit with such terrific force that you could hear the smacking of bodies up in the press box."

A week later, the enthusiasm continued. The ball club went to Green Bay to meet the pathetic Packers. It was their last year before the arrival of Vince Lombardi, who was still an assistant coach for the New York Giants. These Packers would win only one game all year. But they almost beat the Colts.

In the second quarter, Green Bay led 17 to 0. The Colts were being beaten, and beaten up. At halftime, they trailed 17 to 7. Steadman spent the game on the Colts' bench. He saw Unitas conferring with Mutscheller.

"The angle out is open," said the tight end.

"Yeah, but the linebacker's moving out and the safety man is, too," said Unitas. He seemed to have eyes everywhere. "Let's go for the angle-in and try to get 'em."

A few minutes later, the two connected for a fifty-four-yard touchdown. Now it was 17 to 14. With about three minutes remaining, Steve Myhra kicked a tying field goal.

Now the Packers, frustrated at losing a lead that had seemed insurmountable, tried to take it back. Bart Starr threw long. Andy Nelson intercepted and ran behind a convoy of blockers: Marchetti and Lipscomb, knocking down everyone in sight and leading Nelson fifty-two yards for a touchdown. The Colts won, 24 to 17, their third straight, and the kid Nelson was mobbed by his teammates.

FIFTY YEARS LATER, Andy Nelson remembers all of it. He stands in front of an old team photograph of the '58 Colts. The photo hangs on a wall at Andy's Ribs, the restaurant Nelson has owned for the past few decades along Baltimore County's York Road corridor.

"Got a little reminder of it the other day," he says. "Some guys came in here with a piece of the goal post from that day in Yankee Stadium. Wouldn't give me any of it, but they did give me a picture."

"A picture of a piece of a goal post?"

"Yeah," Nelson says. "Heck, I remember when that goal post was going down. They had it down before we even got off the field."

Unprompted, he turns to the old team photo on the restaurant wall and points a finger at one old teammate and then another. Around here, the names and faces are still familiar to everyone of a certain age, like an old high school homeroom shot.

"Shinnick," he says softly. "Gone. Art DeCarlo, gone." He lingers for a moment over each player and gently recites the roll call of the deceased. "Jim Parker, Big Daddy. There's the Horse. And Pellington and Sherman Plunkett. And Unitas. Half the ball club, gone now."

"You look at this a lot?"

"I keep lookin'," says Nelson, "'cause they keep disappearing. Preas just passed, you know?"

No first names are needed. But it was George Preas and Jim Mutscheller and Lenny Moore throwing the key blocks that led Ameche into the Giants' end zone in overtime. The hole was wide enough to slip a sixteen-wheeler through.

"I know," I say. "I saw it in the paper. Hell of a blocker, huh?"

"I'm just thankful I'm still here," says Nelson.

"You look like you could still play. You're still pretty skinny."

"Was six-one, hundred seventy-five," he says.

"I don't get it," I say. "How does a guy as skinny as you stop a guy like Jim Brown? I'm bigger than you, and those guys would have pulverized me."

"I was farm strong," Nelson says. "I was like a piece of wire from all those chores."

He grew up on a cotton farm around Athens, Alabama, a town with about five thousand people. There were thirty-three kids in his high school graduating class. When he arrived at Memphis State for college, he'd never seen a place so big. There were three thousand students there.

When he got to Baltimore, there was more culture shock. His first glimpse of Memorial Stadium was the big intrasquad game. Nelson anticipated a few hundred die-hard fans showing up. When he trotted onto the field, he looked up at more than forty thousand people.

"It scared me," he said. It was the same reaction Unitas had had two years earlier: utter awe. "In college I played before maybe five thousand people. I turned to one of the guys on the team and said, 'Is it always like this?' He said, 'You ain't seen nothing yet.' "

When the ball club went to New York for the first time, Artie Donovan took Nelson to Times Square one night. But he wouldn't let him open his eyes until the right moment, when he could get the full electrical blast.

"Gosh, I couldn't believe it," Nelson said. "I'd never been to too many places."

In college, he never gave pro ball a thought. Football was just a way to get through school on a free ride. Memphis State wasn't big enough to play many big-names schools, but there were a few. They played Kentucky, where Blanton Collier was coach. Collier was friends with Weeb Ewbank and told Weeb about this kid named Andy Nelson, overlooked by everybody. That's how Baltimore drafted him. Memphis State also met the University of Louisville, where Unitas was quarterback.

"I said, 'This guy's something else,' " Nelson remembered. "Not just the arm. He knew everything that was going on on the football field."

When the Colts signed Nelson a year after they got Unitas, John reached out a helping hand. "He knew I was from a small school," Nelson said. "He took me aside and told me what I had to do to make the team. 'They look for aggressive,' he said. 'Play the ball in the air.' Right away, he became one of my best friends on the team."

They were cut from the same mold: tough, wiry kids from small schools whom no one had given much of a chance. Both were married and had a couple of kids, as well.

"Plus," Nelson said, "I was quiet. That's why he liked me."

The Colts roomed Nelson with Milt Davis, a defensive halfback out of UCLA. Davis was a slender, refined black man who'd been raised in a Hebrew orphanage. Big Daddy Lipscomb would wander down to their room. Davis tried, without noticeable success, to straighten out Lipscomb's finances. Nelson marveled at the big man's capacity for liquor and for women.

A year later, Nelson roomed with Steve Myhra whenever the Colts played on the road. Here was the real adjustment. Rooming with Davis was no problem, said Nelson. He'd known black people who worked on his family farm and black ballplayers from sandlot games. He and Davis got along fine.

But Myhra was a nervous wreck. Everybody said so, but Nelson saw it up close. He'd wake up on game days and immediately start talking to himself.

"Warming your voice up?" Nelson would ask.

He roomed with the trembly Myhra the night before the sudden-death game and watched him rush onto the field for the field goal attempt with the seconds ticking away. And he drove home after the game, just the two of them after they had shaken the earth from its orbit, with the cool Unitas.

In New York, they had just changed the world of sports in America. Returning home, they'd been met at Friendship Airport by thirty thousand adoring fans. The team bus barely escaped. When the players were dropped off to get their cars, Unitas drove Nelson home.

"Just the two of you?" I asked.

"Yup."

"What was that like?"

"Not much."

"Did you talk a lot? Did you listen to the radio to hear if they were talking about the game?"

"Nope," Nelson said. "We rode the whole way in silence. We got to my house, and I got out of the car. And John Unitas turned to me and said, 'See you tomorrow.'"

THREE GAMES INTO THE SEASON, the Colts were the only undefeated team in pro football. When they headed for Detroit, they carried their trepidations with them. A year earlier, when everything was going swimmingly, they led the Lions 27 to 3 but gave up four fourth-quarter touchdowns and lost, 31 to 27. They never forgot it. In the newspapers, some writers made reference to a jinx. Gino Marchetti blew up when he heard it. No such thing, he said.

But it was on their mind. Steadman wrote that the Colts "still scream out in their sleep at night with horror shouts of, 'No, no, it can't be true,' whenever they think of last year in Detroit."

But this year was different. Lenny Moore ripped off 50 yards in one run and 136 on just a dozen carries. Unitas hit Berry for 54 yards and Mutscheller for 37 yards and a touchdown. In the owners' box, a nervous Carroll Rosenbloom spread packs of mints, Lifesavers, hard candies, and two brands of cigarettes in front of him. One for the offense, one for the defense. He sat with Don Kellett, the general manager. Kellett paced, while Rosenbloom muttered, "This football just scares the blood right out of you."

He had nothing to worry about. The Colts not only won, 40 to 14, but they beat the point spread on which Rosenbloom had bet a small bundle.

In the next day's *News-Post,* the Swami continued waving pompoms with his game story. "Restraint—yowee!—is needed today," he wrote. "Oh, brother!—in considering the undefeated Colts'—whew!—unprecedented 40 to 14 Lion-taming job—Gimme a C, gimme an O—at Detroit—Gimme an L, gimme a T—before 55,190 unwilling new believers—gimme an S—Yeah, Colts! And what can happen now? Anyone for smelling salts?"

Instead, everybody got a slight touch of controversy.

On the Monday before the Colts met the Washington Redskins, Baltimore's Advocates Club held a luncheon at the Southern Hotel.

Rosenbloom was there, and so was his counterpart, Redskins' owner George Preston Marshall. They were not friends. Marshall thought the Colts were draining attention from his Redskins, and Rosenbloom thought Marshall was a bigot. They were both right.

Marshall was the last man in the league to sign any black ballplayers. Two years earlier, when Steadman was still doing public relations for the Colts, Marshall approached him after a banquet. Steadman remembered him full of venom.

"Where's Kellett?" said Marshall.

"I don't know," said Steadman.

"Where's Rosenbloom?"

"I don't know. He's around here somewhere, Mr. Marshall."

"Well, you'll do," said Marshall. "You tell them I'm never coming back here, never, ever again. The idea, to have a nigger speaking. You don't bring those kinds of people up here to speak to an audience, those are the kind of people you use to clean out the toilet in your bathroom."

The speaker he resented was Lenny Moore.

Now, two years later, Marshall had returned despite all declarations that he wouldn't. This time, it was Rosenbloom addressing the lunch crowd.

"I won't have much to say," Rosenbloom smiled, "because the man I'm sitting with just loves to talk."

"If I had your money, I'd talk more," Marshall snapped.

"If you stopped talking a little, you might make more money," said Rosenbloom.

It went on like this for a few more snipes, and then the Colts' center, Madison "Buzz" Nutter, took the microphone. Nutter was a good-natured storyteller who'd originally tried out with Washington five years earlier but didn't make the team. Now, at the Ad Club luncheon, he laughed about having to hitchhike home. Marshall bolted from his chair and grabbed the microphone.

"This young man is a liar," he said. The audience of five hundred people went silent. Marshall defended himself and his ball club. He said he had loaned several of his players money and didn't charge interest. He said his Redskins were one of the few teams that furnished football shoes for free. He said he had personally paid for his team's civilian outfits: burgundy and gold blazers, gray slacks, and gold ties.

"Twenty-six hundred dollars in all," he said.

Nutter, who was only trying to be funny, stood there in embarrassment. Marshall said, not for the first time, that he would never come back to the Ad Club luncheon again. Then he handed the microphone back to the stunned Nutter.

"I'm sorry. I was only kidding around," Nutter told the crowd. Then he turned to Marshall. "On the other hand," he said, "we'll see you Sunday."

The Ad Club story was widely reported, and Nutter's teammates vowed payback against Marshall. In their pre-game locker room, Marchetti asked the coaches for three minutes of privacy. Voices bounced back and forth across the room. Marshall was out of line, everybody agreed. They wanted revenge.

They got it, 35 to 10. Unitas threw a couple of touchdown passes to Berry. He'd now thrown touchdown passes in twenty straight games, the second highest in league history. Leonard Lyles returned a kickoff 101 yards for a touchdown. He became the first player to run more than a hundred yards for a touchdown twice in the same season. Nutter played the whole game, not mentioning to anyone that he had fractured ribs.

All of this was followed quite avidly, and taken quite seriously, in the daily newspapers. It was all part of the Colts' great crusade. Nutter was now a hero, and so was Rosenbloom, who may have been the luckiest man in North America. He had to be coaxed into buying the ball club five years earlier. Then he put up a small amount of his own money to get 51 percent of it. And now the club's value was increasing with each victory.

Rosenbloom was a Baltimore native who'd built a summer home just off the beach on Margate's Nassau Avenue, in the suburbs of Atlantic City. One of his neighbors there was NFL commissioner Bert Bell, who remembered Rosenbloom from their football days at the University of Pennsylvania, when Bell coached the backfield and Rosenbloom played halfback.

After school Rosenbloom went to work for his father's Marlboro Shirt Company. When the war arrived, he took over the Blue Ridge

Manufacturing Company, which turned out denim clothes used for military uniforms. The money rolled in faster than anyone could count.

When Bell approached him about the Colts, Rosenbloom played coy. But not for long. Purchase price for the team was $200,000, with $25,000 to be paid immediately. Rosenbloom put up $13,000, and four minority partners each put up $3,000. Ponder that number, half a century after the fact: Thirteen grand up front, and a man buys a professional sports franchise.

But Rosenbloom was a guy who needed more. He had money to burn, but he craved action. The talk was all over town that he bet serious money on football. This was spoken with a wink and a nod by people going strictly by twelfth-hand rumor. It was also spoken by two who had a pretty good idea. Weeb Ewbank was one.

"There was a lot of talk about Rosenbloom betting on games," Ewbank told Vince Bagli years later, when Bagli was writing *Sundays at 2:00 with the Baltimore Colts.* "I could never say that he bet on a game because I never talked to him about it. But he had some friends who were big gamblers. All they thought about was the point spread."

One was Constantine "Gussie" Huditean, who claimed for almost fifty years that he knew all about Rosenbloom's bets because he was one of the guys taking them. Huditean was co-proprietor of Gussie's Downbeat, the working-class nightclub at Eastern Avenue and Oldham Street. Some years after the fact, Gussie didn't make a big deal out of it. Rosenbloom was just another customer, albeit a big one. Rosenbloom, he said, bet money on regular season games, and he bet money on the sudden-death game. At Gussie's Downbeat, where the bookmakers gathered on Mondays, the night after Sunday football games, the bettors came from all kinds of backgrounds.

"Who do you know today who don't talk about point spreads?" Huditean asked during one of a score of conversations we had.

"Nobody."

"It was the same way then. Everybody in town."

"Rosenbloom?"

"Every week."

"Big money?"

"Thousands."

"Including the sudden-death game?"

"Of course."

Ewbank heard about it. The Colts were 3½-point favorites to beat the Giants. They disdained a tying field goal in overtime. It would have given them a win but lost on the spread.

"Later," Weeb Ewbank told Bagli, "I heard that one of Carroll's gambling friends complained that a touchdown meant he lost his bet." Rosenbloom never talked about it with Ewbank. But Huditean talked about it with all kinds of people who showed up at his joint.

The bookmakers always came to Gussie's Downbeat to settle up. The co-owner of the joint was Albert Isella, with whom I had lunch every week for thirty years whenever he wasn't locked up somewhere on a gambling charge. He stopped counting the arrests after a hundred or so. Between Isella's stories of the Downbeat, and Gussie's, and those of a dozen others who went there, a picture evolves of the typical Monday night in that autumn of '58 in that legendary joint.

That's the big night of the week, since the bookmakers all settle up their bets from the previous day's action. You walk down a couple of steps off Eastern Avenue and enter a long, narrow place with a small alcove on the left. Actually, you shove your way in and discover a hurricane going on. Here you find The Tilters, with Nicky Fields singing, in front of a small dance floor jammed with people trying to jitterbug. Some of them are neighborhood girls who run what they call "the Circuit": Sweeney's on Greenmount Avenue, the Seagull Inn, The Keystone on Holabird Avenue, the Surf Club on Pulaski Highway, the Hollywood Inn out on Sollers Point Road. Just looking for a good time between graduation from high school and the drudgery of settling down for the long haul. Then a long bar on the left, some booths on the right, and just overhead a bunch of exposed wires and pipes given to leaks from the washtubs occasionally overflowing upstairs in the Chinese laundry. Above the din, you hear the voice of Arky the Knife Sharpener, who's a little theatrical. "Innkeeper," he cries, "food and wine for my people."

The place is designed to hold fifty people, tops, but on Mondays it holds twice that, or maybe more. It's so crowded, sometimes patrons have to walk around the block just to enter the back door and get to the men's room. The regular crowd snacks on dill pickles and hard-boiled eggs for a nickel apiece. There are two or three pinball machines, which Gussie says bring in seventy-five grand a year, except when they're out of commission from two guys busting them during a fist fight. Cigarette smoke fills the air, and always, much talk about the Colts if you can hear it above the band.

Gussie's curly haired and always hyper. He's a Romanian, but everybody thinks he's a Gypsy. He is all movement, all nerves. He's completely goofy, but he's lucky at everything. Plays long-shot bets, they come in. Wins thirty-eight grand in a Vegas card game playing a thousand dollars a hand. In 1958, nobody in east Baltimore plays with that kind of money. Nobody's ever seen so much money. These are people who still can't believe they got through the depression without starving.

In the autumn, between football and the daily number, Gussie's got more action than imaginable. But he's not big enough to take it all. When it gets too much, he lays off with Julius Salsbury, who calls himself "the Lord." The feds are on to him; they've got his telephone tapped. Salsbury knows. When he's talking to Fifi London, who's another bookie, the two of them talk in Yiddish. The feds aren't stupid. They bring in a guy who knows Yiddish and translates.

But this is Gussie's neighborhood. He grew up here, hustling in odd ways. He'd sell his clothes. Or he'd sell his blood. Needed money to go to the racetrack, that's all. And he sold formal suits to undertakers, for use by the dearly departed. If the suits didn't fit quite right, they'd just slice open up the back, and who's to notice?

He served in World War II and then Korea. Won a couple of Silver Stars in Korea but had a somewhat mixed record, owing to a beef with an officer. Wound up in the stockade, where everybody played pinochle and volleyball. Gussie always claimed that when they came to release him, he said, "Wait a minute, we got it too good in here, I don't want to leave."

When he returned to civilian life, Al Isella found him walking down Eastern Avenue. Isella was in the middle of his own legend. He was always getting arrested for bookmaking and then getting released with a fine. But there were too many arrests to put his name on a liquor license, so he enlisted Gussie to take half interest.

Isella was another one whose engine was always running. He arrived in Baltimore from the coal mines of Pennsylvania, having survived a cave-in that trapped him underground for three days and killed his father. The father headed a miners' local. The two of them hollered to each other through the darkness until the old man's voice gave out. In Baltimore, Isella moved into an aunt's apartment on Oldham Street while he worked with sheets of tin at the Sparrows Point steel mill and eventually helped organize a union there. It wasn't easy. One time the company police beat him up for passing out leaflets. Another time, his car was blown up. But there were twenty-five thousand people working there, and slowly they understood the strength of their own numbers. Isella always said the men were scared to buck management but the women never were.

He stayed there from the depression through the war years and befriended an east Baltimore butterball named Dominic "Mimi" DiPietro, who worked as a catcher's helper in the steel mill. Mimi made a buck and a quarter a day during the depression. The heat in the place was brutal. He'd do fifteen minutes on, fifteen minutes off. Then he was promoted. Picked up hot iron with tongs and threw it to a catcher.

"It was so hot," Mimi described it one day, "that you had to wear a mask. I had burnt eyes, a burnt chin. Then my old man got me a job in the hot mill." The father worked for the railroad, twelve hours a day, for seven dollars a week in the depression. "He had to pay fifty bucks to get me my job. He slapped me across the face with the back of his hand and busted my mouth."

"What the hell for?"

" 'Cause I saw him pay the money," said Mimi.

There had to be more to life than this, even for a guy like Mimi, who was a third-grade dropout. He was like all these guys hanging at Gussie's. You get through a depression, you get through a war, you'll do whatever it takes to make a buck, to finally find yourself living a little bit.

For Mimi, it was a little bookmaking, a little loan-sharking, and a lot of mangling the language. The Alistair Cooke of east Baltimore, the wags called him. He thought an intestinal operation involved the removal of testicles. Naturally, being this brilliant, Mimi would one day become a Baltimore city councilman and get himself elected six times. When he gave a speech, he'd wait for a standing evasion, he said. A genius he was not. But he remembered his father paying money to get him a job, and he based his political life on finding jobs for everybody who ever called him. No strings attached.

In their years at the steel mill, Mimi and Al Isella were introduced to the beauty of the three-digit number. This was a time when governments, well under the sway of religious lobbyists, held gambling to be immoral and thus arrested those involved in it. Later, when the government discovered all the money to be made, it cashed in by becoming the biggest bookmaker of them all.

Mimi and Al didn't see themselves as criminals, merely as businessmen who found an opportunity. As it happened, of course, there were criminal connections along the way. Al got to know Meyer Lansky, the famous Jewish gangster. In 1958, on a Saturday morning, Al drove Lansky along Miami Beach's famous Collins Avenue. They pulled up to a red light. Lansky glanced out of his side window, saw a man in a dark suit, and immediately ducked out of sight.

"Get this car out of here," he said.

"I got a red light," Isella said.

"Get this car out of here," Lansky repeated.

"What the hell's going on?" Isella asked as he sped away.

"That guy on the corner," said Lansky. "That was my rabbi. I'm not supposed to be in a car on a Saturday."

By then Isella was pretty big in the numbers business, as was DiPietro. They parlayed this as best they knew how. DiPietro got close to politicians and went to city hall, while Isella had Gussie's Downbeat, where the street-corner types kept piling in on these Monday nights, some identifiable by full name, others fully known only to their bail bondsmen.

Here you could find Robert "Fifi" London, so named because of an affair he once had with a French singer named Fifi D'Orsay when she played Baltimore twenty years earlier. Fifi would bet fifty grand on a race horse but wouldn't spend fifty cents for a good meal. In his whole life, everybody says, he owned only two suits. One week he wears the brown one, the next he wears the blue. But he ran what the feds called a five-million-dollar-a-year bookmaking operation out of a hovel in the 1200 block of North Charles Street.

Then there's Michael "Bo" Sudano, so nicknamed because he has a mustache and a toupee, the world's worst, which makes him look like Mr. Boh, the National Bohemian Beer mascot. The toupee is most crucial. One night at President and Fawn streets, in the midst of a craps game, money is scattered about, and greed is in the air, when suddenly a door is flung open and the police appear.

Bo had eleven hundred-dollar bills in front of him, which he didn't intend to lose. Swiftly, he lifted his toupee, slipped the money underneath, and patted everything back into place. That night, every other player goes broke when the cops take everything, but Bo goes home with his money. He loves telling the story of the wonderful toupee.

"You don't wear it for vanity?"

"Hell, no," Bo says one day. "I was at the Carousel Club one night and the barmaid says, 'I want to run my hands through your hair.' I took it off. I said, 'Here, take it home with you.' "

Tough guys come into Gussie's, too, such as John Iozzi, known as "the Animal," and Gilbert Bowen, known as a psychopath. In a fit of pique one day, he machine-gunned a Fells Point bar. For a living, Bowen robbed people.

"And," Al Isella explained one time, "if he found out you had robbed somebody, and you made a score, he wanted his share.

"On what grounds?"

"On the grounds he wanted it."

Isella said this without any particular indication of judgment. It was just the way certain people lived their lives. You got through the toughest years, and now it was time to cut loose a little. You shot a little dice, you jitterbugged along the Circuit, and you bet a few bucks on a football game. It was all part of the same lifestyle. You talked about it all night long at Gussie's, and at the Hilltop Diner, and a hundred more places, and it felt like the good life.

And then everybody watched what happened to John Unitas against the Green Bay Packers and thought, Why does this always have to happen to Baltimore?

THE LAST RITES

JUST WHEN EVERYBODY was having such a great time, the party seemed ready to end.

On a raw, rain-swept November afternoon at Memorial Stadium the Colts beat the Green Bay Packers 56 to 0. They were up by 20 when Unitas, tackled by the Packers' John Symank, had to be helped off the field. Bruised ribs, the Colts said. This was a lie. Then Unitas was taken to the hospital two times. Just precautionary, the doctors said. This was another lie. Then, everybody said, he had to be given the last rites of the church. And this was taken as utter gospel.

The hit came toward the end of the first half when Unitas ran with the football. Symank drove his knee into Unitas's ribs. Unitas heard somebody say, "How's that feel, you son of a bitch?" He tried to get up but couldn't. Out came the Colts' trainers, Dick Spassoff and Eddie Block. Ewbank looked over at George Shaw. The forgotten man was suddenly remembered. He started throwing warmup tosses on the sidelines. Spassoff and Block tried to get Unitas to his feet. He was having trouble breathing. Three ribs were broken, but nobody knew it yet. His lung was punctured, but nobody even suspected it yet. Ewbank motioned to Shaw: Get in there for Unitas.

The game couldn't have been better. The cold, penetrating rain kept coming down, but the score kept mounting, and nobody in the packed house went home. They were having too much fun. The Colts intercepted five passes. Shaw threw a couple of touchdowns, first to Leonard Lyles, and then to Bert Rechichar. Nobody could believe this. Rechichar was the wild man on the defense, but the game was so completely out of hand that Ewbank was throwing everybody in, and still the scores kept coming.

With less than a minute to play and Baltimore leading by eight touchdowns, the Packers finally got close to the Colts' goal line. In the stands, a chant went up: "Hold that line." In the defensive huddle, Bill Pellington had blood in his eye: "Don't let 'em score," he yelled at his teammates. Don Joyce was going crazy: "Don't let 'em score." The players heard the crowd's insistent chants, and knew they'd stayed through the long afternoon's constant rain, and didn't want to let them down. Donovan looked over at the Packers. Joyce and Pellington were making so much noise, the Packers could hear them screaming.

"The Packers," Donovan remembered years later, "are looking at us like, 'Are you nuts?' "

"I looked up," Pellington said later, "and I saw all these people in the rain."

"Here it is, 56 to 0," said Carl Tassef, the defensive back, "and I don't think anybody in the whole crowd's left."

On the last play, the Packers' Joe Francis got down to the one-yard line, where Pellington wrapped his meaty arms around Francis's neck. Francis got no further.

So everybody went home banged up but happy. "Fortunately," said Alan Ameche, "Unitas isn't hurt seriously." Ameche was hearing what everybody else in the locker room was hearing. The Colts were playing everything down because they didn't want the next opponent, the New York Giants, to know they'd be facing a different quarterback.

In the next day's papers, Unitas's injury was strictly an afterthought. "It has become time," N. P. Clark wrote in his *News-Post* game story, "to break down and admit the Colts have one of the most powerful teams ever put together."

In a column headlined "Heroes in the Stands," Steadman wrote: "Nothing fair-weather about the greatest fans in football. That means

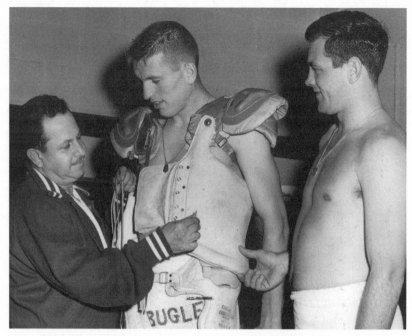

Three weeks after Green Bay's John Symank broke John Unitas's ribs and punctured a lung, Unitas donned a protective vest and returned to action with a flourish. That's trainer Ed Block on the left and halfback L. G. Dupre looking on. *Courtesy Baltimore News-American Collection, Marylandia and Special Collections, University of Maryland Libraries*

you, you and you over there under that funny looking rain helmet . . . the most durable, damp and delirious crowd ever to show up in Memorial Stadium."

But, amid all the hosannas, something had gone wrong.

When Unitas came out of the game, he was taken to Union Memorial Hospital, eight or ten blocks straight down 33rd Street. X-rays indicated broken ribs. Unitas thought: Big deal. He'd played with broken ribs before. The doctors gave him some codeine for the pain, and Unitas went back to the ballpark, where the Colts had now run up the score to 49 to 0. He watched from the sidelines.

When he got home, he had dinner and turned on the television. It was the same way all over America every Sunday at eight o'clock: Ed Sullivan or Steve Allen? Unitas went for Steve Allen. He needed a laugh. He watched Louis Nye and Don Knotts and Tom Poston do their regular Man in the Street routine. John started cracking up. He wasn't a man given to easy laughter, but when it came, it came hard. Now he was laughing so much, his ribs were hurting, and he had to leave the room.

When he tried to go upstairs a few hours later, he started to worry. By the time he got halfway up the steps, he could barely breathe.

The next morning one of the team doctors called. Meet me at the hospital, he said. Right now. And, this time, bring your pajamas.

At Union Memorial, there were more X-rays, more tests.

"You're only operating on one lung," a doctor said. "The other one's collapsed."

In bed, they had him blowing air into tubes to build up strength in the lung. He did this all afternoon. Then, toward evening, another doctor appeared. There was blood around Unitas's lung, he said. They needed to operate.

Now bits and pieces of the news were all over town. The *News-Post* ran a streamer across the top of page 1: "Colts' Unitas Out 4 Weeks." Rumors circulated that John was hurt far worse than the Colts were saying.

The next day Unitas lay in his hospital bed, his chest heavily bandaged, wondering if his career was over. Back to Pittsburgh, back to working construction. Into his room came the two trainers, Dick Spassoff and Eddie Block. They brought a football with them.

"What if I can't throw any more?" Unitas said.

"Sit up," said Spassoff. He handed Unitas the football. "Can you throw me the ball?"

And there they were, the three of them, tossing a football around a hospital room, trying to test Unitas's strength and his flexibility and trying to build his confidence back up.

By Thursday, rumors had taken on a life of their own. Unitas was hurt worse than anyone knew; it was whispered he'd been given the last rites. The bookmakers were going crazy; they didn't know who was quarterbacking, and therefore they didn't know what kind of point spread they needed. Not to mention, was the poor guy alive or dead?

By the end of the week Unitas went home, and everyone in Baltimore prepared not to see him for either the next four weeks or the rest of their lives.

And the Colts got ready for the New York Giants. The timing

couldn't have been worse. The usual inferiority complex, made worse by Unitas's absence. The Yankees had just won another championship. Bob Turley, the fireballer the Orioles had traded away, was the World Series hero. Barely had baseball finished when the football Giants started winning and winning.

They were fighting for first place with the Cleveland Browns. But in many ways they were in a league of their own: in money, in glamour, in big names. Their halfback, Frank Gifford, was a handsome, slashing runner and receiver who could also throw the ball. In his spare time, he wasn't working at Sparrows Point or selling cemetery plots. He was now starring in movies. He and the receiver Kyle Rote were doing television and magazine advertising. So was the middle linebacker Sam Huff. He headed a defense on which nobody moved. A TV network would do a documentary on Huff, called "The Violent World of Sam Huff." He created the violence. They had Andy Robustelli and Rosey Grier and "Little" (260 pounds) Mo Modzelewski on the line and Jim Patton and Emlen Tunnell playing deep. All of these were future Hall of Famers, or close.

Already, this felt like a title game.

"New York, world stronghold of debonair superciliousness, is finally getting steamed up about a football game just like us benighted provincials," wrote N. P. Clark. The Giants said they were flooded with ticket requests and anticipated a crowd of about 70,000 people. In their whole history, the Giants had only once sold out Yankee Stadium. Many of the ticket requests came from Baltimoreans. The newspapers reported about 8,000 people would be going to New York.

At the heart of all the passion now was George Shaw instead of Unitas. For Shaw, after all this time, it was a chance to show how good he might have been. For fans, a chance to see that their football team could continue winning without its leader.

In the first five games of the year, Shaw had played only nine minutes. Now he was leading the Colts into Yankee Stadium for his first start in two years. It turned out to be pretty remarkable, but not enough. He threw two touchdown passes to Lenny Moore and another to Raymond Berry. He hit Leonard Lyles in the end zone, but Lyles dropped the ball.

That was a turning point. With the score tied, 21 to 21, Shaw rolled out to pass at the Giants' twenty-five-yard line. Sam Huff, moving to the outside anticipating a flare pass, intercepted. The Giants drove close enough for Pat Summerall to kick a field goal in the closing three minutes, and New York won, 24 to 21.

Baltimore slipped into a funk. New York, New York. It was still the same old story, and the Colts knew it. "It's tough enough losing," said Alan Ameche, "but when you know that so many people are disappointed because of it, you feel much worse."

Then the Giants were guilty of piling on. In a by-lined piece in the *New York Journal American* the next day, quarterback Charlie Conerly explained the Giants' win: "We out-gutted 'em." The line would stick in the Colts' craw.

Meanwhile, on the train ride back to Baltimore, Shaw buried his head in his hands and blamed himself for Huff's interception. "I'd have given everything I own" to beat the Giants, he said. "The last couple of years sitting on the bench haven't been easy. You watch the rest of the players wanting so much to win. You sit there and hope that when your chance comes, that you can make a contribution. . . . That's all I wanted—just to make a contribution to victory."

Everybody said Shaw was being too hard on himself. Unitas, watching the game at home, thought Shaw had played well. Ewbank praised him. Then everybody, coaches and trainers and doctors, went into panic mode.

On Monday, Unitas went back to the hospital. An orthopedic brace maker constructed some molded aluminum that went from his sternum to his backbone on the left-hand side. They covered it with half an inch of foam rubber on both sides, and a plaster-of-paris cast over that, and attached all of it to Unitas's shoulder pads.

Later that week, barely ten days since the ribs had been broken and the lung punctured and all those rumors about the last rites, he gave it a professional test. He fell down. It felt all right. Then he rolled around. Not bad. Then he took a few hits. Maybe this could work.

"We'll take you to Chicago," said Ewbank.

Chicago was the next game. Shaw would start, but Unitas would stand there on the sidelines, just in case. The Bears were as tough a team as any in football, and the Colts didn't want to risk hurting Unitas any further if they didn't have to. But they wanted a win—and, if Shaw wasn't up to it, they wanted Unitas standing by.

It wasn't exactly a vote of confidence for Shaw. In the locker room before the game, it was the usual scene: Marchetti pacing back and forth. Donovan in the men's room, throwing up the way he did before every game. Big Daddy Lipscomb, more agitated than usual, so tense this time that Lenny Moore saw tears coming out of his eyes.

"Feels like a suicide mission," said Lipscomb. "Either we win or we die. Just like they told us in the marines."

Shaw sat in front of his locker and pondered the obvious. This was the place where his career was blind-sided two years earlier. Here were the Bears, looking to nail him all over again. And there, any time he glanced toward the sidelines, he would find Unitas, waiting to replace him once again.

When the Colts took the field for pre-game practice, Unitas went with them, wearing the full support regalia beneath his uniform. Ewbank took him aside and issued instructions.

"I want you to go out there and throw nothing but long ones," he said. "Just psych the Bears, let 'em see that if you're gonna play, you're gonna play." So Unitas threw the ball long. And the Bears watched.

"You had 'em all looking," Ewbank said when he came back to the bench.

But it was Shaw who played. He missed his first pass, and then another. He saw Unitas standing on the sidelines. He missed four more. The game was slipping away from him. His two offensive guards, Alex Sandusky and Art Spinney, approached him on the sidelines.

"Don't worry about it," Sandusky said.

"You're gonna do it," said Spinney.

The words lifted him. Shaw started connecting. He hit nine passes in a row. When he wasn't passing, he called on Ameche again and again, and the Horse gained 142 yards. Meanwhile the Colts' defense, led by a ferocious Lipscomb, was crushing the Bears.

But then came the replay of 1956. In the third period, Shaw was clobbered and barely made it to the sidelines. Ewbank told Unitas and backup Gary Kerkorian to warm up. Art Spinney looked over at Shaw.

"You could read the expression on his face," Spinney said later. "He

And a miracle it was, as the Colts recovered from a 27 to 7 halftime deficit to defeat the San Francisco 49ers on a freezing Baltimore afternoon. The astonishing victory gave the Colts their first Western Conference title and led to the legendary championship game at Yankee Stadium. *Courtesy Baltimore News-American Collection, Marylandia and Special Collections, University of Maryland Libraries*

was hurt but he wasn't going to leave. He could have taken the easy way out, but he didn't."

Ewbank went to Shaw, but the quarterback cut him short. "I'll be ready," he said. "Let me go back in."

The Colts won, 17 to 0. It was the first time Chicago had been shut out in a dozen years.

When the Colts' plane returned to Baltimore at ten o'clock that night, there were nearly three thousand fans waiting for them at Friendship Airport. The band was there, too, and the cheerleaders with their bare legs in the cold. As the crowd surged toward the taxiing plane, police tried to hold it back. They failed. And this crowd was barely one-tenth the size of the teeming mass that would greet them on the last Sunday in December.

THIS WAS THE YEAR CITY FATHERS, rattled by downtown's decline and the ongoing flight to the suburbs, unveiled their answer: the $127 million Charles Center. It was also the year they grabbed $23 million in federal money to build the Jones Falls Expressway—thus making it easier to leave downtown jobs and head straight for the suburbs.

But the biggest news was the return of Unitas to the Colts. Everybody said Shaw had been fine, but everybody wanted Unitas back in action. There was too much at stake now. They'd blown it in '57, and they didn't want to do it again. They had home games coming against Los Angeles and San Francisco—both explosive teams—and then they had to play each of them on the West Coast to wrap up the regular season.

That was the worry afflicting the whole town. In their entire history, the Colts had won only a single game on the West Coast against these two teams, and by '58 it felt like some eternal hex had been placed on them. So there was no getting around it: the Colts had to win the two homes games and thus clinch the division title before heading west.

Unitas once again donned the protective brace. Everybody knew it, including the Rams. There were newspaper stories and radio broadcasts, and the whole town wondered: Will he still play with his old skills? The Colts were still calling it bruised ribs—not broken—but what would happen if he took a good shot?

The question about his skills was answered on the Colts' first play from scrimmage.

At his own forty-two-yard line, Unitas faded to pass, and Lenny Moore ran six yards downfield and cut to the inside. Unitas pumped as if to throw to him. Moore bolted down the right sideline and disappeared from everybody. Not a soul was near him as Unitas let fly. The ball was right on the money. Fifty-eight yards. One play, one touchdown.

In the press box, against the thunder of the crowd, Chuck Thompson exclaimed to his radio audience, "How rusty can a guy get?"

Unitas lowered his head and trotted off the field. As he reached the sidelines, he heard somebody say, "Were you thinking about the hospital?"

"Never occurred to me," said Unitas.

The Colts won, 34 to 7.

AND SO, ON THE FINAL SUNDAY of November, it came down to the San Francisco game.

The newspaper stories all reflected the general anxiety. The Colts had to win today. It wasn't that way mathematically, but math meant nothing here. This was about destiny. They couldn't win on the West Coast, and everybody knew it, and if they played there for the rest of their lives, they'd probably never win a game there. It was simply the way the football gods had worked things out, and there was no getting around the gods.

Everybody remembered 1957, when the Colts went west in a tie for first and lost both games and lost a division title that seemed within their grasp. The Baltimore curse. In their whole history they'd played eighteen games in California and won exactly once. California had star quality. Baltimore seemed to exist to play supporting parts in other cities' triumphant star turns. The Orioles were consistently awful, and the Colts were better but would surely let us down again. Who did we think we were? We weren't New York, where they took victory for granted. We weren't California, where the world was so glamorous that the football teams seemed casual reflections of the West Coast's good life. We weren't even Cleveland, which had Jim Brown and his football Browns fighting the New York Giants for the Eastern Division title. We were just scruffy Baltimore with people working on assembly lines and cargo docks, and standing in front of blast furnaces, and in the midst of trying to feel hopeful, we knew we were truly at home with defeat. Victory was for other people. This was the dread that filled each of us when the Colts met the 49ers.

And nothing that happened for the first half of football changed anyone's mind.

The day was bone-chill freezing. Twenty-two degrees at game time, and sixteen before it was over. People with tickets piled on all the clothes they could find. Men accustomed to wearing jackets and ties to football games—many still dressed that way in '58—now wore hooded sweatshirts beneath their overcoats, and women wore babushkas and boots. When they got to their seats, they looked for something to holler about. The temperature kept dropping, and the Colts went from bad to worse. The 49ers' Y. A. Tittle found his receivers ridiculously open, and Joe Perry and Hugh McIlhenny ran with the football

The scoreboard tells part of the tale. The Colts rallied for four second-half touchdowns to beat San Francisco. But the delirious crowd on the Memorial Stadium turf tells the rest of it: sheer joy in a town that hadn't tasted a big-league title of any kind since the turn-of-the-century Orioles. *Courtesy Baltimore News-American Collection, Marylandia and Special Collections, University of Maryland Libraries*

without apparent resistance. When Bill Gattus and Reds Hubbe circled the field to lead cheers, almost nobody had the heart to cheer back.

With two minutes left in the half, San Francisco led 20 to 7. At the Colts' bench, Ewbank told Unitas, "We're playing terrible. Keep it on the ground and we'll go in and straighten this out at halftime." Unitas listened, nodded his head, and then went in and threw the football. His arm was hit as he let go. The 49ers linebacker Matt Hazeltine intercepted and ran for a touchdown. When the Colts went to their locker room, Andy Nelson heard some of the 49ers taunting, "Not today, baby." His teammates all heard scattered boos around the ballpark, and it stunned them.

In the stands, people wondered if they should stay or go home. They were freezing. They were too cold and miserable even to talk to each other. In the Colts' locker room, players sat silently. Unitas had thrown seventeen passes in the first half and completed only five. Twenty-eight yards passing, that's it. He hadn't thrown a touchdown pass. He'd thrown one in twenty-two consecutive games, one shy of the league record. Did he care? When a reporter asked him about it before the game, he snapped, "Statistics are for losers."

Now he sat silently, wondering what in the world might work in the second half. The backfield coach, Charlie Winner, leaned over and talked with him. "Pick them to pieces with short passes," he said. "Angle in, angle out, hooks." The line coach, Herman Ball, mentioned a few running plays that might work.

Then Ewbank, never a great one for pep talks, stepped in front of the locker room blackboard. He wrote: "4 TDs."

"That's all?" Donovan thought sardonically. He turned to Marchetti and muttered, "What, are you kidding me? Four touchdowns, and hold those guys scoreless?"

"The way they're running at us?" Marchetti muttered. "Who's he kidding?"

Ewbank said, "The test of a champion is whether he can come back."

Donovan remembers a knock on the locker room door. A time-keeper, telling Ewbank, "Five more minutes, coach." He remembers Ewbank turning to his team and saying, "You guys want to win?"

"What the hell you think we're here for?" Donovan said.

There were 57,557 people in the stands that day, and everybody who didn't have a ticket had a radio. There was no television for the home games. But you heard Chuck Thompson over the air with his voice rising, and sometimes you heard cheering so loud that Thompson's cries were all but drowned out.

It wasn't very dramatic at first. A steady, solid drive. Fifteen plays. Unitas hits five of six passes. Ameche bulls his way into the end zone. With seven minutes left in the third quarter, it's 27 to 14. So there's a moment's glimmer of hope.

Then the moment passes. The Colts get the ball back and Unitas fumbles. You can hear the groans over the radio. Jerry Tubbs recovers for San Francisco on the Colts' twenty-three-yard line. If the 49ers score here, it's all over. On third down, Tittle fades to pass. He looks for R. C. Owens, who can outleap everybody. The play's called an Alley-Oop. Tittle sees Owens, but he doesn't see Gino Marchetti bearing down on him. Gino gets Tittle's hand. The pass comes up short.

The Colts' safety, rookie Ray Brown, cuts across the end zone and intercepts. In the midst of a massive stadium roar you can hear the small sighs of relief from everyone.

Now, on the Colts' first play from scrimmage, Unitas tells Mutscheller to look for a quick pop pass. But when Mutscheller gets to his spot, he's got a linebacker all over him. So he keeps on going. Unitas looks his way and sees nobody's there. But maybe he hears a voice because Mutscheller's hollering to him for everything he's worth: "John, John, I'm open." Unitas looks long. There's Mutscheller. A leaping catch, a fifty-yard gain. They're at the 49ers' thirty-yard line. A kind of delirium has swept over the whole ballpark: Are we seeing what we think we're seeing here? This is Baltimore: Does a whole city dare to dream that its ship might finally arrive?

On a long third-down play, Unitas throws to Moore in the flat. On sheer determination Lenny gets a first down. Then Unitas calls on Ameche. Twice he follows Jim Parker and Art Spinney, and then, on a third straight call, he follows George Preas and Alex Sandusky into the end zone. Across the ballpark, they're howling to the heavens. We're into the fourth quarter now, and the Colts still trail. But there's hope: it's 27 to 21. After such a catastrophic first half, how has such a miracle occurred?

Another touchdown could mean not only a tie but the lead. Because, back in the first half, Ordell Braase reached up and blocked a 49ers extra point attempt. And there's more happiness: Pittsburgh has upset the Chicago Bears. When the numbers are posted, the ballpark erupts. Strangers are jabbing at each other and pointing to the scoreboard: "You see this? Look at this." They can't wait to show each other: if the Colts win, the title's all theirs; the Bears can't even get a tie.

The next time they get the ball, there's barely time for anyone to breathe. One play, and the earth slips off its axis. At the twenty-seven-yard line Unitas hands to Moore, who sweeps left. He's got Berry and Spinney in front of him as he nears the line of scrimmage. Berry, who's down to 180 pounds this late in the season, flattens a 230-pound linebacker and then sprints off to try to catch Moore. Lenny sees a lane open wide, but he's got 49ers pressuring him toward the sidelines. So he changes direction. Ameche cuts off a linebacker. Moore's yelling out loud at himself, "Run, Lenny, run." Without losing speed he cuts toward the center of the field, where he sees Mutscheller and Preas knocking people down. George Preas, the tackle! And he's fifty yards downfield, knocking a couple of tacklers off their feet! Moore twists away from two or three other guys. He cuts back toward the sidelines, where Berry's caught up with him and throws another block as Moore, with more tacklers chasing after him, simply outruns everybody. A seventy-three-yard touchdown.

They've done it. On this gray, freezing, late Baltimore afternoon, people are screaming to the sun gods. There must be windows rattling from the noise. Fans have come down out of the stands, and they're ringing the field. Reds and Gattus are down there hugging each other. The cops are trying to hold everybody back, but they've got no chance at all. Go try to hold back the tide. Moore's come back to the bench, where his teammates are all over him. His head's spinning. Ewbank's yelling to his guys, "Now we gotta hold 'em. Now we gotta hold 'em." But the Colts are barely listening. The Fat Ass Squad, the guys like Donovan and Parker and Sherman Plunkett, are running out to block for the extra point. With Steve Myhra, it's never a sure thing.

He hits it. Colts, 28 to 27. Suddenly the temperature's gone up forty degrees. It's balmy in Baltimore. Reds and Gattus are hollering, "Gimme a C," and a tidal wave roars back. In the broadcast booth, Chuck Thompson's trying to stay focused, trying to let the game speak for itself. Next door Steadman's thinking, I've gotta be in that locker room when it's over. This isn't just about football—it's about a team, and a city, finally tasting victory.

But the 49ers aren't finished. Now they're moving the ball. The old dreads creep back into the crowd. Tittle gets them as far as the Colts' forty and seems to have something going. But when he tries to pass again, Carl Tassef intercepts. The crowd's lost its collective mind now. What do the Colts do, try to run the clock down, or go for another score? They're only up by a point, and that'll never last against these 49ers.

Unitas, never one to play it safe, starts throwing. Where does he get his nerve? He hits Mutscheller; he hits Berry. They get to the 49ers' nineteen-yard line, where it's fourth down and a yard to go. With time out Unitas heads for the sidelines to talk to Ewbank. He might as well talk to a wall. In the heat of battle Weeb's brain has locked.

As Unitas approaches the sidelines, Donovan sidles close enough to hear. Unitas wants to know if the Colts should try a field goal, run the ball, or pass?

"What have you got for me, Weeb?" Unitas says.

"Nothing," says Ewbank. "What have you got?"

"If I had something, I wouldn't have come to you," says Unitas.

Ewbank is all aflutter now. He starts to move away from Unitas; John follows him. "If you got something, use it," Weeb says. "Run the ball. Or throw to Berry. Unless you got something else."

Unitas shakes his head, goes back in and calls Berry's number. On fourth and one, he hits him in the end zone for a clinching touchdown.

ON PAGE 1 of the next day's *News-Post* Alexander Gifford will write, "Ten thousand slightly mad Baltimoreans swept onto the stadium turf and there was nobody to say them nay. They picked up everybody they could lift and bore them happily aloft . . . and in the stands the remainder of the 57,557 who saw the struggle of giants watched in high approval of the disorder below as fans overran the helpless grinning policemen. On each sideline the crowd stood, 10 or 12 deep. Then it only deepened. Came 58 seconds to play, and now Milt Davis intercepted. The big countdown began, getting louder by the second. The sideliners weren't human—they were a wave that swept forward and engulfed the team. They got Dupre up on their shoulders. They tried for Daddy Lipscomb and Myhra, but they were too much to lug. But they finally got Gino Marchetti up, and Ray Berry, and headed for the exits."

It was delirium. As Mutscheller ran for the locker room, he thought he might be trampled. He saw a little boy fall down and feared the kid would be crushed. George Preas scooped him up and carried him off the field. An exhausted Berry thought he wouldn't make it to the locker room without getting killed. There were fans wrapping their arms around Ameche, or trying to, and they pounded on Unitas's helmet. But John kept his head down, the standard Unitas posture. Another day at the office.

It was bedlam in the locker room. Steadman stood in a corner and took in the whole scene for the next day's paper. Donovan and Spinney, who'd arrived here with the original Colts squad and suffered through the worst of it, hugged each other and sobbed openly.

"Look at my father," cried Alex Sandusky. "He's as happy as I am."

Ameche, spotting Moore across the crowd, hollered, "I'd give my right arm to run like you. You're too much."

"Baby, hell of a block," Moore yelled back. "Yeah, baby, when you threw that block, the whole lane opened up."

"Lenny took off like he was running for the First National Bank," said George Shaw.

"Fantastic," Mutscheller kept saying. "Like something you'd read in a story book."

Years later Donovan remembered finding a telephone and calling the Bronx in the midst of the madness. "I told my mother I'd call her if we won," he said. "I talked about ten minutes' overtime, and she's crying, and my sister's crying, 'cause it's the first championship I ever played in from all the years since I started on a cinder field at P.S. 8 in the Bronx."

Unitas, wrapping an arm around Moore in the locker room, said, "All we gotta do is work together."

"And we always will, baby," Moore said. He looked around the room and spotted George Preas and said, "Something in my mind kept repeating, 'Go, Lenny, go. You gotta make it.' That's what I wanted to do. To make it. Downfield I saw that blue shirt. That's when I cut across, to get behind the blue shirt. Yeah, the cat in the blue shirt was George Preas." The big lineman, fifty yards downfield. "How do you like that?"

"I'm so happy I don't know what to do with myself," said Art Spinney.

"I never played so hard in my life," said Berry, slumped forward.

Years later, Andy Nelson remembered standing in the locker room shower, with the last of the day's bitter cold still on his skin, and even though the shower's needles were hitting him like razor cuts, "it never felt so good."

In the *News-Post* the next day Steadman wrote, "You can get flowery and sentimental over the Baltimore Colts. In harsh reality, they are just a gang of professional football players representing a city known as Baltimore in a state called Maryland. But, no, the Baltimore Colts are more than that. Call them a way of life. To some of the faithful they really and truly are. . . . They have become a vehicle for much that's good in a world which is cynical, gruff and at times without understanding."

As he stood there in the Colts' locker room, Steadman saw Carroll Rosenbloom with tears in his eyes. "Suddenly," John wrote, "you thought of Willie the Rooter and how happy he would have been."

WHEN IT WAS OVER, it was the usual. In the places like Gussie's Downbeat, all the people hoisted their drinks and called out cheers for the Colts. Then they wondered what the point spread would be. In the places like the Hilltop Diner, they talked about the Colts all night long. In every neighborhood in town boys raced out of their houses with footballs and looked for their friends. It was cold out, but it didn't matter. It was getting dark, but it didn't matter. Their imaginations were on fire, and they wanted to be like the Baltimore Colts.

The next week the team went to Los Angeles. Sure enough, they lost. The score was 30 to 28. The week after that, they went to San Francisco. Sure enough, they lost. The score was 21 to 12. The West Coast curse was still there.

Everyone in town heaved a sigh that they'd beaten the 49ers at home for the clincher. These losses didn't matter, did they? Did they? And then they all went back to their standard emotion, which was enormous worry, since losing two in a row to end the regular season naturally seemed a portent of traditional, inevitable Baltimore disaster to come.

A TOWN WITHOUT FOREPLAY

NOW SOME ENORMOUS SHUDDER seemed to run through the entire city. Wait a minute—we're really going through with this? Baltimore playing for a championship in front of the whole damned country? It didn't compute. Every fall America had the ritual of turning on television to hear Mel Allen bring us the Yankees winning another baseball World Series. It was the only way many of us had ever known life and was therefore the way we secretly assumed it would always be. New York wins, everybody else loses. That was our destiny. So why should a football game against New York be any different?

John Unitas had never even seen New York until four years earlier. He walked along Broadway gawking at the tall buildings. He had a couple of dollars in his pocket and slept on the floor of a fleabag hotel room a bunch of guys chipped in to afford. Andy Nelson had never seen New York until Donovan, the Bronx native, took him to Times Square. Nelson stood there with his mouth open.

Now this seemed symbolic of how the whole town felt. We weren't New York, the city against which every other city was measured. We were gawkers at the occasion of our own unanticipated success. We were just Bawlamer, where the only national champion was duckpin bowling's Toots Barger. Some of the old-timers were still talking about Wee Willie Keeler hitting 'em where they ain't for the turn-of-the-century Orioles, or maybe Joe Gans, the great boxer who grew up in east Baltimore and beat up guys around town for five bucks a match. Let us play for the duckpin bowling title, or the world championship of eating steamed crabs. *Then* we'd feel at home. But this was football, and it was New York, and a professional championship was bigger than anything we'd ever known.

And so, as the town closed in on the championship game, an atmosphere slowly crept in. It was somewhere between terrific elation and nervous unreality, covered with a thin, artificial veil of pugnacity: We'll show those stuffy New Yorkers. We're a town of tough people; we're not scared. This was mostly a bluff.

Along with the usual municipal self-consciousness, we carried all kinds of embarrassments and insecurities to the national stage. It wasn't just the football game; it was a reminder of our entire lives. New York had the Statue of Liberty and the Empire State Building as its great landmarks. Baltimore had the Bromo Seltzer tower. New York had Mickey Mantle in center field. Baltimore had Willie Tasby, who played one overcast afternoon in his stocking feet because he feared his spikes might attract lightning. New York had Ed Sullivan on Sunday night television. Baltimore insiders were proud because we had one of Sullivan's minor players, an advertising pitchman named Ad Wienert, who called himself Lee Stevens when he took the train up to New York every week to do a live thirty-second commercial on Sullivan's show. Lee Stevens, who was he kidding? The implication was: If you were from Baltimore, you couldn't even travel under your own name in the big city. New York had Sugar Ray Robinson at Madison Square Garden. Baltimore had Don Joyce and Big Daddy Lipscomb wrestling for a few bucks at the rickety Coliseum. New Yorkers like Jackie Gleason and Joe DiMaggio hung out at the famous saloon owned by the colorful Toots Shor. Baltimore's only Toots was Barger.

In '58 Baltimore had three daily newspapers, pretty good, but New York still had seven or eight. There were newspaper kiosks on every corner. In Baltimore a young guy with dreams of becoming a sports writer could go to Abe Sherman's kiosk, located outside the Calvert Street Courthouse, and pick up most of the New York papers just to

Colts' fans hoping for championship-game tickets at Yankee Stadium line up in the December chill. An estimated twelve thousand purchased tickets and headed for New York via bus and train and the New Jersey Turnpike. *Courtesy Baltimore News-American Collection, Marylandia and Special Collections, University of Maryland Libraries*

read what the gods of journalism were turning out. There was Red Smith in the *Herald Tribune* and Dick Young in the *Daily News*. The *New York Post*, when it was still a real newspaper, had Jimmy Cannon. Or maybe you tried to figure out the locutions of Murray Kempton's political columns. You didn't exactly know what he was saying, but you knew he was smart, and so you felt a little better about yourself just for trying to figure him out. You liked the Baltimore columnists, but you knew the New York guys were really big league.

Writing still counted for something in '58. It wasn't just the newspaper types, either. Everybody had heard about the Beatniks, who were living in downtown New York in a place called Greenwich Village and writing all kinds of explosive material. Those of us just starting to get serious about our reading, and our latent rebelliousness, liked some of the things they were saying. But we suspected they were going to get yelled at by the authorities. Some of their writing you couldn't buy in Baltimore without the cops swooping down on you. But you could read reports about it in places like *Life* magazine, and in the midst of the sleepy, complacent Eisenhower years it was clear something was happening up there that was changing perceptions about life's possibilities.

To a lot of young people, wondering why the adults seemed so uptight, the Beats seemed to be sounding a call to arms. They were telling us to cast off the old, safe, conservative ways. We wanted to—but where would we put it all, all those hangups, all those rules and restrictions handed to us like religious pronouncements? And how would we explain to friends who'd think we were weird if we did?

Seen from the city of Baltimore two hundred miles to the south, New York in 1958 seemed like another world altogether, a mecca of rich sophisticates (or wannabes) headed out for an evening at the Copa in their tuxedos and evening gowns. In Baltimore, the Buddy Deane girls had to wear veils over their bare shoulders to please the local clergy. In New York, the evening gowns would be strapless, and not a clergyman in sight dared utter a syllable of complaint.

New York was where Bruce Jay Friedman would write a native son's appreciation and call it "New York—A Town without Foreplay."

"Approaching, say, from the Queensboro Bridge at 59th Street," wrote Friedman, "the buildings appear majestic, confident, imperious, like players in some magnificent backfield or, for the more extravagant, like sentries at the gates of Olympus." It made New Yorkers feel as if nowhere else in the world could possibly matter.

"There was a country out there," Friedman wrote. "You knew it because Jimmy Stewart movies took place in it. Someone's uncle moved out to California for his health and there had to be a Detroit, unless the Tigers were kidding around, secretly holed up in Washington Heights when they weren't playing the Yankees. But for all practical purposes, America was New York City. And if there was life beyond its boundaries, you required some real proof before you'd buy it. . . . Couldn't New York, if it got its back up, break off from the rest of the country, start an army and put on one hell of a show if it came to war? What an army. Not since the French wore red knickers at the Marne. Might not win, but they'd look good goin' down."

New York meant sophisticated theater. In Baltimore, the locals pronounced it "thee-A-tur." That year on Broadway, the stars included

Claudette Colbert and Charles Boyer, Henry Fonda and Anne Bancroft, Alfred Lunt and Lynn Fontaine, Joseph Cotton and Arlene Francis, Carol Lawrence and Larry Kert, Cyril Ritchard, Judy Holliday, Robert Preston, Colleen Dewhurst, Lillian Gish, Zero Mostel. These were all famous names, and New Yorkers seemed to have them living right in their own neighborhoods. Our local entertainment was Miss Nancy on *Romper Room.*

You wanted serious drama that our schoolteachers told us about, New York in '58 had *Look Back in Anger* and *Long Day's Journey into Night* and *Look Homeward, Angel* and *The Crucible* and *The Dark at the Top of the Stairs* and *Waiting for Godot.* You wanted musicals, it had *The Music Man* and *Bells Are Ringing* and *Three-Penny Opera* and *West Side Story* and *My Fair Lady.*

New York in 1958 meant chic Manhattan supper clubs. In Baltimore, we had supper at home. If we wanted sophisticated entertainment while we dined, we watched Huntley and Brinkley with the evening news. Or, if the little kids managed to prevail on programming, there was a local actor named Richard Dix, dressed up as a character called Officer Happy, who introduced old Laurel and Hardy movies.

At Manhattan's Blue Angel the comic Shelley Berman shared the bill that fall with singer Bobby Short. Mike Nichols and Elaine May played the Latin Quarter. Gordon MacRae sang at the Waldorf-Astoria and Harry Bellafonte at the Empire Room. At the New York City Ballet, they were dancing Swan Lake.

On Buddy Deane's program, they would soon be dancing the boogaloo.

On The Block, Irma the Body danced about and removed her bloomers for the sophisticates.

New York took its fame, and its famous people, for granted. Baltimore once had Babe Ruth, but he left early and made his name with the Yankees. Baltimore produced Thurgood Marshall, the future Supreme Court justice who had just helped desegregate the schools. But he hated Baltimore for making him feel like a second-class citizen. Billie Holiday lived in Baltimore as a kid, but when she came back later, the heroin dealers gravitated toward her to keep her habit going. Poor Billie couldn't even stay at a decent hotel. She'd bunk at the apartment of Harley Brinsfield, who played her records on his radio jazz program every night.

New York not only had the baseball Yankees, who won every year—they had the football Giants, the glamour team of the National Football League. They were different from the Colts. Unitas had put in his time at the steel mill, and Marchetti had set pins at a bowling alley. The Giants' Frank Gifford was cutting movie deals. Jim Parker was selling cemetery plots, and Big Daddy and Joyce were wrestling fraudulent fat guys. The Giants' Gifford and Kyle Rote were on television in coats and ties. The Colts' biggest media gig was Lenny Moore's: he worked at a low-wattage Baltimore radio station six days a week when the team wasn't practicing. Donovan was running from bar to bar hustling booze. The Giants' quarterback, Charlie Conerly, lined up a national endorsement deal with Marlboro cigarettes. Mutscheller was breaking into the insurance business while Gifford was doing Jantzen sportswear ads. Madison Avenue loved the Giants, understood in their bones that something sexier than baseball, something more energetic, was going on in the country and here were the ballplayers who could be the face of the new action.

One thing the Giants did not have was the Colts' fans: maybe, we secretly figured, we could outshout 'em. The Giants' fans were knowledgeable, and they liked the action, but they did not approach the game the same as the Colts' faithful.

"No mother ever took her children to her breast as old Bawlamer, Merlin (as we pronounced it) embraced the Colts," native son Frank Deford would write. "It wasn't just that they played on Sundays and thus finally made us 'big leaguers' in the eyes of the rest of a republic that was rapidly becoming coaxial-cabled together. No, the Colts were just folks, all around town, at crab feasts and bull roasts and what-have-you. Why, I knew I could go a few blocks to Moses's Sunoco station on York Road and see a bunch of Colts there, hanging out, kicking tires. Had I had a good enough fake I.D., I could've even gotten into Sweeney's, up Greenmount Avenue, and drunk beer with them. The Colts were real people, so we loved them even more as they went on their merry way to becoming champions of the world."

Gifford and Rote and Conerly? They were there to admire in their new Jantzen sweaters. Unitas and Gino and Artie? Have a beer, pal.

Three years earlier, when the Giants were still playing in the Polo Grounds, they drew seven thousand people for a game against the

Cardinals. Seven thousand, *announced*. They blamed it on rain. Hell, when the Colts played Green Bay in that near hurricane, they filled the ballpark, and everybody stayed until the end.

When they met the Colts in the sudden-death game, the crowd was 64,185. That was several thousand below capacity. And that's with 12,000 Colts fans who made the trek up from Baltimore. Everybody blamed the empty seats on a New York newspaper strike. Please. They needed a newspaper to know there was a pro football championship game that day?

But it was one more sign of the richness of New York life. New Yorkers could take it or leave it. Baltimore had the Colts, and New York had a smorgasbord of delights from which to choose.

They'd also been here before. Two years earlier the Giants had beaten the Chicago Bears, 47 to 7. By '58 they'd developed maybe the best defense in the league. The entire year, they gave up only 103 points.

While the Colts were spending their last two weeks on the West Coast, going through the motions and getting themselves throttled by the Rams and the 49ers, the Giants were playing remarkable football.

Trailing the defending champion Cleveland Browns by a game in the final week of the regular season, they played them at Yankee Stadium. On the first play from scrimmage, the incomparable Jim Brown went sixty-five yards for a touchdown. It was the last time he got anywhere. Sam Huff was all over Brown the rest of the day. Cleveland couldn't run and couldn't pass. New York rallied to tie the game, 10 to 10. Then, aiming through a blizzard so heavy that it obliterated yard markers, Pat Summerall kicked a winning field goal from somewhere out around midfield.

That set up a rematch for the division title, and this time the Giants won, 10 to 0. They didn't have much offense, but they didn't need it. Nobody moved the ball on the Giants. Jim Brown couldn't do it. Why would John Unitas? He was back in action, but he was wearing that brace to protect his broken body.

So there it was. The usual. New York had everything. And behind our public bravado we were suitably intimidated by the incomparable city and its ferocious football team.

IN BALTIMORE THAT FINAL FULL WEEK of December 1958, the talk was all football and all points spreads. For people who didn't bet money, the point spread seemed a barometer of how the true insiders viewed the game. For those who bet, it was a chance to put their money where their dreams were. Everybody was an expert, and almost everybody wanted a piece of the action. The Colts were a religion, but they were also a chance to make a slight killing. Or, in the case of Carroll Rosenbloom, a killing big enough to stir his blood.

The word was all over town that Rosenbloom was betting big on this one. But Gussie Huditean knew it for a fact, or claimed that he did, and who was to say no? Through the years, Gussie would sometimes say the figure was $17,000 and sometimes $25,000. Who knows what it really was?

Officially, the NFL was against gambling, since the nation's leaders, and its clergy, still regarded all gambling (except church bingo) as a sin, and football wanted a clean bill of health like baseball. The league knew that the slightest hint of gamblers fixing even a single contest would wipe out all confidence in the legitimacy of the sport, and the league.

But the NFL couldn't entirely outrun its own history and its own cast of characters. The league had nervously survived a small scandal in the 1940s, suspending two players who admitted they'd been approached by gamblers.

But the problem was more insidious than that. Gambling money had helped build the league. The Giants' owner Tim Mara had been a bookmaker at Saratoga Racetrack. The Steelers owner Art Rooney owned a horse track, and the Chicago Cardinals owner Charles "Blue Shirt Charlie" Bidwill made his money printing parimutuel tickets. Bell, summertime neighbors with Rosenbloom, knew that gambling existed and also knew these were strong, willful men who were not going to be told what to do. So he didn't pretend naïveté.

His position was: The league will keep an eye on gambling and therefore make certain nothing happens that involves the play on the field. For individuals such as Rosenbloom, the message was clear: Be discreet. So he was. As Gussie Huditean told the story for the rest of his life, he and Rosenbloom met every week, and Rosenbloom discreetly made his bets. And then Gussie couldn't wait to tell everybody who walked into his joint.

And if you ask any of the surviving Baltimore Colts if Rosenbloom's betting affected their play, or the ball club's strategy, in even the slightest measure in the championship game, they will wither you with looks of sheer contempt. This was the moment of their lives, untainted by the financial whims of Rosenbloom or anyone else.

SUDDEN LIFE

EARLY ON THE GRAY MORNING of December 28, 1958, Bill Gattus makes his way to Baltimore's Pennsylvania Train Station with the things most precious in his life. He has his Baltimore Colts helmet, which he will wear on his head for the rest of the day and hold in his possession for the rest of his life. He has his saxophone to play music on the train. He has his beer, some of which he will drink on the way to New York and some which he will store in a locker at the New York train station in order not to be parched on the train ride home. He carries tickets for himself and fifteen of his friends, and they hop on the special trains with thousands of others from Baltimore, and now begins the delirium.

It comes from all parts of town. Twelve thousand will ride the trains, the buses, and the highways to New York. Gattus brings folks from his North Point Road bar in Dundalk, and Reds Hubbe's got his gang from Highlandtown and Fells Point. From northwest Baltimore entire squadrons of regulars from the Hilltop Diner have tickets. Gussie's Downbeat will be a little empty because so many are heading for the Bronx, bookmakers included. Here's half a dozen guys piling into the train with an outsize pair of women's bloomers, maybe six feet

wide, bearing the message, "Colts Will Kick the Pants Off Giants."
They're scrambling in with guys who came off the Bethlehem Steel
night shift out at Sparrows Point, along with downtown judges, aluminum siding salesmen, schoolteachers, and obstetricians who've
given strict instructions to women not to have any babies today. And
here's the Colts band, decked out and already tootling through the
aisles. "Let's go you Bawlamer Colts / And put that ball across the
line . . . "

It goes this way for four hours across two hundred miles of Pennsylvania Railroad track. Gattus plays his saxophone and marches through
the rattling cars, and everybody sings along. Reds is leading cheers.
Members of the Colts band divide up, a few sax players here, a couple
of trombones and a trumpet there, and they're passing the hat after
each musical rendition. As is some guy with an accordion. When he's
not playing the Colts song, he's playing polkas. And people are still
yelling, "Gimme a C" all the way through Delaware and Pennsylvania
and Jersey.

When they pause to catch their breath, it's the same conversation in
every car. They're wondering about the weather. Or they're wondering
if their seats will be any good. And they're wondering if Unitas's ribs
can hold up under that cage he's worn since the Green Bay game.

Some of 'em, they're reading the morning paper. At the top of the
front page, a headline says: "It's the Payoff, Colts Are Rarin' to Go."
That's the story they're all devouring. The other stuff, who cares?
"Cuba Moves to Halt Rebel Drive," says one story. In four years Cuba
brings us to the brink of nuclear annihilation, but, right now: What's
Cuba? "Ike Leads Most Admired List," says another headline. It's the
annual Top Ten list: Eisenhower, Churchill, Albert Schweitzer, Billy
Graham, Truman, gimme the rest of the names some other time, will-
ya? Right now, just gimme a C.

Maybe they scan the TV page, just to see what they're missing.
Robert Frost's answering questions on *Meet the Press*. The world still
thinks poetry worthy of the idiot box. CBS is showing a documentary on Woodrow Wilson and the League of Nations. Tough taking a
pass on that one, huh? Maybe the kids will watch *Lassie*. The preview
looks real promising: "Lassie's love for Timmy conquers the dog's fear
of insects."

These things exist in some other world.

This moment has stunned Baltimoreans. It's not that they've waited for it their entire lives—they never in their lives anticipated such a thing could actually happen to them. This kind of moment was always some other city's, some other kind of people's. And now that it's arrived in their own lives, they're determined to play it out for all it's worth, since who knows if it'll ever come their way again.

So they get to New York and spill out of the trains like an army advancing on its vocal cords.

"Gimme a C," somebody's always yelling.

"C!"

"Gimme an O."

"O!"

New Yorkers don't know what to make of this.

Gattus in his Colts helmet's still playing his sax, and the fellow with the accordion hasn't let up. The guys with the six-foot women's bloomers unveil them in the train station. Some of the crowd walks up 42nd Street, still calling out cheers, still singing, "Let's go you Bawlamer Colts." Most of 'em go down into the subways, where they're still cheering. New Yorkers shrug their shoulders: "Crazy people, who needs 'em?" New Yorkers, they're used to people like this; hell, they're used to game days like this: the championship of this, the championship of that. Big deal, they've been here before.

It doesn't matter. For the Baltimore people it feels like a holiday. For a lot of them, it feels like they're taking over the town. They've stepped off the assembly line and into a kind of giddy group anarchy. It feels like they're part of an invasion force occupying the biggest city in the world. It feels like nothing they've ever known. They're trying to take away what seems to belong by birthright to all of New York: championships, bragging rights, that smug sense of New Yawk superiority. They want to know what it feels like themselves for once in their overlooked lives.

THE TIMES HADN'T YET changed on December 28, 1958.

The highest-priced championship game ticket was $10 then, instead of the $600 it would cost for a Super Bowl seat half a century later. For the '58 game there were thirty minutes of pre-game television chat, instead of two weeks. Nobody imagined awakening at dawn on a Super Bowl Sunday for a twelve-hour televised sunrise service of video clips and pre-game analysis, not when they had actual lives to live. It was a championship game that afternoon at Yankee Stadium, but it was still just a football game. The Colts band performed at halftime, not Michael Jackson. No fleet of Air Force jets roared across the ballpark, symbolically linking patriotism and military might with a game in which the Bomb is thrown. The Colts' cheerleaders wore antlers on their head, indicating the lingering Christmas spirit, instead of prancing around with their chests hanging out like national monuments. And nobody set off fireworks when it was over.

It wasn't a cultural event—it was a contest they were playing four days before the college bowl games. Now *those* were considered big to most Americans (as witness the host of the Tournament of Roses Parade, Ronald Reagan). Baseball, too, was considered far bigger. Until this hour the NFL could only dream of making its mark on the national psyche the way baseball had. If this was the last pro football game of the year, it signaled to many Americans that only six weeks remained until spring training when we could talk about the real national pastime.

Or so we called it until this hour.

Colts' fans thought the game was the biggest thing in their lives; people in New York saw it as one more signal of their town's continuing greatness. For the rest of the country, the game was a slight diversion, something to tune in on a cold winter afternoon if they had nothing better to do. The pros were still everybody's afterthought.

These were grown men playing a football game for money. Some of them had fought in a world war, and they were hoping to earn a few thousand extra dollars for a new car or a down payment on a house. All of them would go back to their regular jobs when the game was over. A championship game today, a real job on Monday.

Nobody imagined the game that was coming, or its reverberations.

FROM THE CONCOURSE PLAZA HOTEL you can walk to Yankee Stadium. Artie Donovan knew the way. He'd grown up in the Bronx and played his high school ball there and occasionally took the subway down to the hotel after he came home from the war. The American Legion held

A ticket to the '58 Colts-Giants championship game: $10. It seemed like a lot of money back then. Half a century later, a Super Bowl ticket could cost $600, and scalpers were getting even more. *Courtesy Baltimore News-American Collection, Marylandia and Special Collections, University of Maryland Libraries*

dances there. "We'd steal pitchers of beer off the tables," he remembered years later.

Now, on the afternoon before the championship game, he and a couple of teammates took a little stroll from their hotel down to the stadium. This was his town; he felt like a hero here. Outside the ballpark, under the El, lots of people milled about. Some of them recognized Donovan and started calling out to him.

"You're gonna get killed tomorrow," one man cried.

"I hope this team's better than the one you played on at St. Michael's," yelled another.

Donovan loved it.

"Ah, we're gonna stick it up your ass tomorrow," he hollered back.

He giggled and moved on. But he thought about all the years he'd been playing football games. Going all the way back to St. Michael's, in the old neighborhood, he'd never been on a championship team. Played on some dogs, but never in his life a winner. He walked back to the hotel. Ewbank was keeping close tabs on everybody, but Donovan slipped up to his old neighborhood around 202nd Street and bought a couple of pizzas and sneaked them back to the room. "Best pizza in town," he told Art Spinney, his roommate. The two of them dug in. When they heard a knock on the door, Donovan said, "Put the pizza under the bed." He didn't feel like sharing.

Spinney, who'd been his teammate back at Boston College, was showing some jitters. Donovan wasn't. He always saved his nervousness for the locker room. He never played a game his whole life without first throwing up in the toilet.

A few doors down the hotel corridor, John Unitas studied his play-book. Raymond Berry did, too. A few doors from them, Steve Myhra did not. The guy's such a nervous wreck, he left Baltimore and forgot to bring the damned book. If Weeb finds out, he's in major trouble. Andy Nelson watches him pace their room and figures it's the usual Myhra jitters. But he doesn't know the half of it.

Myhra's telephoned a guy back in Baltimore named Eddie Veditz, who rents him a few rooms during the season. The playbook's there. Veditz's brother-in-law, Joe Perzynski, will drive up from Baltimore for the game. He works the night shift in the hot strip mill at Sparrows Point. He gets off at three in the morning. Veditz gives the playbook to Perzynski, who'll try to get it to Myhra Sunday morning. As if, by then, he'll have any use for it anyway.

By morning everybody's wired.

Donovan's down in the hotel lobby just after dawn with Bert Rechichar and Jack Call. Early mass. Others go for a short walk around the hotel. Get a feel for the weather, stretch the legs. A little warmer than expected. A ten o'clock team breakfast, where Ewbank talks briefly, nothing inspirational. He's saving that for later: his Knute Rockne moment. He tells them to go to the sixth floor of the hotel to get their knees and ankles taped. It's tedious stuff, until Donovan shows up. He's wearing nothing but his undershorts.

"Look at this," he announces. He points to a small hole in his shorts. "I feel like I'm gonna be so rich today that here's what I'm gonna do."

He puts one finger in the torn spot and pulls away. The shorts come asunder. With laughter filling the room, here come Big Daddy Lipscomb and Bert Rechichar, singing two different songs loudly and off-key. Rechichar sings, "You got the whole world championship in your hands."

Out in the hall, Steve Myhra bumps into a guy he's never seen before. It's Joe Perzynski, who's arrived with Myhra's missing play-book. "I showed it to the Giants first," Perzynski says. "You don't mind, do you?" Myhra smiles wanly at the jest. Just what he needs, a joker when his nerves are coming undone.

In the taping room, most of the day's tension's still covered by a veil of jauntiness. Lenny Moore walks in talking music. Jim Parker sits in a chair, which collapses, setting off howls of laughter. Steadman stands in a corner of the room, quietly taking notes. In these days, a sports writer still has such access.

Soon the mood starts to darken. When the ballplayers gather in the hotel lobby and somebody cracks a joke, nobody laughs. They're watching people on the street head for the ballpark. They've been waiting a long time for this, and now it's starting to feel very real.

Jim Parker starts pacing the lobby, and everybody backs away. Years later Mutscheller remembers, "We always joked that you had to stay out of Parker's way on game day because he was so worked up, he kept bumping into people."

By 12:30 they're on their way to the stadium in two buses. Back in Baltimore, schoolboys are throwing footballs around, trying to burn off energy, trying to kill time until something connected to the game comes on the TV set. Right now it's the usual Sunday fare for 1958: *Lamp unto My Feet. Faith for Today. Life Is Worth Living.* Against the Colts, such programs haven't got a prayer.

In the locker room, as everyone slowly dresses, Don Shinnick mutters, "I think we're ready to explode." Carroll Rosenbloom makes his way around the room, wishing each player luck. He's got none of his gambling friends with him this time, and nobody mentions any point spreads. It'd be like betting on casualty figures in a war zone.

In Baltimore housewives leaf through the morning paper: The government says the U.S. population's now reached 175 million. White Coffee Pot's got two all-meat crab cakes for seventy-five cents. Louella Parsons says Debbie Reynolds gave birth to a little boy and she and her husband, Eddie Fisher, named him Todd, after Mike Todd, the producer whose plane just went down. Such a lovely gesture, the housewives think; what special friends they must be with Todd's widow, the lovely Elizabeth Taylor.

In New York the Colts cheerleaders walk onto the field, and they're greeted by the boos of Giants' fans. "The first time on record that a pretty girl was ever booed in this town," the Hearst columnist Bob Considine will write.

Then the Colts come out.

They file out for their pre-game warmups to the sound of anticipated boos, but something else, as well: loud cheers. It comes mostly from the two end zones, where Baltimoreans are sitting. Gattus is up there

Baltimore's favorite moment of 1958, as captured that winter by the distributors of National Bohemian Beer. That's Alan Ameche in sudden-death overtime, plunging through a hole as wide as the New York subway system, with Lenny Moore opening up half the line for him while John Unitas looks on.
Courtesy Louis Rebuck Jr.

leading his gang, and Reds has his gang. People have unfurled Colts banners here and there. They're ducking various flying objects hurled at them by Giants' fans. And the band's already struck up the fight song. For the players, it feels pretty good; they're not alone in the big city.

When they get back to the locker room, the outside world is blocked out entirely. Ewbank closes the door and tells everybody to sit still. Fifty years later many of the surviving Colts could still remember Weeb's words, though Donovan was an exception.

"I was in the bathroom throwing up," he remembers.

Berry recalls pieces of it. "To be honest with you," he says so many years later, "the thing I remember most about that pep talk was the sound of Donovan throwing up in the bathroom. It sounded like somebody goosing a hippopotamus."

He also remembered being surprised by Ewbank's passion.

"He starts going around the room, and I remember thinking I didn't expect anything like this."

Ewbank told Berry, "Nobody wanted you in the draft." He'd been a twentieth-round selection.

He told Unitas, "Pittsburgh didn't want you, but we picked you off the sandlots." He told Lenny Moore, "You can be as good as you want to be." He told Lipscomb, "The Rams didn't want you." He told Andy Nelson, "They said you couldn't play pro ball." He told Ameche, "The Giants say you're not as good as Jim Brown." He told Mutscheller, "They said you could never play in this league."

He went around the room like this, slowing the world down for a few moments to let each player realize how far he had come and the odds he'd beaten. And how this was the day to prove everybody wrong who'd ever said they weren't good enough.

They had one more motivation. Ewbank posted copies of the *New York Journal American* from midseason. They all knew what it said. It was Charlie Conerly's remark after the Giants beat the Colts: "We out-gutted them."

By this time, the line was burned into their brains.

THE GAME ITSELF was not the greatest ever played until the hour grew quite late.

But its impact on professional football, and on the American sporting culture, was breath-taking. And its emotional impact on Baltimore lingers half a century later, when aging men still choke up when they hear the playing of the Colts fight song or see that picture of Ameche with his head down. It's not only a touchdown he's scoring; it's the birth of a generation finally feeling terrific about itself.

But until the tension of those final two minutes of regulation play and the eight minutes, fifteen seconds of overtime that followed, it was only a football game and no particular piece of history.

First the Giants had the ball, and Marchetti had the Giants. He deflected a pass on the game's first play. On the second play he nearly sacked starting quarterback Don Heinrich. On the third he and Donovan forced Heinrich to throw early and off-target.

But then came a series of blunders: first Unitas fumbled. Then the Giants' Mel Triplett fumbled. Then Unitas threw an interception.

Later in the quarter Myhra tried an easy field goal. He missed. He got another shot because the Giants were off-side. He missed again, when Sam Huff blocked it. Pat Summerall kicked a Giants field goal for a 3 to 0 lead, and that's how the first quarter ended. No legends, no memories to savor for the ages. A football game.

And, just off camera, a slight comic opera.

Donovan had a visitor. Sitting right there on the Colts' bench, an old family friend, John Brady, a captain in the New York Police Department. He's got a whiskey bottle in his hand, and he's drinking away. Every time Donovan comes off the field, Brady's telling Artie what he's doing wrong.

"John, Jesus, leave me alone, I got enough troubles," Donovan hollers.

Ewbank spots this lunatic. He turns to a nearby uniformed cop.

"Get rid of this guy," he says.

But Brady's not only a cop—he's head of police protection for the game.

"Coach," says the cop, "you go before him. Because he's Jesus Christ."

In the second quarter the blundering continues. Tackle Ray Krouse hits Gifford and knocks the ball loose. Lipscomb falls on it at the Giants' seventeen. In five plays, Ameche plunges over from the one. Colts 7, Giants 3.

But then more blunders: The Colts' Jackie Simpson fumbles a punt. The Giants' Gifford fumbles again. Two plays, two fumbles. Not the stuff of greatness.

But now the Colts begin to look like the Colts.

On third down from their nineteen, Unitas pitches to Ameche for ten yards. Moore zigs and zags for ten more. They're finding a rhythm now. From midfield Unitas looks to throw. Nobody open. So he runs for sixteen yards. Three plays later, it's classic Unitas to Berry, with Raymond cutting between Emlen Tunnell and Patton for the touchdown.

Now, that was more like it. When the Colts reached the locker room a minute later, they had a 14 to 3 halftime lead.

In Baltimore, people heaved the day's first small sighs of relief. In scores of smoky street-corner bars where patrons gathered around TV sets, they ordered rounds of celebratory drinks. Hey, somebody's always warning, don't get ahead of yourself—it ain't over yet. In the Yankee Stadium stands, Gattus and Reds led cheers among the Colts fans and ducked all flying objects heaved their way. In the Colts' locker room, Ewbank said, "Forget the score. You've got to play as if you're two touchdowns behind. We need two more scores." At this moment, it sounds pretty easy; the first thirty minutes feels like the beginning of a blowout.

We pick it up midway through the third quarter, when Unitas rifles a pass to Jim Mutscheller. He leaps and collides with Jimmy Patton as they reach for the ball. Mutscheller lands on his head but some-how makes the catch. As he stands up, dazed, he mutters, "Where am I?" He's at the Giants' twenty-seven-yard line. Then Unitas throws to Berry and to Moore. A sweet inevitability seems to be sinking in. First down at the three.

For the rest of their lives the Colts speak in one voice: If they score here, the game will be a blowout. But they do not score. Three running plays get them to the one. On fourth down, they wave off a field goal attempt. Myhra's tried two already, and two failed. They're down near the baseball home plate. The crowd noise makes it tough to hear. In the huddle, Unitas calls "428." He expects the Giants to bunch up the mid-dle of the line, and 428 will cross them up. It's a pitch to Ameche, who's to sweep right and throw the ball to Mutscheller in the end zone.

But Ameche never hears the "4" in front of the "28." When he sees Mutscheller, Jim's alone in the end zone, going, "Alan, Alan." Ameche thinks: What's he doing there when he should be blocking? The moment's hesitation costs him: Cliff Livington hits him from his blind side and dumps him for a four-yard loss. Giants' ball. The sta-dium erupts.

Now the game turned. Conerly found Kyle Rote over the middle. Rote caught the ball at the Colts' forty-five and cut through Carl Tassef and Milt Davis. When he got to the Colts' twenty-five, Andy Nelson hit him and knocked the ball loose. There it was, bouncing free in little clouds of dust on the stadium floor while spectators screamed their heads off. Alex Webster, trailing the play, scooped it up and never broke stride. Behind him came Tassef. It's a foot race to the goal line. Webster's knocked out of bounds at the two-yard line. The play cov-ered eighty-six yards, including all bounces.

Two plays later Mel Triplett ran it in. Instead of a 21 to 3 Colts lead, it was 14 to 10.

On the Baltimore bench, Marchetti tried to calm everyone. "It's all right," he said, marching up and down. "A fluke, a fluke. It's never gonna happen again. Come on, we're dominating."

Not for long. When the Giants got the ball back, Conerly passed to Bob Schnelker twice and then to Gifford for a touchdown. What the hell happened? Just like that, the Giants lead, 17 to 14.

In Baltimore, the reaction is simple. it's as though failure itself has walked into the room like a familiar face, and everyone declares: Yes, yes, of course, we've been expecting you.

This is New York, and we are merely Baltimore. We know in our hearts that our football team is better than anybody on the planet's, and we know that this no longer matters. We've been propped up to show our physical superiority only to make New York's storybook comeback even more heroic. It is their eternal destiny. We are merely Baltimore, and they are mighty New York. We are people who work on assembly lines and shipping piers, and New Yorkers are people who rule the world. For New York teams, the gods of sport always manage to work the proper angles.

Never mind that fourteen minutes remain in the fourth quarter: the handwriting's on the wall. In the Yankee Stadium press box, John Steadman tells himself, "There's still plenty of time." But he notices, for the first time in his life, an intense pressure building in his chest.

As the hour grows late, the stadium lights go on. On television the field looks a little haunted. Unitas, back to work, hits a few passes. But the drive stalls, and another field goal attempt fails. This one, by Bert Rechichar. Now the temperature's dropping, and patches of ice form on the turf. The players on the sidelines drape capes around their shoulders and blow on their hands to try to warm them. The stadium is so barren of grass that every time the players move they churn up more clouds of dust. In front of the Baltimore bench Donovan and Marchetti stand next to each other.

"If we lose this," Donovan says, "it's a travesty. We're so much better than them, and here we are fighting for our lives."

"You're right, Fatso," says Marchetti.

The next time they get the ball, momentary hope is snatched away

The Toast of the Town. That's Baltimore mayor Tommy D'Alesandro Jr. beaming in the Colts' locker room after the championship victory, with *(left to right)* Steve Myhra, John Unitas, and Alan Ameche. That's a soda bottle in Ameche's hand. It was the only celebratory drink available. *Courtesy Baltimore News-American Collection, Marylandia and Special Collections, University of Maryland Libraries*

again. The gods are great teases. Unitas throws the bomb, and Lenny Moore reaches over Lindon Crow to catch it at the one-yard line. But the referees say he's out of bounds, and Moore's objections get him nowhere. After that, knowing Unitas has to pass on every play, the Giants' linemen come roaring after him. On consecutive plays, he's thrown for big losses by Robustelli and Modzelewski.

A great mournfulness now covers all homes in Baltimore. The angel of death has come to visit. How did they let this get away? With the clock moving toward the two-minute mark, the Giants have the ball. Can't somebody stop the damned clock? Webster carries, then Gifford. Third and four at the Giants' forty. If they make the first down here, they run out the clock for sure. There is universal trembling in every living room in the Baltimore area, and Steadman in the press box wonders again about the pain in his chest. In their end-zone seats, the Colts fans are imploring their defense to hold tight.

The Giants send Gifford sweeping right. He gets three yards and he gets two feet. But then he runs into Marchetti and Pellington and

Donovan, followed by Lipscomb. Big Daddy lands on Gino's ankle. In the tangle of blockers and tacklers and ball carrier, Gifford calls out, "First down, I made it."

"Will you shut up," Donovan says. "You didn't make it."

Marchetti's crying, "My ankle . . . my ankle."

One of the Giants snaps, "Get up, Marchetti, the play's over."

"I can't," Gino says. "My ankle."

The right one's broken. The referees are trying to measure for a first down. The men with a stretcher are trying to cart Marchetti off. The Giants are yelling first down, and the Colts are saying no. The ball game's on the line, right here. Steadman, looking down from the press box, jots a line in his notebook, which he will keep to the end of his life: "Short by a foot," it says. A few days later, the Giants' own movies will verify this.

"He's short," the referees finally signal. And this time it's the Giants' complaints that go nowhere.

"Kick the ball, young man," Coach Jim Lee Howell tells his punter, Don Chandler.

Meanwhile six guys are trying to haul the huge Marchetti down the sidelines to the locker room. He won't go. "Put me down here," he says. He wants to see the game. He wants his teammates to see that he's still here, he's their captain, he's not deserting them. Up in the stands the Baltimore fans are chanting, "Gino, Gino, Gino." He's the gladiator who refuses to fall on his shield.

"Gino, Gino, Gino."

The raw theatrics are powerful. Up in the press box Steadman, thirty-one years old, the son of a fireman who died young of a heart attack, now believes he's having one of his own. It's the same feeling in homes all over Baltimore. But Steadman believes he's not going to leave the ballpark alive.

In their final possession, the Colts don't have the luxury of emotion.

The Giants punt, and the Colts take over on their own fourteen-yard line. The Giants' end zone is eighty-six yards away, barely visible in the falling dusk. The clock shows one minute and fifty-six seconds left. As Berry runs onto the field, he thinks, "We've blown the darned game. We should have put it away." But the thought stays with him only a moment. For him, and for all of them, the training takes over. In the huddle, Unitas is cool as ever. He is twenty-five years old and three years removed from a semi-pro league where he made six bucks a game on a field littered with glass and oil slicks, and now this gutsy kid is about to move the world.

On first down, he throws long for Mutscheller, who's covered by two Giants. Incomplete. At least it stops the clock. On second down, incomplete to L. G. Dupre. As Berry goes back to the huddle, he's thinking, "Why is John throwing to Dupre?" In the press box Jack Mara, who runs the Giants, gets up and leaves. He's convinced it's over, and he's headed for the locker room to congratulate his team. The Giants' fans are pummeling each other in happiness. The Baltimore fans are disconsolate. Out there in the end-zone seats they're throwing things at Bill Gattus, trying to hit his Colts helmet. But he'll never take it off.

Along the sidelines, Donovan's muttering a prayer. Our Lady of Victory, please help us. Anybody, please do something. He's thinking of all those humiliating losses through the years. He's thinking of all the teams he's played on, and not once a champion. He's thinking he's been coming to Yankee Stadium since boyhood, watching his father referee boxing, watching the Yankees win their pennants. Finally, here's his moment in history, and it's about to pass him by.

On third and ten, all hope fading, Unitas drops back to pass again. The din in Yankee Stadium is deafening. Unitas throws hard and low to Lenny Moore along the right sidelines. Moore grabs it off his shoe tops. Needed ten yards. Got eleven. First down. The clock seems to be sprinting toward closing time.

Another pass to Dupre, incomplete again. So now it's second down, at the twenty-five-yard line, and under ninety seconds left. In the huddle, Unitas calls a ten-yard square-in to Berry. The Giants will be guarding the sidelines. It's the play Raymond will describe in the hotel room fifty years later. There's the big Giants' linebacker Harland Svare, and he's right in Raymond's face. There's no way Raymond can run the route. They've got that backup plan, which he and Unitas worked out maybe two years earlier for this situation.

But they haven't talked about it in God knows how long.

And so, in the dusk and chaos of Yankee Stadium, Berry looks down the line of scrimmage and tries to catch Unitas's eye. He's thinking, "I hope John remembers." Unitas looks Berry's way, thinking, "I hope Raymond remembers."

Berry fakes left and hopes Svare will follow him. He does. Berry quickly knifes back to the right, ducking under Svare toward the middle of the field. Unitas snaps the pass to him. Raymond's got it around the thirty-eight. He's hit by big Cliff Livingston but somehow bounces off him, spins completely around, and with dust flying everywhere keeps on going as five or six of the Giants converge on him step for step.

But they don't catch him until he's reached midfield.

The clocks shows sixty-four seconds are left. In Baltimore living rooms they're screaming as though they've got seats on the fifty-yard line. Now Berry has Karl Karilivacz covering him. He's backed off; he's giving Raymond room to maneuver in close. Unitas throws short again. Berry's got ten yards, takes a solid hit, but carries it five more. First down at the thirty-five. But they're out of time-outs, and the clock's still racing along. Nobody in America has ever seen a football team make so much yardage under so much pressure in so little time. They don't even have time for huddles; in Baltimore everybody's yelling for them to line up fast, line up fast, as though their voices can be heard two hundred miles away. Unitas looks once more for Berry. Raymond's got it again. This time he's at the fifteen, takes a couple of shots, fights forward for a few more yards.

"Kicking team," Ewbank's yelling. Berry, exhausted, breathless, barely makes it to the sidelines before he collapses near the bench. "Kicking team, kicking team."

That means Myhra. It's come down to the nervous wreck to try to save the day. It's come down to a field goal, when they've already missed three of them today. It's Myhra, and he's running out there thinking, "I better not miss this one." George Shaw's running out to hold the snap. He's thinking, Don't drop it, don't drop it. Donovan and Parker, members of the Fat-Ass Team, the big buffaloes who block for field goal attempts, line up next to each other at the line of scrimmage.

On the sidelines, Andy Nelson's thinking, "Come on, Steve, calm down, just this once."

Shaw's drawing an X in the dirt, where he wants to spot the ball.

Along the line of scrimmage, everybody's hollering at somebody. Parker's yelling at Donovan, and Donovan's yelling at Parker. "Tighten up the line," somebody's yelling, "tighten up the line."

"Shut up," Donovan cries.

"I'm nervous," Parker cries back.

"Tighten up the line."

"Shut up, shut up." Donovan hollers again.

The next thing Donovan knows, he's knocked backward and can't see a thing through the tangle of bodies. Myhra's leg swings forward. As the kick sails toward the uprights, the clock says seven seconds are left. When Donovan looks up, he sees Myhra leaping in the air with both arms extended.

It's the mirror image of the thing happening in living rooms all over Baltimore.

It's 17 to 17.

It must be some kind of an illusion.

AND NOW WHAT?

In Baltimore, we're collapsed in our living rooms, still digesting the miracle of the last drive when Chuck Thompson and Chris Schenkel are explaining what comes next on our televisions. This is all new territory. Along the sidelines at Yankee Stadium, it's a mystery to the ballplayers, too. Half a dozen Colts start walking off the field. They think the game's over and it's ended in a tie.

"Where you going?" one of the assistant coaches yells at them.

"Game's over," Andy Nelson tells him.

"We're gonna play some more," the coach says. "Sudden death."

Nelson's never even heard the phrase before this.

"What do you mean?"

"We're gonna play it off. First team that scores wins the game."

Sure enough, out there in the dusk at midfield they're calling for the captains. That means Marchetti. But Gino's gone—he's still lying on his stretcher on the sidelines. The Colt crowd's still yelling, "Gino, Gino, Gino." Unitas takes Gino's place at midfield now, and they flip a coin to see who'll receive. Giants win. They score, they win. Simple as that. Unitas lopes back to the sidelines, where Ewbank's got everybody gathered around him.

"Block and tackle," he hollers through the crowd noise. "When we get the ball, we gotta hold it. Here's our chance to win it for Gino."

It's just words lost in the dark until he gets to the part about Marchetti.

"Yeah, for Gino," they answer Weeb.

From the Giants' twenty, Gifford tries the right side. Ordell Braase's in for Marchetti, so the Giants think they can beat him. They get four yards. Johnny Sample's now playing defensive back for Milt Davis, whose bad ankle has finally given way. Sample's thinking, God, don't make me the goat of the game. Conerly thinks he can beat Sample. He throws, and it's incomplete. On third and six Conerly tries to pass again. His receivers are all covered, so he runs. Shinnick and Pellington bring him down a foot short of a first down. The Giants have to punt. The Colts take over at their own twenty-one.

From their end-zone seats the Baltimore crowd's yelling, "Get it for Gino." He's still lying on his stretcher. There's this dying warrior there, and they're torn between caring about him and not wanting to miss a moment of the action. The championship's on the line, the temperature's dropping, and now the trainers are worried Marchetti's starting to go into shock.

Unitas gives to L. G. Dupre.

Marchetti won't listen to the trainers, so now the cops have come over to lend their authority.

Dupre gets ten yards.

As the Colts huddle up, the cops are giving Marchetti orders. When this crowd spills out of the stands, they won't be able to protect him, so he's gotta get out of here.

Unitas, impatient, throws long to Moore. Lindon Crow knocks it down.

Marchetti gives one last glance at the action. "Jesus," he mutters. The trainers lift Gino off the ground. The Baltimore people are still hollering his name. This is torture. They'll carry him to the locker room, where there's more torture. Gino's got to lie there on a table with no radio or TV and try to figure out what the hell the noise above him means.

Out there it's third and seven. Unitas flips a screen pass to Ameche out in the flat. The Giants are playing too far back. By inches, the Horse makes the first down. Now, down in his underground bunker,

Marchetti hears a new round of cheers, too loud, must mean something bad for the Colts.

It does. Modzelewski's buried Unitas, making it third and long. What's left in John's bag of tricks now? He looks long for Moore. Lenny's covered. Unitas shifts direction, heads left to buy time, and spots Berry. But John's not satisfied. He wants Raymond deeper, and waves his left hand to tell him, and then throws the ball. Berry's got it along the left sidelines. He's got Karilivacz clinging to his ankle, and Raymond's trying to yank it away when two other Giants come up to help. But it's a first down at New York's forty-four.

When Berry gets back to the huddle, he needs an oxygen tent. He loves Unitas's next call. It's Fifteen Sucker, a fullback trap play. It takes Raymond out of the heart of the action. He figures he can catch his breath. The play's an old one: the left guard Spinney takes one step back, as if to block for a pass, and lets the Giants' Modzelewski rush Unitas. But Spinney will suddenly stop and drive low and hard into Mo while the other guard, George Preas, takes out linebacker Sam Huff. And Ameche will run.

It's the other play Berry will talk about fifty years later in his hotel room—the play they'd run for four years and never gained more than two yards. He's supposed to block Jimmy Patton, the New York defensive back. But Raymond figures the play's going nowhere, so it's his brief moment to pace himself. He gives Patton a slight brush block, but nothing more.

And the next thing he knows, Spinney and Preas have opened up huge holes, and Ameche's out in the open. The Horse is churning up the middle, ten yards, twenty yards, who knows how far he might go? Until that damned Patton, left alone by Berry, races up to pull Ameche down from behind. The play will haunt Raymond for a long time: If only he'd blocked Patton seriously and taken him out of the play, maybe Ameche goes all the way to the end zone.

But it picks up twenty-three yards and another first down at the twenty-one.

Now the wheels are turning everywhere. Ewbank's wondering, Do we play it safe and go for a field goal now? Is he kidding? Who's supposed to kick it, Myhra? They got lucky the last time; they can't press their luck again. Should they play it safe and run the ball?

Not Unitas. He calls on the exhausted, embarrassed Berry again. This time a slant, and this time Raymond takes it down to the eight-yard line.

And then, just like that, the world goes blank. Across America the television sets tuned to the game display nothing at all. The screens are all dark. Fifty years later Baltimoreans will still ask each other, Remember when the TV went out? All around town, all around America, they're turning their sets on and off, they're checking their electrical plugs, they're pounding their fists against the sides of the sets.

Nothing helps.

"Where's the radio? Where's the goddamned radio?"

Somebody in New York leaned on a cable or stepped on an outlet. Fifty years later, it's still not clear. In Baltimore, everybody's gone into panic mode. Just when it looks like we finally might win something, the gods won't let us gaze into the Promised Land from our living rooms.

But there's a break in the action. Some idiot's run out onto the field, and three New York City cops are trying to chase him down. The guy's not bad. He's at the forty, he's at the thirty. He kills enough time that they figure out the problem back in the control room, and the TV sets come back on all over the whole country.

Just in time for Ameche to get a yard. Even here, even seven or eight measly yards from triumph, a sense of woe creeps into Baltimore blood. We've been here before, haven't we? This looks like the third quarter drive, the one that stalled at the goal line with three straight runs. We're not going through that again, are we?

Unitas has a better idea. The crowd's hot with passion, and John's icy and calculating. When he gets to the line of scrimmage, he sees something that nobody else sees. Usually it's the Giants' strong safety, Emlen Tunnell, covering Mutscheller. This time it's the linebacker Cliff Livingston. He's trying to take away any inside moves. So Unitas checks off. He wants Mutscheller to run a diagonal out. The only one over there is Lindon Crow, and Crow's got all he can handle trying to watch Lenny Moore.

With the Giants braced for a run, Unitas drops to pass. How do you like this guy's moxie? He pump-fakes, then delicately lofts a floater toward the sidelines. There's Mutscheller down near the goal line, but there are so many bodies down there, ballplayers and sideline hang-ers-on, that who the hell knows what happened? Did he catch it? Did he score? There's only one TV angle, and it tells us nothing. But finally there's the referee's signal. Mutscheller caught it, all right, but the field's frozen down there, and he fell out of bounds at the one.

Close enough. So close that people in Baltimore can now imagine the previously unimaginable.

In the huddle Unitas says, "Sixteen Power." It's about as basic as football gets. It goes back to Rockne's era. It goes back to schoolboys drawing plays in the dirt. It's Ameche with Preas and Mutscheller in front of him, wiping out the interior of the Giants' front line, and Moore taking out anybody on the outside. It's the kind of football they've been running since the age of the cardboard helmet.

And yet it's the beginning of the Great Change. As Unitas looks over center, he can see Huff and Modzelewski and Jim Katcavage. But if he lifts his head above them, just beyond the upper facade of Yankee Stadium, that's the future out there, and it's arriving right now with the whole country watching.

A sport has been transposed. Baseball, once the national pastime, is suddenly perceived as slow and sleepy. A professional football league created in a garage in Canton, Ohio, is on its way to the very heart of American sporting culture. A game designed for coal miners will now be covered by the dust of pure gold.

And so Ameche runs. Oh, boy, does he run. Head down, legs churn-ing, a hole opens so wide he plunges through the air, his body bounc-ing twice as he hits the ground. He lands in the end zone. He lands in the American future. He's still lying there, his body cupped around the ball, when they're pouring all over him, swarms of people who have jumped down from the stands. Some kid swipes the ball, and Buzz Nutter's gotta swipe it back. Ameche can't get out of the end zone. A whole bunch of Baltimore people lift him up on their shoulders, and already the goal post's coming down, and the Colt band's going up and down the field like it's marching into Rome.

Just off the Colts' main locker room Marchetti hears the noise and knows it's over now. But he doesn't know which way. He's stretched out on a trainer's table, in a room not much bigger than a walk-in closet. The waiting's killing him. He hears the sound of a bunch of cleats clacking atop cement, and a door's opening. There's Jim Parker. He's wrapping his arms around Gino.

"World champions," Parker says. "How you feeling?"

"I'd have broken the other ankle if I knew it'd mean this much," Gino says. His hair's flopped down over his forehead, and the trainers are starting to cut his uniform from his body, but he's beaming as Ameche charges in and hands him the game ball.

"The happiest man who ever broke an ankle," says Dr. Erwin Mayer, the team doctor.

"Who out-gutted who?" Art Spinney's yelling.

"I guess their hearts weren't as big as their mouths," Buzz Nutter says.

"Where's the beer?" Donovan yells. But there is none. Some Nehi Orange, he'll remember for years to come. He never gets over it. World War II veterans, and they're celebrating with Nehi Orange.

Never mind.

"It was the greatest," declares the mayor of Baltimore, Tommy D'Alesandro, smiling broadly as he walks around the locker room littered with towels and tape and discarded uniforms. He knows what this means to his struggling city. "The greatest."

Berry heads straight for the lavatory. Something happened to him out there today, and he needs to think about it by himself. Years later he says, "I never was a person who gave God much thought. Religion was habit, that's all. It was tradition and habit, but I never tried to communicate with God, I didn't know you could. But the day was overwhelming, and I just had the sense that God had been involved in it, big-time. I wasn't a person who prayed. But I sat down, and I was thunder-struck. God did that. That's what I said to myself."

When he reaches the locker room, he hears Don Shinnick's voice: "How 'bout the prayer, guys?"

And there they are. Lenny Moore, who played most of the game with a cracked rib, bows his head and crouches on one knee. He's next to Shinnick, who's slumped on a little stool by his locker. Tassef and Spinney are kneeling nearby, and there's Berry, the only one standing in the whole group, his helmet in his hand, thinking, "What in the world went on out there?"

Out on the field, Baltimore fans are down on their knees, too, but they're pulling up clumps of grass, scooping up dirt. This is hallowed ground now, and they want it sanctified. Some of 'em are still down there in the end zone. They're fighting for pieces of the goal post, trying to get a few slivers. One guy's got a splinter in his finger. It's enough, he says, marching off happily. Or they're dancing in circles, like schoolkids playing Ring Around the Rosey. Or they're hollering and hooting, no particular words, just some primeval howls to the heavens.

It's the same outside the stadium. Gattus in his Colts helmet, crying out, "Johnny U, Johnny U," has been hoisted onto shoulders as though he scored the winning touchdown. From Yankee Stadium to Penn Station, his feet will not hit the ground.

The train ride back to Baltimore's different from the one up.

When all the people get to the trains, they're exhausted. A couple try getting up cheers, but it's too much. Enough to bask in the win, to ask each other who's the biggest hero, Unitas or Berry or Myhra or maybe Ameche. Some folks sit there in a kind of stupor. Some of the band members strike up the fight song, but it's too late. Everybody's spent. It's as though they played every down themselves.

Jim Henneman's one of the passengers. He's a young sports writer at the *News-Post*. He turns to a pal and says, "I'll tell you one thing. There ain't gonna be many people at the airport when the Colts get in, 'cause everybody's on this train."

Oh, but he's wrong about that.

"THEY JUST WANTED SOMEBODY
TO BE HAPPY WITH"

IN BALTIMORE some of us ran to the streets, and some of us ran to the airport, and then everybody met at the television set.

On the streets we did the thing schoolboys always did after a Colts game. We gathered with our friends and threw a football around and talked about the thing we had just witnessed. It was cold outside, and it didn't matter. It was getting dark, and it didn't matter. Some of us just threw the ball back and forth. Some of us ran pass patterns in the street or the backyard or the schoolyard down the block. Maybe the greatness we had seen on television could be transferred by some kind of osmosis to our own scrawny bodies. Anything imaginable was possible now.

And then we heard the call from our mothers, not for dinner this time but to come quickly to the television set because we wouldn't believe what was happening out at Friendship Airport.

The whole world seemed to have landed there.

THE BALL GAME IN YANKEE STADIUM ended a few minutes before five, and by five the first cars from Baltimore arrived at the airport. By six o'clock more than 1,000 people were there, and the numbers kept

Baltimore's old Friendship Airport, as thirty thousand ecstatic fans surround the bus carrying the world-champion Baltimore Colts and hundreds of thousands more watched from their TV sets. Having survived football's version of sudden death, the overwhelmed Colts now wondered if they'd survive their fans' hysteria. *Baltimore News-American Collection, Marylandia and Special Collections, University of Maryland Libraries*

growing. The Colts weren't due until ten of eight. As Alexander Gifford wrote in the next day's *News-Post,* after he beheld the entire gathering spread before him, "It was a mob, a happy bunch of semi-lunatics carrying signs, carrying babies, and some of them just carrying on."

All over the Baltimore area people stood in their living rooms with their mouths open and envied the collective insanity on their television sets.

There were thousands of human beings splayed all over the airport, and all over its runways, as if waiting to cradle in their arms any incoming flights. There were boundary lines, but these were ignored. There were two dozen Pinkerton guards and who knows how many police, but they were ignored. The original 1,000 people became 10,000 and then 20,000. They filled up the airport garage and then an auxiliary garage. Then the 20,000 became 30,000. When the garages overflowed and the long road into the airport backed up, people parked their cars along the highway. And they walked the rest of the way to the airport, and it was too late now for them to hear the announcers on the radio stations saying anybody thinking about going to the airport should turn around and go home.

It wouldn't have mattered; this was their moment.

People on the tarmac unfurled their banners: "Champs," some of them read. Whenever a light appeared in the distant sky, cheers went up, and the crowd edged toward the runway and then retreated in disappointment when it wasn't the Colts coming in.

"Gimme a C," they were crying.

Then they listened for the echoes.

And people stood there in their living rooms and still could not believe the sea of humanity on their television screens.

The ball club's plane was ten minutes outside Baltimore when general manager Don Kellett emerged from the cockpit with a message from the pilot: There was a problem on the ground. There were 30,000 people at the airport, and they were out on the tarmac and out of control. He told this to Rosenbloom and Ewbank. He said airport officials were suggesting an act of sanity and self-preservation: the plane should bypass Baltimore and head to Washington instead.

No chance, the Colts said. They understood the moment and its meaning. This was the municipal love affair in its grandest hour. It was a generation of people who'd been told they were a nowhere town, third-rate to imperious New York and second-rate to self-important Washington just down the highway. And now their great affection for a football team had suddenly turned them all into America's darlings.

"We're going to Baltimore," Kellett told the pilot.

As the plane circled the airport, the ballplayers gazed out their windows and looked for the crowd somewhere below. In living rooms everywhere the sportscaster Joe Croghan stood before a WBAL-TV camera atop a platform set up to interview the players. He had no chance at all.

The plane landed in a dark and distant corner of the airport grid and rolled to a stop without approaching the terminal. Two police cars and two buses drove out to meet it.

"Let me tell you what we've got," said Captain Carl Kunaniec. As the players climbed onto the two buses, Kunaniec described the mayhem awaiting them. "We've never seen anything like it," he said.

In our living rooms we heard none of this, but we didn't need to. Television had never given us raw pictures like this. We were accustomed to watching ball games inside prescribed dimensions, with prescribed rules. Or we watched scripted moments inside meticulously lighted studios. We saw little children playing on *Romper Room,* or teenagers dancing to rock and roll on Buddy Deane. Or we saw Toots Barger throwing a bowling ball down a narrow alley. All of it, inside controlled environments. Later we would see tall buildings in New York blown apart in our living rooms, and car bombs exploding somewhere in the Middle East. But this was only 1958, when we saw an anchorman sitting at a desk delivering the 7:23 news every night, seven minutes of a talking head with an occasional photograph next to him, and we found even this tiny event remarkable.

But we had never seen a massive crowd surging everywhere, unscripted, unchoreographed, erasing all previous boundaries of television, and of human experience, right here in our homes.

The first police car, lights blinking, attempted to escort the first bus toward the terminal. It was Moses trying to part the Red Sea and failing. The bus was quickly drowning in bodies. The driver slowed down to avoid running over people. The second bus driver, seeing the trouble, turned around and managed an end run around the roaring crowd.

The first bus could not escape. Dozens of fans climbed atop the roof, standing and squatting while the crowd surrounded them. Steadman was inside with the players. The bus was stopped cold.

"They'll tear us to pieces," Ewbank said.

"Do you think we'll get out of here alive?" said the linebacker Leo Sanford.

The fans were screaming out players' names and howling just to hear themselves howl, as if telling the heavens themselves, Look who's down here. Against all odds, and all previous history: Just look.

Some stood atop the police cruiser. The roof began to crumble. Atop the roof of the bus some people leaned over the sides and tried to look in the windows. As quickly as police pulled them down, they were replaced by others.

"Are they drunk?" a player asked Steadman.

No, John told him, they were just happy. John understood. They'd never had a moment like this their whole life; nor did they expect another ever again.

On the TV platform Croghan cut his microphone cord. While the camera continued to capture the sweep of the crowd, he climbed down atop his remote van. No words were necessary, even if they could have been heard. And this, too, became a message: television was visual. Supply the right pictures, and words cease to matter.

People gaped at all of this from the safety of their homes, and some cursed themselves for not being in the airport crowd.

Steadman, inside the bus, would write, "There was no semblance of sanity, much less order. . . . The players watched in disbelief at what was going on around them and listened to the pounding on the roof. Waves of men, women and children would race, for no apparent reason, in one direction and then again, for no apparent reason, rush back to where they had been only a minute before."

Finally, as if exhaustion had overcome them simultaneously, the crowd began to melt slowly back. Some sense of order was finally arriving. The bus driver, Dana DeLisle, with police cars leading and following, sped to a distant parking lot by a building that appeared to be a church or a school. The players sat back in their seats and laughed with relief as police reached up to the roof of the bus and pulled down fourteen boys who'd held on during the high-speed trip.

Steadman watched as the boys came down. When the cops admonished them for their foolishness, John overheard one of the kids say, "Mister, I want to meet some Colts." Unitas and Sanford walked over. They shook the boys' hands. The police whispered to Rosenbloom that no charges would be pressed against them.

"I don't care if they do lock me up," one of them cried. "I just met some of the Colts."

That's what everybody wanted.

That, and one thing more. The bus driver, Dana DeLisle, glancing back toward the 30,000 at the airport who were finally beginning their journeys home, said, "They just wanted somebody to be happy with."

For this brief moment, in the evening's glow of December 28, 1958, that's what everyone got. They had stepped away from the loneliness of the assembly line and the isolation of neighborhoods divided by race and religion and economics and found thousands of people to be happy with.

Up on the roof of that battered bus, and the airport grounds all around it, was Baltimore thrown together. The photos were right there in the newspapers the next day, to reinforce it for everybody: Whatever our separate lives, whatever our diverse backgrounds, we really were part of each other's worlds. This giddy madness was the opening of a door. We had stepped out of the shadows of our separateness and found ourselves having the time of our lives together.

And the moment stayed with us forever.

NOTE ON SOURCES

CHAPTER 1. THE LOST CITY

Much of Chapter 1 comes from being part of the original cast. I was there for many of the Colts games and saw many more on television and listened on the radio to Chuck Thompson. I watched the Sunpapers Bowling Tournament every year. I went to the local movie theaters. I was in the city's public schools when the Colts were the constant conversation. This was supplemented by reading accounts in the Baltimore daily newspapers of that year.

The accounts of 1958 east Baltimore are drawn from many conversations through the years with Bill Gattus and Reds Hubbe, with Senator Barbara Mikulski and with Father Lou Esposito, with Charley Eckman and Gus Hansen, with Mimi DiPietro and Al Isella, with Gene Raynor and Michael "Bo" Sudano, and from my own newspaper reporting over many subsequent years.

The accounts of 1958 south Baltimore are drawn from many conversations through the years with Joe DiBlasi and Dominic Leone and from my own newspaper reporting through the years.

The accounts of 1958 northwest Baltimore are drawn from living there from that era until the present day.

The accounts of John Unitas's funeral come from my reporting that day.

CHAPTER 2. "JUST LOOK AT THOSE AWFUL PEOPLE"

Accounts of the life of John Steadman come from my thirty-four-year friendship with Steadman. Those conversations include many accounts of life at the *News-Post*. Accounts of Chuck Thompson's life come from many conversations with Thompson and from his autobiography, *Ain't the Beer Cold!* (Chuck Thompson with Gordon Beard, Diamond Communications, 1996).

Accounts of the Colts come from interviews with John Unitas, Art Donovan, Alan Ameche, Lenny Moore, Raymond Berry, Jim Parker, Jim Mutscheller, Andy Nelson, Ordell Braase, and Sisto Averno.

Accounts of Reds Hubbe and Bill Gattus come from interviews with Hubbe and Gattus. Accounts of Carroll Rosenbloom's betting come from Constantine Huditean, Al Isella, and John Steadman.

CHAPTER 3. THE HOMELY GIRL

Accounts of Mayor Tommy D'Alesandro Jr.'s life, and the Jack Pollack connection, come from interviews with his son, Mayor Tommy D'Alesandro III and from John Pica Sr.

Accounts of the blizzard of 1958 come from newspaper accounts of that week and also from several interviews through the years with Baltimore Vice Squad's Lieutenant George Andrew and from numerous conversations with Philip "Pacey" Silbert and with Daniel "Nookie the Bookie" Brown. The Bowie Racetrack account comes from Silbert and Brown and Jesse Bondroff and from a February 17, 1958, *Baltimore Sun* account, "5,000 Fans Evacuated from Bowie by Train."

Mark Kram's description of Baltimore is drawn from his October 10, 1966, account for *Sports Illustrated*, "A Wink at a Homely Girl."

Accounts of the *Romper Room* show come from my own observations of the program. Likewise, accounts of *The Buddy Deane Show* come from my observations—plus interviews through the years with Deane, with Royal (Parker) Pollokoff, with John Waters, and with numerous Committee members.

John Goodspeed's account of Baltimore during the World War II years comes from an October 1987 piece, "Boomtown," in *Baltimore* magazine.

Accounts of Baltimore public schools' integration come from interviews with Tommy D'Alesandro III, from Kenneth Durr's *Behind the Backlash: White Working-Class Politics in Baltimore, 1940–1980* (University of North Carolina Press, 2003), and from *Toward Equality: Baltimore's Progress Report*, by Edgar Jones and Jack Levin (Sidney Hollander Foundation, 1960).

CHAPTER 4. "WAY YOU CHUCK 'EM IN, HON"

Accounts of John Unitas's life come from interviews through the years with Unitas and with John Ziemann, Mike Gibbons, Lenny Moore, Art Donovan, Jim Mutscheller, Alan Ameche, Jim Parker, John Mackey, Raymond Berry, and John Steadman.

The account of Reggie Jackson trying out for the Leone's baseball team comes from Joe DiBlasi.

CHAPTER 5. FATHER RAYMOND BERRY

Accounts of Raymond Berry's career come from interviewing Berry.

Accounts of northwest Baltimore come from a variety of sources, including the author's own recollections; interviews with Lenny Moore, Joel Kruh, Ron Sallow, Stan Nusenko, Harvey Hyatt, Henry Leikach, Bruce Kobin, Barry Director, and Phil Rubinstein; and a February 14, 1958, *Baltimore Jewish Times* account, "Town Topics," on the changing racial dynamics in the city's Ashburton neighborhood.

Accounts of the Buddy Deane Committee rules come from Committee member Carl Parks.

Accounts of Bert Rechichar and Buddy Young's relationship come from John Steadman.

Other accounts of the era come from newspaper accounts noted in the text.

CHAPTER 6. LENNY AND BIG DADDY

Accounts of the Orioles' racial makeup come from John Steadman, former Oriole Joe Durham, and examinations of Orioles' rosters. Accounts of the city's racial divide come from Jones and Levin's *Toward Equality: White Working-Class Politics in Baltimore, 1940–1980.* Accounts of America's racial divide come from contemporary newspaper stories and from a December 5, 1958, *U.S. News & World Report* story, "Latest Problem for Cities in North: 'Blockbusting,' " and from the author's own recollections.

Accounts of Lenny Moore and Gene "Big Daddy" Lipscomb come from interviews with Moore and with John Steadman. Game accounts come from the reporting of John Steadman and N. P. Clark in the *News-Post,* plus the author's own observations.

CHAPTER 7. THE AUTUMN RITUALS

Accounts of south Baltimore come from Joe DiBlasi.

Accounts of northwest Baltimore come from interviews through the years with Donald Saiontz, Barry Levinson, Leonard "Boogie" Weinglass, and Richard Sher.

Game accounts come from Steadman, N. P. Clark, and the *Sun*'s Jesse Linthicum.

The account of George Marshall's rant about Lenny Moore comes from John Steadman. Accounts of Marshall's outburst with Rosenbloom come from Steadman's *Football's Miracle Men* (Pennington Press, 1959).

Accounts of Rosenbloom's gambling come from Constantine Huditean, Al Isella, John Steadman, and Weeb Ewbank's recollection in *Sundays at 2:00 with the Baltimore Colts*, by Vince Bagli and Norman Macht (Tidewater Publishers, 1995).

Accounts of the characters at Gussie's Downbeat come from conversations with Huditean, Isella, Gene Raynor, Gus Hansen, John Vicchio, Art Donovan, Mike Curtis, Pacey Silbert, Jesse Bondroff, Mimi DiPietro, and Michael "Bo" Sudano.

The rest of the chapter comes from conversations with Andy Nelson.

CHAPTER 8. THE LAST RITES

Accounts of John Unitas's injury come from interviews with Unitas, Colts physician Dr. Erwin Mayer, Art Donovan, John Ziemann, and John Steadman and a Q&A with Unitas in Lou Sahadi's *Johnny Unitas: America's Quarterback* (Triumph Books, 2004).

Conversations with George Shaw and game accounts of the Colts-Giants regular-season game come from Steadman's *Football's Miracle Men* and from his contemporary newspaper accounts.

Accounts of Chuck Thompson's description of Unitas's return—"How rusty can a guy get?"—come from the author's distinct recollection.

Accounts of the 49ers game and the postgame locker room come from the author's recollection; from conversations with Unitas, Donovan, Moore, Parker, Mutscheller, Nelson, and Berry; from Steadman's *News-Post* account, "We Got Up to Win Like a Champion"; and from Steadman's *Football's Miracle Men.*

CHAPTER 9. A TOWN WITHOUT FOREPLAY

Accounts of 1958 Baltimore come from the author's personal recollections.

Descriptions of New York come from Bruce Jay Friedman's "New York: A Town without Foreplay," written for *Playboy* magazine (December 1971), and from 1958 theater coverage in the *New Yorker* magazine.

Frank DeFord's account comes from his September 11, 2002, *Sports Illustrated* story, "The Best There Ever Was!"

Accounts of pro football gambling come from Michael MacCambridge's *America's Game: The Epic Story of How Pro Football Captured A Nation* (Anchor Books, 2004).

CHAPTER 10. SUDDEN LIFE

Accounts of December 28, 1958, off-field action come from conversations with Bill Gattus, Reds Hubbe, Joe Perzynski, Joe DiBlasi, John Steadman, N. P. Clark, Jim Henneman, Unitas, Donovan, Berry, Mutscheller, Parker, and Nelson, plus contemporary newspaper accounts by Cameron Snyder in the *Baltimore Sun* and N. P. Clark, Steve O'Neill, and Steadman in the *News-Post* and the author's own observations.

Game accounts come from those men, plus stories in the *News-Post* on December 29, 1958, and Steadman's *The Greatest Football Game Ever Played* (Press Box, 1988), plus the author's own observations.

CHAPTER 11. "THEY JUST WANTED SOMEBODY TO BE HAPPY WITH"

Accounts come from the author's recollections of the mad television scene from Friendship Airport and from interviews with Steadman, Unitas, Nelson, Gus Hansen, and Joe Croghan, plus December 29, 1958, *News-Post* newspaper accounts and Steadman's *The Greatest Football Game Ever Played.*